American Religion,
American Politics

90-95, 146-153, 206-219

American Religion, American Politics

An Anthology

Edited by

Joseph Kip Kosek

With a foreword by Jon Butler

Yale UNIVERSITY PRESS

New Haven and London

Published with assistance from the foundation established in memory of
Amasa Stone Mather of the Class of 1907, Yale College.

Yale University Press books may be purchased in quantity for educational, business, or
promotional use. For information, please e-mail sales.press@yale.edu (U.S. office) or
sales@yaleup.co.uk (U.K. office).

Set in Sabon type by Newgen North America.
Printed in the United States of America.

Library of Congress Control Number: 2016956026
ISBN: 978-0-300-20351-6 (paperback : alk. paper)

A catalogue record for this book is available from the British Library.

This paper meets the requirements of ANSI/NISO Z39.48-1992 (Permanence of Paper).

10 9 8 7 6 5 4 3 2 1

For Ellie, Charlotte, and Theo

Contents

Foreword

Jon Butler

Religion and politics were the subjects you weren't supposed to bring up at Thanksgiving dinner. Why not? Aren't they the most interesting, the topics that provoke the most discussion, the ones that get the juices flowing?

Those are the reasons, of course.

Still, why, and why in America? Don't we have separation of church and state?

William James, the American philosopher, explained why religion raised the discussion stakes. Religion concerns "the inner dispositions of man . . . his conscience, his deserts, his helplessness, his incompleteness." It is "the primordial thing."

Virginia's James Madison, the Founding Father and fourth president of the United States, explained why politics roiled discussions. Politics beget government, "the essence of Government is power, and power, lodged as it must be in human hands, will ever be liable to abuse."

James and Madison describe the implications of religion and politics, but what do we mean by "religion" and by "politics"? The concepts have never not been debated, and modern scholars have only added new voices to old. James helps on a conception of religion. He described it as the "feelings, acts, and experiences" individuals have "in relation to whatever they may consider the divine." And the divine? Some would describe it as the transcendent, that which is permanent, timeless, standing outside and beyond the human, God.

Politics? It is far more than government, which is just its modern instrument. The classic concept comes from Aristotle's treatise, *Politics*. For Aristotle, it concerned what the Greeks called the "polis," the

community: what falls under the community's purview, who constitutes the community, and how the community's authority is distributed and exercised, the latter involving government in modern terms.
Politics is life. It is especially about the ways individuals, families, and
groups live life in relationship to others, to the whole.

Transcendence, life, and power. With subjects like these, the drum-
sticks could be dangerous.

But why should discussions of religion and politics at an American
Thanksgiving become so heated when the Constitution seems crafted
to avoid them? Unlike the founding documents of many modern societies, the original U.S. Constitution contained no reference to religion
except in Article 6, which stipulates, "no religious test shall ever be
required as a Qualification to any Office or public Trust under the
United States." The words "under the United States" limited the prohibition only to federal, not state, offices, but the stipulation might be
thought to defuse many American controversies about religion and
politics, if not all.

Seemingly more definitive is the First Amendment to the Federal
Constitution, ratified in 1791. It famously asserted rights of free
speech, the press, assembly, and petitioning government. But it opened
with a sweeping statement about religion and politics:

> Congress shall make no law respecting an establishment of religion,
> or prohibiting the free exercise thereof; or abridging the freedom of
> speech, or of the press; or the right of the people peaceably to assem-
> ble, and to petition the Government for a redress of grievances.

Yet far from settling matters, the First Amendment raised questions
about religion and government, just as it raised questions about free
speech, freedom of the press, free assemblage, and petitioning for
grievances. Many always have been general. How far do these stipula-
tions go? How strictly should they be interpreted? Are they absolute?
Do other rights compete?

But some questions have been very specific. What does "establishment" mean? What qualifies as "religion"? How free is "free exercise"? Some questions also have come from later assertions made
about the First Amendment, most notably one by Thomas Jefferson.
In a letter written to Connecticut Baptists in 1802 Jefferson argued
that the Amendment built "a wall of separation between church and
state," a phrase so mellifluous that it has come to seem like part of
the Amendment itself—even cited in some U.S. Supreme Court opinions—although it has no legal standing.

Jefferson, in haste or with craft, changed the First Amendment's phrasing from a law banning "an establishment of religion" to one erecting "a wall of separation between church and state," the reference to "church" especially circumscribing the subject with much greater specificity.

Intriguingly, the U.S. Supreme Court has never defined "religion." Justices have used the term routinely, as they obviously must. But they have never crafted a legal definition of "religion" or determined which religion or religions might claim protections of the First Amendment, especially the protection given "free exercise."

The reason is not hard to fathom. The American record of spawning new faiths (Spiritualism, Mormonism, Adventism, Jehovah's Witnesses, Christian Science, New Thought, Pentecostalism, the Native American Church, Reconstructionist Judaism, the Nation of Islam, and Scientology) and all the time importing more (Catholics, Swedenborgians, Muslims, Hindus, Buddhists, Confucianists, Sikhs, Daoists, Jains, Taoists, and Rastafarians, among others) would bring any constraining legal definition of religion immediately to its knees.

America's unprecedented religious pluralism thus helps explain why controversies about "establishment" never have focused on the term's traditional meaning: government support for a single religion—the Catholic Church or the Church of England, for example.

Instead, "establishment" controversies have focused on broad practices involving religion, required by law or government regulation, that many religious and nonreligious people have found offensive, and an effort to "establish" religion broadly but not a specific religion. In the nineteenth century these included disputes about which Bible, Protestant or Catholic, might be used in compulsory Bible readings in publicly supported schools, and in the twentieth century they have concerned the compulsory Bible readings themselves, compulsory school prayers, and requirements to salute the American flag.

First Amendment arguments about "free exercise" often have a grittier feel and have brought the Court to setting limits on religiously founded behavior. The Court effectively outlawed Mormon polygamy in 1878, distinguishing between belief and action, and in 1990 it upheld Oregon's ban on peyote, used in the services of the Native American Church, because the ban was directed broadly at a drug, not at a religion.

The legal arguments over free exercise, important in their own terms, also illuminate the extraordinary way religion has engaged the whole of American life—of what Aristotle considered "politics." Even a minimalist reading of America's national struggles and controversies will find religion critical to their very core. Three examples illustrate how.

Our long, still debilitating struggle over slavery and race invoked religion at the heart of the matter. Every side in the struggle took religion as a proof-text. Advocates constantly quoted the Bible to justify and condemn slavery, racial superiority and inferiority, and racial separation and integration. So central were the religious claims about these subjects and so strongly held, with such deep cultural resonance, that any historian would be hard pressed to determine how these controversies could have played out absent the catalyst of religion and politics.

Religious language also stood at the center of America's deepest political arguments about foreign policy and war from the American Revolution forward. God has fought on every side and supported and opposed every American intervention, including even World War II. The terrorist events of September 2001 inspired responses that were unique to the moment yet embedded inside a long national history of religious support for and against American foreign policy and military intervention and action from the Civil War to the Spanish-American War to the war in Vietnam.

Finally, many struggles about religion have become particularly contentious because their specifically religious elements have challenged Americans' historical identities as a people, individually and collectively. Catholics and Mormons allegedly owed allegiance to religious institutions and their leaders, not to the nation. Non-Protestant immigrants, especially Catholics, Jews, and, more recently, Muslims, Hindus, and Sikhs, have challenged America's reputed core culture. New and revisionist theologies have indeed wrought intellectual and social tension inside religious groups but in good part because they also have confronted political issues, certainly women's traditional roles and racial boundaries, controversial in American culture far beyond the religious sanctuary.

Thomas Jefferson's 1802 letter assuring Connecticut Baptists that the First Amendment erected a "wall of separation between Church & State" might seem to have underestimated the future relationship between religion and politics in America. Perhaps Jefferson proved more prescient later. In the mid-1810s Jefferson began collecting the sayings of Jesus in a little book he termed the "Philosophy of Jesus." Jesus's ethical teachings, as well as those of Epicurus and Plato, fascinated him, and he discussed them and the problems of religion and politics with some regularity up to his death in 1826. Americans have never stopped.

Acknowledgments

My most substantial debt is to the students and graduate teachers in my "U.S. Religion and Politics" course at George Washington University. Many of the readings in this anthology first appeared on our class syllabus, and many of the ideas were worked out in lively exchanges during class meetings and office hours. The Young Scholars in American Religion program at Indiana University–Purdue University Indianapolis profoundly shaped my sense of how to conceptualize and teach American religion. At Yale University Press, Sarah Miller encouraged me that this unusual project would be worthwhile. She and Ash Lago managed the publication process with empathy and efficiency. Anonymous reviewers were exceedingly generous with comments and criticism that improved the final product immeasurably. Matthew Sutton gave advice from his experience editing an outstanding documentary history of the religious right. Muriel Moore provided tireless research assistance tracking down historical texts. I am deeply grateful that Anne and I share an interest in exploring and debating big ideas. I dedicate this book to our children, with hope.

American Religion,
American Politics

Introduction

This book brings together two subjects, religion and politics, that might seem to have little to do with each other. Religion reaches toward the transcendent, expressing a belief in supernatural beings and powers that intervene in human affairs. Politics, on the other hand, is oriented toward this world, a process of making decisions in groups that relies on pragmatic compromise to distribute power and resources. Religion claims ultimate loyalty, while politics creates ever-shifting alliances. If religious believers have often condemned the political arena as a cesspool of corruption and dishonesty, political philosophers have often distrusted religion as a seedbed of narrow-minded fanaticism.

Despite this apparent dichotomy, Americans have throughout their history also seen religion and politics as deeply intertwined. Upon reflection, this is not surprising, for the two realms have some things in common. Both assert the authority to guide and even coerce the behavior of individuals, both claim to offer solutions to the challenges of living together in communities, and both generally promote some version of a greater good that extends beyond narrow self-interest. Religious people have brought their faith commitments to politics, as when Martin Luther King, Jr. insisted that Christian conceptions of divine justice required the extension of political equality to African Americans. Conversely, political developments have shaped the character of religious groups, as when Unites States Muslims were pressured to articulate their loyalty to the nation in the wake of the al Qaeda attacks of September 11, 2001. In short, the relationship of religion and politics has framed some of the most urgent questions about American democracy.

American Religion, American Politics is an anthology of significant writings on these two subjects from the colonial period to recent times. Rather than offering a comprehensive prescription for our public life, the book presents an extended conversation. Often the authors in these pages disagree with each other, and readers will undoubtedly disagree with some of them as well. As editor, I have sought to produce not a theological treatise but a useful text for the academic study of American religion. That kind of study tries to leave aside questions of ultimate meaning, at least provisionally, to treat religion as a product of human history and culture. My goal is to have readers understand the range of debates over religion and politics and to encourage them to work out their own interpretations based on their interests and the expectations of their particular disciplines.

This book has the word "religion" in its title, but it is emphatically not for believers only. The issues in these pages confront readers of all spiritual and political persuasions. For example, anyone, religious or not, concerned about the protection of civil liberties has to reckon with the Supreme Court's decisions in the 1940s regarding Jehovah's Witnesses, a small apocalyptic sect that refused to salute the flag or participate in other patriotic rituals. Anyone interested in the long history of feminism will find it useful to work through the critiques of Christian patriarchy by Frances Willard and Elizabeth Cady Stanton. Anyone studying the ethical concept of the just war will gain insight from Reinhold Niebuhr's searching analysis of the sometimes conflicting requirements of love and justice. In other words, the readings have been chosen to highlight religion as a force in its own right and also as a site for discussing a wide range of ostensibly secular subjects.

The conception of "politics" in the volume has a similarly capacious scope. Some of the texts reprinted here are obviously political: presidential speeches, laws, and Supreme Court decisions, to name a few. Yet to restrict politics to the official operations of government would present an impoverished view, one that would miss many of the most pressing issues in American history and culture. Therefore, this volume also includes many representatives of major social movements, people who never held elective office but who expressed ideas that shaped the power dynamics of the nation's public life. For instance, John Shelby Spong's endorsement of gay marriage may seem at first to deal only with the behavior of individuals in the privacy of their bedrooms. However, the LGBT rights movement (like feminism before it) showed marriage to be also a public legal construction, one that became the site of intense political debate leading up to the landmark 2015 *Obergefell v. Hodges* decision, which legalized same-sex unions. Politics, then, is not only what the president or Congress does; it is also the activity of lesser-known pressure groups that can, over time, change the government from the outside.

Although this volume covers a wide range of subjects, it returns throughout to three interrelated themes, common problems that persist across historical eras. The first theme deals with the scope of religious freedom and religious toleration, values inextricably linked to the First Amendment's religion clauses: "Congress shall make no law respecting an establishment of religion, or prohibiting the free exercise thereof." With this bold statement, the founders made a significant break with the colonial model of religious establishment, the framework of government-supported churches that had reigned in Europe for hundreds of years and in the New World colonies as well. Following in the spirit of the First Amendment's imperative, ordinary Americans transformed the spiritual landscape in the first half-century of the nation's life, flocking to fledgling evangelical denominations such as the Methodists and Baptists and starting a dizzying array of brand-new groups. The legal and social shift to acceptance of religious diversity signaled the acceleration of a distinctly American experiment.

Religious freedom, though, had important limits. Even after the Bill of Rights was ratified, individual states maintained their official support of churches (Massachusetts did not end the practice until 1833, the last state to do so). Furthermore, Protestant Christianity constituted in many ways an unofficial establishment despite the First Amendment's claims, a phenomenon criticized by the freethinker and suffragist Elizabeth Cady Stanton, who appears in this volume. For most of American history, Protestants dominated the leadership of the country's economic, political, and educational institutions. Blasphemy and obscenity laws were used throughout the nineteenth century to enforce specifically Protestant ideas about God and morality. Even as the boundaries of religious toleration have expanded in the twenty-first century, opinion polls still consistently show that large numbers of Americans would refuse on principle to vote for a presidential candidate who was an atheist. The story of religious freedom, then, is a story of continuing expansion and, at the same time, persistent barriers to inclusion.

The second theme of the book addresses religion's role as an ethical compass for public life. What should religious people do about racial slavery, or global warfare, or homosexuality? And is religion a trustworthy guide to public morality in the first place? Such ethical questions often played out less in the legal realm than in the arena of social reform and dissent across the political spectrum. This anthology therefore includes selections from figures inside and outside government who developed moral visions of the good society and launched moral protests against perceived obstacles to it. This kind of religious politics goes back to the Puritan John Winthrop, a dissenter from the Church of England who admonished his fellow settlers to create a new community "knitt together" by Christian love. It continues through the most contemporary readings in the book, including Wendell Berry's insistence on a religious respect for human limits in an age of ecological devastation.

The third major center of gravity, which intermingles with the first two, is about the character of the American nation. Is it Christian, inclusively religious, secular, or something else? What does it mean to assign the nation a religious identity? Would that identity be a description of what America is, or rather a hope (or a fear) concerning what it might become? Over and over, conceptions of nationalism have been tied up with ideas about God, faith, and sacred history. The most famous example in this volume is Abraham Lincoln's second inaugural address, in which the president grimly suggested that the carnage of the Civil War was a divine judgment on the country, North and South, for the social sin of slavery. Nearly a century later, a Washington, DC minister named George Docherty proposed, more optimistically, that religion was central to America's success and that the phrase "under God" ought to be added to the Pledge of Allegiance to recognize this fact. Whether commentators wanted to rebuke the United States or celebrate it, they often understood it as having religious meaning and significance.

Of course, this book can hardly present a full survey of American religion and politics. By its nature, it focuses on the ideas of elites. Even those authors who are not presidents or ministers were sufficiently educated to be able to write coherently and obtain a hearing from their audiences. Readers need to be aware, therefore, of the rich worlds of "lived religion" and "infrapolitics" that scholars have emphasized in recent studies. Lived religion refers to the practice of faith, especially as that practice diverges from official theological tenets, while infrapolitics names the subtle everyday struggles for power that operate beneath the organized world of parties, elections, and marches. I have tried to balance authors in the rarefied worlds of national government with those, less eminent, who connect at some level to broader social movements and shed light on the politics of dissent. Still, much of American religion and politics operated beneath the radar of expressly articulated thought.

All this is to say that *American Religion, American Politics* is an invitation to further study and reflection. It is a starting point for understanding one of the most important and exciting conversations in American history, a conversation that began before our nation's founding and continues today. These texts are important for believers and atheists, for Republicans, Democrats, and independents. I hope that readers, regardless of their religious or political allegiances, will use these selections to deepen their understanding of America's history and future.

I

———◆———

Religious Establishment and Religious
Freedom in Early America

M ost European rulers, Protestant as well as Catholic, governed according to the model of religious establishment,
which held that a state ought to have an officially sanctioned faith. After all, how could people live together in political community if they disagreed on ultimate questions about God and His
will? Against this system of established religion, however, emerged
a theory of toleration that sought an end to the religious violence
that establishment had fomented. The English political theorist John
Locke's 1689 *Letter Concerning Toleration* exemplified the shifting
attitude toward religious freedom. "The Church it self," Locke wrote,
"is a thing absolutely separate and distinct from the Commonwealth,"
so citizens were entitled to equal protection under the law even if their
faiths were different. Though Locke's conception of toleration was
limited (it did not, for instance, extend to unbelievers), it marked a
move away from the assumption that each state needed absolute religious unity. The first documents in this chapter show how Britain's
New World colonies were shaped both by the tradition of religious
establishment and by the newer ideas of religious toleration.

Unlike the early colonists, many of the founders of the United
States doubted that religious establishment was necessary. They were
constrained in part by American political realities: the newly independent nation was simply too religiously diverse for any one group to
claim official status. Yet Thomas Jefferson, James Madison, and others were motivated by principle as well. They drew on theology and
political theory to show that religious diversity might be permitted
to the benefit of church and state alike. That idea was first enshrined
in Article VI of the Constitution. The only substantive mention of

6

religion in the original document, it stipulated that "no religious Test" could be required to hold national office.

More important were the religion clauses of the First Amendment: "Congress shall make no law respecting an establishment of religion, or prohibiting the free exercise thereof." This was a sweeping statement of religious liberty, one that went well beyond European or colonial experience. To be sure, it was also vague and elusive: the amendment did not define what counted as "religion," nor did it prohibit individual states from keeping their own religious establishments (which some did, for a time). Still, these sixteen words make up one of the most audacious and significant elements of the American experiment.

JOHN WINTHROP,
"A MODELL OF CHRISTIAN CHARITY" (1630)

For a long time, Americans have found in the Puritan colonists the best and worst of the nation's subsequent political culture. These English radicals insisted on the need to "purify" the Christian religion of idolatry and corruption. Although Henry VIII had broken with the Catholic Church during the Protestant Reformation and established the Church of England, subsequent changes following this rift did not go nearly far enough for the Puritans. Eventually some of the dissenters fled England to make a new start on the American continent, founding Plymouth Colony in 1620 and Massachusetts Bay Colony in 1630. Subsequent admirers have celebrated the Puritans as bold exemplars of rebellious independence, while detractors have pointed out that the new settlers believed not in freedom for all but only for the practitioners of their specific faith.

John Winthrop (1588–1649) was the most important leader of the early Puritan settlements in the New World. The first governor of Massachusetts Bay, Winthrop wrote the sermon excerpted here (tradition holds that he composed it aboard the ship *Arbella*) to lay out his vision of a Christian community held together by bonds of love. As a political authority, Winthrop balanced these high ideals with attention to practical economic and diplomatic issues and kept the settlement going during its difficult early years. He also enforced religious orthodoxy, most famously by banishing Anne Hutchinson from the colony during the Antinomian controversy of 1636–37.

In recent decades the status of the Puritans as quintessential American precursors has faded. To many twenty-first-century observers, the relatively homogeneous society of Winthrop's "city on a hill" no longer seems like a useful or desirable metonym for the multireligious, multicultural United States. That said, "A Modell of Christian Charity" continues to resonate, both for its compelling call to place the public good above individual self-interest and for its hints of the intolerance and injustice that political groups can perpetuate.

John Winthrop, "A Modell of Christian Charity"

GOD ALMIGHTY in his most holy and wise providence, hath soe disposed of the condition of mankind, as in all times some must be rich, some poore, some high and eminent in power and dignitie; others mean and in submission.

The Reason hereof.

1 *Reas.* First to hold conformity with the rest of his world, being delighted to show forth the glory of his wisdom in the variety and difference of the creatures, and the glory of his power in ordering all these differences for the preservation and good of the whole; and the glory of his greatness, that as it is the glory of princes to have many officers, soe this great king will haue many stewards, Counting himself more honoured in dispensing his gifts to man by man, than if he did it by his owne immediate hands.

2 *Reas.* Secondly that he might haue the more occasion to manifest the work of his Spirit: first upon the wicked in moderating and restraining them: soe that the riche and mighty should not eate upp the poore nor the poore and dispised rise upp against and shake off theire yoake. 2ly In the regenerate, in exerciseing his graces in them, as in the grate ones, theire love, mercy, gentleness, temperance &c., in the poore and inferior sorte, theire faithe, patience, obedience &c.

3 *Reas.* Thirdly, that every man might have need of others, and from hence they might be all knitt more nearly together in the Bonds of brotherly affection. From hence it appears plainly that noe man is made more honourable than another or more wealthy &c., out of any particular and singular respect to himselfe, but for the glory of his creator and the common good of the creature, man. Therefore God still reserves the propperty of these gifts to himself as Ezek. 16.17. he there calls wealthe, *his gold and his silver*, and Prov. 3.9. he claims theire service as his due, *honor the Lord with thy riches* &c.—All men being thus (by divine providence) ranked into two sorts, riche and poore; under the first are comprehended all such as are able to live comfortably by their own meanes duely improved; and all others are poore according to the former distribution. There are two rules whereby we are to walk one towards another: Justice and Mercy. These are always distinguished in their act and in their ob-

ject, yet may they both concurre in the same subject in eache respect; as sometimes there may be an occasion of showing mercy to a rich man in some sudden danger or distresse, and alsoe doeing of meere justice to a poor man in regard of some perticular contract &c. There is likewise a double Lawe by which wee are regulated in our conversation towardes another; in both the former respects, the lawe of nature and the lawe of grace, or the morrall lawe or the lawe of the gospell, to omitt the rule of justice as not propperly belonging to this purpose otherwise than it may fall into consideration in some perticular cases. By the first of these lawes man as he was enabled soe withall is commanded to love his neighbour as himself. Upon this ground stands all the precepts of the morrall lawe, which concernes our dealings with men. To apply this to the works of mercy; this lawe requires two things. First that every man afford his help to another in every want or distresse. Secondly, that hee performe this out of the same affection which makes him carefull of his owne goods, according to that of our Savior, (Math.) *Whatsoever ye would that men should do to you.* This was practised by Abraham and Lot in entertaining the angells and the old man of Gibea. The lawe of Grace or of the Gospell hath some difference from the former; as in these respects, First the lawe of nature was given to man in the estate of innocency; this of the Gospell in the estate of regeneracy. 2ly, the former propounds one man to another, as the same flesh and image of God; this as a brother in Christ allsoe, and in the communion of the same Spirit, and soe teacheth to put a difference between Christians and others. *Doe good to all, especially to the household of faith*; upon this ground the Israelites were to putt a difference betweene the brethren of such as were strangers though not of the Canaanites.

3ly. The Lawe of nature would give no rules for dealing with enemies, for all are to be considered as friends in the state of innocency, but the Gospell commands loue to an enemy. Proofe. *If thine Enemy hunger, feed him; Love your Enemies, doe good to them that hate you.* Math. 5.44.

[. . .]

The deffinition which the Scripture giues us of loue is this. *Love is the bond of perfection,* first it is a bond or ligament. 2ly it makes the worke perfect. There is noe body but consists of partes and that which knitts these partes together, giues the body its perfection, because it makes eache parte soe contiguous to others as thereby they doe mutually participate with each other, both in strengthe and infirmity, in pleasure and paine. To instance in the most perfect of all bodies; Christ and his Church make one body; the severall partes of this body considered a parte before they were united, were as disproportionate and as much disordering as soe many contrary quallities or elements, but when Christ comes, and by his spirit and loue knitts all these partes to himselfe and each to other, it is become the most perfect and best proportioned body in the world, Eph. 4.16.

Christ, by whome all the body being knitt together by every joint for
the furniture thereof, according to the effectuall power which is in the
measure of every perfection of partes, a glorious body without spott or
wrinkle; the ligaments hereof being Christ, or his love, for Christ is love,
1 John 4.8. Soe this definition is right. *Love is the bond of perfection.*
      [. . .]
   It rests now to make some application of this discourse, by the present
designe, which gaue the occasion of writing of it. Herein are 4 things to
be propounded; *first* the persons, 2ly the worke, 3ly the end, 4thly the
meanes. 1. For *the persons.* Wee are a company professing ourselves fellow members of Christ, in which respect onely though wee were absent
from each other many miles, and had our imployments as farre distant,
yet wee ought to account ourselves knitt together by this bond of loue,
and, live in the exercise of it, if wee would have comforte of our being
in Christ. This was notorious in the practise of the Christians in former
times; as is testified of the Waldenses, from the mouth of one of the adversaries *Aeneas Sylvius* "mutuo ament pere antequam norunt," they use
to loue any of theire owne religion even before they were acquainted with
them. 2nly for the *worke* wee have in hand. It is by a mutuall consent,
through a speciall overvaluing providence and a more than an ordinary
approbation of the Churches of Christ, to seeke out a place of cohabita-
tion and Consorteshipp under a due forme of Government both ciuill
and ecclesiasticall. In such cases as this, the care of the publique must
oversway all private respects, by which, not only conscience, but meare
civill pollicy, dothe binde us. For it is a true rule that particular Estates
cannot subsist in the ruin of the publique. 3ly The *end* is to improve our
lives to doe more service to the Lord; the comforte and encrease of the
body of Christe, whereof we are members; that ourselves and posterity
may be the better preserved from the common corruptions of this evill
world, to serve the Lord and worke out our Salvation under the power
and purity of his holy ordinances. 4thly for the *meanes* whereby this
must be effected. They are twofold, a conformity with the worke and end
wee aime at. These wee see are extraordinary, therefore wee must not
content ourselves with usuall ordinary meanes. Whatsoever wee did, or
ought to have, done, when wee liued in England, the same must wee doe,
and more allsoe, where wee goe. That which the most in theire churches
maintaine as truthe in profession onely, wee must bring into familiar
and constant practise; as in this duty of loue, wee must loue brotherly
without dissimulation, wee must loue one another with a pure hearte fervently. Wee must beare one anothers burthens. We must not looke onely
on our owne things, but allsoe on the things of our brethren. Neither
must wee thinke that the Lord will beare with such faileings at our hands
as he dothe from those among whome wee have lived; and that for these
3 Reasons; 1. In regard of the more neare bond of mariage between him

and us, wherein hee hath taken us to be his, after a most strickt and peculiar manner, which will make them the more jealous of our loue and obedience. Soe he tells the people of Israell, *you onely have I knowne of all the families of the Earthe, therefore will I punishe you for your Transgressions.* 2ly, because *the Lord will be sanctified in them that come neare him.* We know that there were many that corrupted the service of the Lord; some setting upp altars before his owne; others offering both strange fire and strange sacrifices allsoe; yet there came noe fire from heaven, or other sudden judgement upon them, as did upon Nadab and Abihu, whoe yet wee may think did not sinne presumptuously. 3ly When God gives a speciall commission he lookes to have it strictly observed in every article; When he gave Saule a commission to destroy Amaleck, Hee indented with him upon certain articles, and because hee failed in one of the least, and that upon a faire pretense, it lost him the kingdom, which should have beene his reward, if hee had observed his commission. Thus stands the cause betweene God and us. We are entered into Covenant with Him for this worke. Wee haue taken out a commission. The Lord hath given us leave to drawe our own articles. Wee haue professed to enterprise these and those accounts, upon these and those ends. Wee have hereupon besought Him of favour and blessing. Now if the Lord shall please to heare us, and bring us in peace to the place we desire, then hath hee ratified this covenant and sealed our Commission, and will expect a strict performance of the articles contained in it; but if wee shall neglect the observation of these articles which are the ends wee have propounded, and, dissembling with our God, shall fall to embrace this present world and prosecute our carnall intentions, seeking greate things for ourselves and our posterity, the Lord will surely breake out in wrathe against us; be revenged of such a [sinful] people and make us knowe the price of the breache of such a covenant.

Now the onely way to avoyde this shipwracke, and to provide for our posterity, is to followe the counsell of Micah, *to doe justly, to love mercy, to walk humbly with our God.* For this end, wee must be knitt together, in this worke, as one man. Wee must entertaine each other in brotherly affection. Wee must be willing to abridge ourselves of our superfluities, for the supply of other's necessities. Wee must uphold a familiar commerce together in all meekeness, gentlenes, patience and liberality. Wee must delight in eache other; make other's conditions our oune; rejoice together, mourne together, labour and suffer together, allwayes haueving before our eyes our commission and community in the worke, as members of the same body. Soe shall wee *keepe the unitie of the spirit in the bond of peace.* The Lord will be our God, and delight to dwell among us, as his oune people, and will command a blessing upon us in all our wayes. Soe that wee shall see much more of his wisdome, power, goodness and truthe, than formerly wee haue been acquainted with. Wee shall finde that the God of Israell is among us, when ten of us shall be able to resist a thousand of our enemies; when hee shall make us a prayse and glory that men shall say of succeeding plantations, "the Lord make it likely that of *New England*." For wee must consider that wee shall be as a citty upon a hill. The eies of all people are uppon us. Soe that if wee shall deale falsely with our God in this worke wee haue undertaken, and soe cause him to withdrawe his present help from us, wee shall be made a story and a by-word through the world. Wee shall open the mouthes of enemies to speake evill of the wayes of God, and all professors for God's sake. Wee shall shame the faces of many of God's worthy servants, and cause theire prayers to be turned into curses upon us till wee be consumed out of the good land whither wee are a goeing.

I shall shutt upp this discourse with that exhortation of Moses, that faithfull servant of the Lord, in his last farewell to Israell, Deut. 30. *Beloued there is now sett before us life and good, Death and evill, in that wee are commanded this day to loue the Lord our God, and to loue one another, to walke in his wayes and to keepe his Commandements and his Ordinance and his lawes*, and the articles of our Covenant with him, that *wee may liue and be multiplied, and that the Lord our God may blesse us in the land whither wee goe to possesse it. But if our heartes shall turne away, soe that wee will not obey, but shall be seduced, and worshipp and serue other Gods*, our pleasure and proffitts, *and serue them*; it is propounded unto us this day, *wee shall surely perishe out of the good land whither wee passe over this vast sea to possesse it.*

Therefore lett us choose life that wee, and our seede may liue, by obeyeing His voyce and cleaveing to Him, for Hee is our life and our prosperity.

Source

John Winthrop, "A Modell of Christian Charity," Collections of the Massachusetts Historical Society (Boston, 1838), 3rd series 7:31–48.

Hanover Historical Texts Project: http://history.hanover.edu/texts/winthmod.html

Further Reading

Bercovitch, Sacvan. *The Puritan Origins of the American Self*. New Haven: Yale University Press, 1975.

Hall, David D. *A Reforming People: Puritanism and the Transformation of Public Life in New England*. New York: Knopf, 2011.

Morgan, Edmund. *The Puritan Dilemma: The Story of John Winthrop*. Boston: Little, Brown, 1958.

Valeri, Mark R. *Heavenly Merchandize: How Religion Shaped Commerce in Puritan America*. Princeton: Princeton University Press, 2010.

MARYLAND ACT CONCERNING RELIGION (1649)

The middle colonies featured a level of religious diversity and a degree of religious toleration not seen in the Puritan settlements of New England. William Penn, the Quaker founder of Pennsylvania, welcomed a variety of religious groups to his colony. The first Jews in the New World arrived at New Amsterdam (later New York) in 1654. The colony of Maryland, from which this reading comes, was founded by the Catholic Cecilius Calvert, known also as Lord Baltimore, as a refuge for his coreligionists. In short, one finds in the middle colonies glimmers of the multireligious society that the modern United States would eventually become.

The Act Concerning Religion, often called the Maryland Toleration Act, has a complicated political history that reflects the possibilities and limits of religious freedom in the colonial era. Though Maryland was ruled by Catholics, their status was precarious as colonial leaders in an outpost of a nation with an established Protestant church. So although the document protects a range of religious views, it was understood in its time to be especially important to ensure the survival of the English Catholic minority. Catholics were right to be worried: the Act Concerning Religion was repealed, then reinstated, then repealed again in the wake of the Glorious Revolution of 1688, which marked a final victory of Protestants over Catholics in the struggle for the English throne.

Modern readers will likely be struck first by the narrowness of the toleration envisioned here. The act remains well within the reigning concepts of religious establishment that defined seventeenth-century theories of government. Only in the political and philosophical ferment following the American Revolution would a more robust model of religious freedom take hold.

Maryland Act Concerning Religion

Forasmuch as in a well governed and Christian Common Weath matters concerning Religion and the honor of God ought in the first place to bee taken, into serious consideracion and endeavoured to bee settled, Be it therefore ordered and enacted by the Right Honourable Cecilius Lord Baron of Baltemore absolute Lord and Proprietary of this Province with the advise and consent of this Generall Assembly:

That whatsoever person or persons within this Province and the Islands thereunto belonging shall from henceforth blaspheme God, that is Curse him, or deny our Saviour Jesus Christ to bee the sonne of God, or shall deny the holy Trinity the father sonne and holy Ghost, or the Godhead of any of the said Three persons of the Trinity or the Unity of the God-head, or shall use or utter any reproachfull Speeches, words or language concerning the said Holy Trinity, or any of the said three persons thereof, shalbe punished with death and confiscation or forfeiture of all his or her lands and goods to the Lord Proprietary and his heires.

And bee it also Enacted by the Authority and with the advise and assent aforesaid, That whatsoever person or persons shall from henceforth use or utter any reproachfull words or Speeches concerning the blessed Virgin Mary the Mother of our Saviour or the holy Apostles or Evange-lists or any of them shall in such case for the first offence forfeit to the said Lord Proprietary and his heirs Lords and Proprietaries of this Prov-ince the summe of five pound Sterling or the value thereof to be Levyed on the goods and chattells of every such person soe offending, but in case such Offender or Offenders, shall not then have goods and chattells sufficient for the satisfyeing of such forfeiture, or that the same bee not otherwise speedily satisfyed that then such Offender or Offenders shalbe publiquely whipt and bee imprisoned during the pleasure of the Lord Proprietary or the Lieutenant or cheife Governor of this Province for the time being. And that every such Offender or Offenders for every sec-ond offence shall forfeit tenne pound sterling or the value thereof to bee levyed as aforesaid, or in case such offender or Offenders shall not then have goods and chattells within this Province sufficient for that purpose then to bee publiquely and severely whipt and imprisoned as before is expressed. And that every person or persons before mentioned offending herein the third time, shall for such third Offence forfeit all his lands and Goods and bee for ever banished and expelled out of this Province.

And be it also further Enacted by the same authority advise and assent that whatsoever person or persons shall from henceforth uppon any oc-casion of Offence or otherwise in a reproachful manner or Way declare call or denominate any person or persons whatsoever inhabiting, resid-ing, traffiqueing, trading or comerceing within this Province or within any the Ports, Harbors, Creeks or Havens to the same belonging an herit-ick, Scismatick, Idolator, puritan, Independant, Prespiterian popish prest, Jesuite, Jesuited papist, Lutheran, Calvenist, Anabaptist, Brownist, Anti-nomian, Barrowist, Roundhead, Separatist, or any other name or terme in a reproachfull manner relating to matter of Religion shall for every such Offence forfeit and loose the somme of tenne shillings sterling or the value thereof to bee levyed on the goods and chattells of every such Of-fender and Offenders, the one half thereof to be forfeited and paid unto the person and persons of whom such reproachfull words are or shalbe spoken or uttered, and the other half thereof to the Lord Proprietary and his heires Lords and Proprietaries of this Province. But if such person or persons who shall at any time utter or speake any such reproachfull words or Language shall not have Goods or Chattells sufficient and overt within this Province to bee taken to satisfie the penalty aforesaid or that the same bee not otherwise speedily satisfyed, that then the person or persons soe offending shalbe publickly whipt, and shall suffer imprisonment without baile or maineprise [bail] untill hee, shee or they respectively shall satisfy the party soe offended or greived by such reproachfull Language by asking him or her respectively forgivenes publiquely for such his Offence before the Magistrate or cheife Officer or Officers of the Towne or place where such Offence shalbe given.

And be it further likewise Enacted by the Authority and consent aforesaid That every person and persons within this Province that shall at any time hereafter prophane the Sabbath or Lords day called Sunday by frequent swearing, drunkennes or by any uncivill or disorderly recreacion, or by working on that day when absolute necessity doth not require it shall for every such first offence forfeit 2s 6d sterling or the value thereof, and for the second offence 5s sterling or the value thereof, and for the third offence and soe for every time he shall offend in like manner afterwards 10s sterling or the value thereof. And in case such offender and offenders shall not have sufficient goods or chattells within this Province to satisfy any of the said Penalties respectively hereby imposed for prophaning the Sabbath or Lords day called Sunday as aforesaid, That in Every such case the partie soe offending shall for the first and second offence in that kinde be imprisoned till hee or shee shall publickly in open Court before the cheife Commander Judge or Magistrate, of that County Towne or precinct where such offence shalbe committed acknowledg the Scandall and offence he hath in that respect given against God and the good and civill Governement of this Province, And for the third offence and for every time after shall also bee publickly whipt.

And whereas the inforceing of the conscience in matters of Religion hath frequently fallen out to be of dangerous Consequence in those commonwealthes where it hath been practised, And for the more quiett and peaceable governement of this Province, and the better to preserve mutuall Love and amity amongst the Inhabitants thereof, Be it Therefore also by the Lord Proprietary with the advise and consent of this Assembly Ordeyned and enacted (except as in this present Act is before Declared and sett forth) that noe person or persons whatsoever within this Province, or the Islands, Ports, Harbors, Creekes, or havens thereunto belonging professing to beleive in Jesus Christ, shall from henceforth bee any waies troubled, Molested or discountenanced for or in respect of his or her religion nor in the free exercise thereof within this Province or the Islands thereunto belonging nor any way compelled to the beleife or exercise of any other Religion against his or her consent, soe as they be not unfaithfull to the Lord Proprietary, or molest or conspire against the civill Governement established or to bee established in this Province under him or his heires. And that all and every person and persons that shall presume Contrary to this Act and the true intent and meaning thereof directly or indirectly either in person or estate willfully to wrong disturbe trouble or molest any person whatsoever within this Province professing to beleive in Jesus Christ for or in respect of his or her religion or the free exercise thereof within this Province other than is provided for in this Act that such person or persons soe offending, shalbe compelled to pay trebble damages to the party soe wronged or molested, and for every such offence shall also forfeit 20s sterling in money or the value thereof, half thereof for the use of the Lord Proprietary, and his heires Lords and Proprietaries of this Province, and the other half for the use of the party soe wronged or molested as aforesaid, Or if the partie soe offending as aforesaid shall refuse or bee unable to recompense the party soe wronged, or to satisfy such fyne or forfeiture, then such Offender shalbe severely punished by publick whipping and imprisonment during the pleasure of the Lord Proprietary, or his Lieutenant or cheife Governor of this Province for the tyme being without baile or maineprise.

And bee it further alsoe Enacted by the authority and consent aforesaid That the Sheriff or other Officer or Officers from time to time to bee appointed and authorized for that purpose, of the County Towne or precinct where every particular offence in this present Act conteyned shall happen at any time to bee committed and whereupon there is hereby a forfeiture fyne or penalty imposed shall from time to time distraine and seise the goods and estate of every such person soe offending as aforesaid against this present Act or any part thereof, and sell the same or any part thereof for the full satisfaccion of such forfeiture, fine, or penalty as aforesaid, Restoring unto the partie soe offending the Remainder or overplus of the said goods or estate after such satisfaccion soe made as aforesaid.

The freemen have assented.

Source

Maryland Act Concerning Religion, The Avalon Project, Yale Law School, Lillian Goldman Law Library: http://avalon.law.yale.edu/18th_century/maryland _toleration.asp

Further Reading

Bonomi, Patricia U. *Under the Cope of Heaven: Religion, Society, and Politics in Colonial America.* New York: Oxford University Press, 1986.

Curran, Robert Emmett. *Papist Devils: Catholics in British America, 1574–1783.* Washington: Catholic University of America Press, 2014.

Farrelly, Maura Jane. *Papist Patriots: The Making of an American Catholic Identity.* New York: Oxford University Press, 2012.

WILLIAM PENN,
*FRAME OF GOVERNMENT OF PENNSYLVANIA
AND LAWS AGREED UPON IN ENGLAND* (1682)

The contradictions in the life of the English Quaker leader William Penn (1644–1718) continue to fascinate scholars and students of history. Although Quakers emphasized the virtues of peace and harmony, Penn seemed to relish insulting and humiliating his theological opponents. His brash defense of his renegade faith brought down the wrath of the established Church of England and led to a prison sentence in the Tower of London. Quakerism also stressed simplicity, yet Penn lived the lavish life of a gentleman, incurring ruinous debts in the process. Penn's desire for religious freedom and his need for money led him to found the New World colony of Pennsylvania.

These excerpts from the *Frame of Government* shed light on Penn's conception of religion in the new settlement. The full document lays out a broader system of government for Pennsylvania and has been considered one of the founding texts of American democracy. As in the Maryland Toleration Act, the religious freedom envisioned here is narrow by modern standards, owing much to the model of religious establishment that dominated European politics. Even Penn, a member of a radical dissenting group, worked within that model.

Penn ultimately counted his colonial venture a failure. It never became a Quaker spiritual idyll, nor did it make its founder very much money (he continued to have financial troubles and even served a stint in debtors' prison). Still, Penn's challenge to Anglican spiritual authority makes him an important figure in the colonial world of religion and politics.

William Penn, *Frame of Government of Pennsylvania
and Laws Agreed Upon in England*

The frame of the government of the province of Pensilvania, in America: together with certain laws agreed upon in England, by the Governor and divers freemen of the aforesaid province. To be further explained and confirmed there, by the first provincial Council, that shall be held, if they see meet.

THE PREFACE
When the great and wise God had made the world, of all his creatures, it pleased him to chuse man his Deputy to rule it: and to fit him for so

great a charge and trust, he did not only qualify him with skill and power, but with integrity to use them justly. This native goodness was equally his honour and his happiness, and whilst he stood here, all went well; there was no need of coercive or compulsive means; the precept of divine love and truth, in his bosom, was the guide and keeper of his innocency. But lust prevailing against duty, made a lamentable breach upon it; and the law, that before had no power over him, took place upon him, and his disobedient posterity, that such as would not live comformable to the holy law within, should fall under the reproof and correction of the just law without, in a Judicial administration.

This the Apostle teaches in divers of his epistles: "The law (says he) was added because of transgression." In another place, "Knowing that the law was not made for the righteous man; but for the disobedient and ungodly, for sinners, for unholy and prophane, for murderers, for whoremongers, for them that defile themselves with mankind, and for man-stealers, for lyers, for perjured persons," &c., but this is not all, he opens and carries the matter of government a little further: "Let every soul be subject to the higher powers; for there is no power but of God. The powers that be are ordained of God: whosoever therefore resisteth the power, resisteth the ordinance of God. For rulers are not a terror to good works, but to evil: wilt thou then not be afraid of the power? do that which is good, and thou shalt have praise of the same." "He is the minister of God to thee for good." "Wherefore ye must needs be subject, not only for wrath, but for conscience sake."

This settles the divine right of government beyond exception, and that for two ends: first, to terrify evil doers: secondly, to cherish those that do well; which gives government a life beyond corruption, and makes it as durable in the world, as good men shall be. So that government seems to me a part of religion itself, a filing sacred in its institution and end. For, if it does not directly remove the cause, it crushes the effects of evil, and is as such, (though a lower, yet) an emanation of the same Divine Power, that is both author and object of pure religion; the difference lying here, that the one is more free and mental, the other more corporal and compulsive in its operations: but that is only to evil doers; government itself being otherwise as capable of kindness, goodness and charity, as a more private society. They weakly err, that think there is no other use of government, than correction, which is the coarsest part of it: daily experience tells us, that the care and regulation of many other affairs, more soft, and daily necessary, make up much of the greatest part of government; and which must have followed the peopling of the world, had Adam never fell, and will continue among men, on earth, under the highest attainments they may arrive at, by the coming of the blessed Second Adam, the Lord from heaven. Thus much of government in general, as to its rise and end.

For particular frames and models, it will become me to say little; and comparatively I will say nothing. My reasons are:

First. That the age is too nice and difficult for it; there being nothing the wits of men are more busy and divided upon. It is true, they seem to agree to the end, to wit, happiness; but, in the means, they differ, as to divine, so to this human felicity; and the cause is much the same, not always want of light and knowledge, but want of using them rightly. Men side with their passions against their reason, and their sinister interests have so strong a bias upon their minds, that they lean to them against the good of the things they know.

Secondly. I do not find a model in the world, that time, place, and some singular emergences have not necessarily altered; nor is it easy to frame a civil government, that shall serve all places alike.

Thirdly. I know what is said by the several admirers of monarchy, aristocracy and democracy, which are the rule of one, a few, and many, and are the three common ideas of government, when men discourse on the subject. But I chuse to solve the controversy with this small distinction, and it belongs to all three: Any government is free to the people under it (whatever be the frame) where the laws rule, and the people are a party to those laws, and more than this is tyranny, oligarchy, or confusion.

But, lastly, when all is said, there is hardly one frame of government in the world so ill designed by its first founders, that, in good hands, would not do well enough; and story tells us, the best, in ill ones, can do nothing that is great or good; witness the Jewish and Roman states. Governments, like clocks, go from the motion men give them; and as governments are made and moved by men, so by them they are ruined too. Wherefore governments rather depend upon men, than men upon governments. Let men be good, and the government cannot be bad; if it be ill, they will cure it. But, if men be bad, let the government be never so good, they will endeavor to warp and spoil it to their turn.

I know some say, let us have good laws, and no matter for the men that execute them: but let them consider, that though good laws do well, good men do better: for good laws may want good men, and be abolished or evaded [*invaded* in Franklin's print] by ill men but good men will never want good laws, nor suffer ill ones. It is true, good laws have some awe upon ill ministers, but that is where they have not power to escape or abolish them, and the people are generally wise and good: but a loose and depraved people (which is the question) love laws and an administration like themselves. That, therefore, which makes a good constitution, must keep it, vie: men of wisdom and virtue, qualities, that because they descend not with worldly inheritances, must be carefully propagated by a virtuous education of youth; for which after ages will owe more to the care and prudence of founders, and the successive magistracy, than to their parents, for their private patrimonies.

These considerations of the weight of government, and the nice and various opinions about it, made it uneasy to me to think of publishing the ensuing frame and conditional laws, forseeing both the censures, they will meet with, from melt of differing humours and engagements, and the occasion they may give of discourse beyond my design.

But, next to the power of necessity, (which is a solicitor, that will take no denial) this induced me to a compliance, that we have (with reverence to God, and good conscience to men) to the best of our skill, contrived and composed the frame and laws of this government, to the great end of all government, viz: To support power in reverence with the people, and to secure the people from the abuse of power; that they may be free by their just obedience, and the magistrates honourable, for their just administration: for liberty without obedience is confusion, and obedience without liberty is slavery. To carry this evenness is partly owing to the constitution, and partly to the magistracy: where either of these fail, government will be subject to convulsions; but where both are wanting, it must be totally subverted; then where both meet, the government is like to endure. Which I humbly pray and hope God will please to make the lot of this of Pensilvania. Amen.

[. . .]

LAWS AGREED UPON IN ENGLAND, &C.

[. . .]

XXXIV. That all Treasurers, Judges, Masters of the Rolls, Sheriffs, Justices of the Peace, and other officers and persons whatsoever, relating to courts, or trials of causes or any other service in the government; and all Members elected to serve in provincial Council and General Assembly, and all that have right to elect such Members, shall be such as possess faith in Jesus Christ, and that are not convicted of ill fame, or unsober and dishonest conversation, and that are of one and twenty years of age, at least; and that all such so qualified, shall be capable of the said several employments and privileges, as aforesaid.

XXXV. That all persons living in this province, who confess and acknowledge the one Almighty and eternal God, to be the Creator, Upholder and Ruler of the world; and that hold themselves obliged in conscience to live peaceably and justly in civil society, shall, in no ways, be molested or prejudiced for their religious persuasion, or practice, in matters of faith and worship, nor shall they be compelled, at any time, to frequent or maintain any religious worship, place or ministry whatever.

XXXVI. That, according to the good example of the primitive Christians, and the case of the creation, every first day of the week, called the Lord's day, people shall abstain from their common daily labour, that they may the better dispose themselves to worship God according to their understandings.

XXXVII. That as a careless and corrupt administration of justice draws the wrath of God upon magistrates, so the wildness and looseness of the people provoke the indignation of God against a country: therefore, that all such offences against God, as swearing, cursing, lying, prophane talk-ing, drunkenness, drinking of healths, obscene words, incest, sodomy, rapes, whoredom, fornication, and other uncleanness (not to be repeated) all treasons, misprisions, murders, duels, felony, seditions, maims, forc-ible entries, and other violences, to the persons and estates of the inhabi-tants within this province; all prizes, stage-plays, cards, dice, May-games, gamesters, masques, revels, bull-battings, cock-fightings, bear-battings, and the like, which excite the people to rudeness, cruelty, looseness, and irreligion, shall be respectively discouraged, and severely punished, ac-cording to the appointment of the Governor and freemen in provincial Council and General Assembly; as also all proceedings contrary to these laws, that are not here made expressly penal.

Source

William Penn, *Frame of Government of Pennsylvania and Laws Agreed Upon in England*, The Avalon Project, Yale Law School, Lillian Goldman Law Library: http://avalon.law.yale.edu/17th_century/pa04.asp#1

Further Reading

Dunn, Richard S., and Mary Maples Dunn, eds. *The World of William Penn.* Philadelphia: University of Pennsylvania Press, 1986.

Frost, J. William. *A Perfect Freedom: Religious Liberty in Pennsylvania.* New York: Cambridge University Press, 1990.

JAMES MADISON, "MEMORIAL AND REMONSTRANCE AGAINST RELIGIOUS ASSESSMENTS" (1785)

In the heady years between the Declaration of Independence in 1776 and the ratification of the federal Constitution in 1789, each state cre-ated its own political charters. These documents reveal that the con-cept of religious establishment, though weakening, was still very much alive. Some states had a system of "multiple establishment," in which citizens could be taxed to support one of a number of authorized churches, while officeholders were often required to declare their be-lief in some combination of God, Jesus, and the Christian scriptures.

In the powerful state of Virginia, the defenders of religious es-tablishment debated advocates for a more thoroughgoing religious freedom. The conflict came to a head with legislator Patrick Henry's proposal for a tax to subsidize "teachers of the Christian religion." Christianity, Henry asserted, "hath a natural tendency to correct the morals of men, restrain their vices, and preserve the peace of society."

His bill was quite mild, favoring the general category of "Christians" rather than a specific church, but it still provided state support for religion.

James Madison fought vigorously to defeat Henry's bill. Once allies in the cause of independence, these two eminent politicians became fierce rivals after the war. Madison was a chief architect of the federal Constitution, while Henry adopted a staunch anti-Federalist position. They battled, too, on the subject of religion. Eventually Henry's plan went down to defeat, and Thomas Jefferson's Act for Establishing Religious Freedom in Virginia became law in 1786. In many ways, the debate in Virginia provides a window onto the logic of the First Amendment to the Constitution.

Madison's *Memorial and Remonstrance*, originally published anonymously during the debate over Henry's plan, still stands as one of the most penetrating arguments for religious freedom in American history. Madison was deeply influenced by the Enlightenment, the intellectual movement that sought to elevate reason as a guide to human affairs. While French Enlightenment thinkers developed an intense hostility to religion, the English and Scottish Enlightenments more often sought to harmonize reason and faith, an approach that was influential among the founders. Madison's writing here bears some similarities to John Locke's 1689 *Letter Concerning Toleration*, a key Enlightenment text that extolled tolerance as a possible way out of England's destructive wars of religion. In addition, *Memorial and Remonstrance* shows Madison's general concern for the dangers of unchecked power, a theme seen also in the Federalist Papers that he authored.

James Madison, "Memorial and Remonstrance against Religious Assessments"

We the subscribers, citizens of the said Commonwealth, having taken into serious consideration, a Bill printed by order of the last Session of General Assembly, entitled "A Bill establishing a provision for Teachers of the Christian Religion," and conceiving that the same if finally armed with the sanctions of a law, will be a dangerous abuse of power, are bound as faithful members of a free State to remonstrate against it, and to declare the reasons by which we are determined. We remonstrate against the said Bill,

1. Because we hold it for a fundamental and undeniable truth, "that Religion or the duty which we owe to our Creator and the manner of discharging it, can be directed only by reason and conviction, not by force or violence." The Religion then of every man must be left to the conviction and conscience of every man; and it is the right of every man to

exercise it as these may dictate. This right is in its nature an unalienable right. It is unalienable, because the opinions of men, depending only on the evidence contemplated by their own minds cannot follow the dictates of other men: It is unalienable also, because what is here a right towards men, is a duty towards the Creator. It is the duty of every man to render to the Creator such homage and such only as he believes to be acceptable to him. This duty is precedent, both in order of time and in degree of obligation, to the claims of Civil Society. Before any man can be considered as a member of Civil Society, he must be considered as a subject of the Governour of the Universe: And if a member of Civil Society, who enters into any subordinate Association, must always do it with a reservation of his duty to the General Authority; much more must every man who becomes a member of any particular Civil Society, do it with a saving of his allegiance to the Universal Sovereign. We maintain therefore that in matters of Religion, no mans right is abridged by the institution of Civil Society and that Religion is wholly exempt from its cognizance. True it is, that no other rule exists, by which any question which may divide a Society, can be ultimately determined, but the will of the majority; but it is also true that the majority may trespass on the rights of the minority.

2. Because if Religion be exempt from the authority of the Society at large, still less can it be subject to that of the Legislative Body. The latter are but the creatures and vicegerents of the former. Their jurisdiction is both derivative and limited: it is limited with regard to the co-ordinate departments, more necessarily is it limited with regard to the constituents. The preservation of a free Government requires not merely, that the metes and bounds which separate each department of power be invariably maintained; but more especially that neither of them be suffered to overleap the great Barrier which defends the rights of the people. The Rulers who are guilty of such an encroachment, exceed the commission from which they derive their authority, and are Tyrants. The People who submit to it are governed by laws made neither by themselves nor by an authority derived from them, and are slaves.

3. Because it is proper to take alarm at the first experiment on our liberties. We hold this prudent jealousy to be the first duty of Citizens, and one of the noblest characteristics of the late Revolution. The free men of America did not wait till usurped power had strengthened itself by exercise, and entangled the question in precedents. They saw all the consequences in the principle, and they avoided the consequences by denying the principle. We revere this lesson too much soon to forget it. Who does not see that the same authority which can establish Christianity, in exclusion of all other Religions, may establish with the same ease any particular sect of Christians, in exclusion of all other Sects? that the same authority which can force a citizen to contribute three pence only of his property for the support of any one establishment, may force him to conform to any other establishment in all cases whatsoever?

4. Because the Bill violates that equality which ought to be the basis of every law, and which is more indispensible, in proportion as the validity or expediency of any law is more liable to be impeached. If "all men are by nature equally free and independent," all men are to be considered as entering into Society on equal conditions; as relinquishing no more, and therefore retaining no less, one than another, of their natural rights. Above all are they to be considered as retaining an "*equal* title to the free exercise of Religion according to the dictates of Conscience." Whilst we assert for ourselves a freedom to embrace, to profess and to observe the Religion which we believe to be of divine origin, we cannot deny an equal freedom to those whose minds have not yet yielded to the evidence which has convinced us. If this freedom be abused, it is an offence against God, not against man: To God, therefore, not to man, must an account of it be rendered. As the Bill violates equality by subjecting some to peculiar burdens, so it violates the same principle, by granting to others peculiar exemptions. Are the Quakers and Menonists the only sects who think a compulsive support of their Religions unnecessary and unwarrantable? Can their piety alone be entrusted with the care of public worship? Ought their Religions to be endowed above all others with extraordinary privileges by which proselytes may be enticed from all others? We think too favorably of the justice and good sense of these denominations to believe that they either covet pre-eminences over their fellow citizens or that they will be seduced by them from the common opposition to the measure.

5. Because the Bill implies either that the Civil Magistrate is a competent Judge of Religious Truth; or that he may employ Religion as an engine of Civil policy. The first is an arrogant pretension falsified by the contradictory opinions of Rulers in all ages, and throughout the world: the second an unhallowed perversion of the means of salvation.

6. Because the establishment proposed by the Bill is not requisite for the support of the Christian Religion. To say that it is, is a contradiction to the Christian Religion itself, for every page of it disavows a dependence on the powers of this world: it is a contradiction to fact; for it is known that this Religion both existed and flourished, not only without the support of human laws, but in spite of every opposition from them, and not only during the period of miraculous aid, but long after it had been left to its own evidence and the ordinary care of Providence. Nay, it is a contradiction in terms; for a Religion not invented by human policy, must have pre-existed and been supported, before it was established by human policy. It is moreover to weaken in those who profess this Religion a pious confidence in its innate excellence and the patronage of its Author; and to foster in those who still reject it, a suspicion that its friends are too conscious of its fallacies to trust it to its own merits.

7. Because experience witnesseth that ecclesiastical establishments, instead of maintaining the purity and efficacy of Religion, have had a

contrary operation. During almost fifteen centuries has the legal establishment of Christianity been on trial. What have been its fruits? More or
less in all places, pride and indolence in the Clergy, ignorance and servil-
ity in the laity, in both, superstition, bigotry and persecution. Enquire of
the Teachers of Christianity for the ages in which it appeared in its greatest lustre; those of every sect, point to the ages prior to its incorporation
with Civil policy. Propose a restoration of this primitive State in which
its Teachers depended on the voluntary rewards of their flocks, many of
them predict its downfall. On which Side ought their testimony to have
greatest weight, when for or when against their interest?

8. Because the establishment in question is not necessary for the support of Civil Government. If it be urged as necessary for the support of
Civil Government only as it is a means of supporting Religion, and it be
not necessary for the latter purpose, it cannot be necessary for the former.
If Religion be not within the cognizance of Civil Government how can
its legal establishment be necessary to Civil Government? What influence
in fact have ecclesiastical establishments had on Civil Society? In some
instances they have been seen to erect a spiritual tyranny on the ruins of
the Civil authority; in many instances they have been seen upholding the
thrones of political tyranny: in no instance have they been seen the guardians of the liberties of the people. Rulers who wished to subvert the public liberty, may have found an established Clergy convenient auxiliaries.
A just Government instituted to secure & perpetuate it needs them not.
Such a Government will be best supported by protecting every Citizen in
the enjoyment of his Religion with the same equal hand which protects
his person and his property; by neither invading the equal rights of any
Sect, nor suffering any Sect to invade those of another.

9. Because the proposed establishment is a departure from that generous policy, which, offering an Asylum to the persecuted and oppressed
of every Nation and Religion, promised a lustre to our country, and an
accession to the number of its citizens. What a melancholy mark is the
Bill of sudden degeneracy? Instead of holding forth an Asylum to the persecuted, it is itself a signal of persecution. It degrades from the equal rank
of Citizens all those whose opinions in Religion do not bend to those of
the Legislative authority. Distant as it may be in its present form from the
Inquisition, it differs from it only in degree. The one is the first step, the
other the last in the career of intolerance. The magnanimous sufferer under this cruel scourge in foreign Regions, must view the Bill as a Beacon
on our Coast, warning him to seek some other haven, where liberty and
philanthrophy in their due extent, may offer a more certain repose from
his Troubles.

10. Because it will have a like tendency to banish our Citizens. The
allurements presented by other situations are every day thinning their
number. To superadd a fresh motive to emigration by revoking the liberty

which they now enjoy, would be the same species of folly which has dishonoured and depopulated flourishing kingdoms.

11. Because it will destroy that moderation and harmony which the forbearance of our laws to intermeddle with Religion has produced among its several sects. Torrents of blood have been spilt in the old world, by vain attempts of the secular arm, to extinguish Religious discord, by proscribing all difference in Religious opinion. Time has at length revealed the true remedy. Every relaxation of narrow and rigorous policy, wherever it has been tried, has been found to assuage the disease. The American Theatre has exhibited proofs that equal and compleat liberty, if it does not wholly eradicate it, sufficiently destroys its malignant influence on the health and prosperity of the State. If with the salutary effects of this system under our own eyes, we begin to contract the bounds of Religious freedom, we know no name that will too severely reproach our folly. At least let warning be taken at the first fruits of the threatened innovation. The very appearance of the Bill has transformed "that Christian forbearance, love and charity," which of late mutually prevailed, into animosities and jealousies, which may not soon be appeased. What mischiefs may not be dreaded, should this enemy to the public quiet be armed with the force of a law?

12. Because the policy of the Bill is adverse to the diffusion of the light of Christianity. The first wish of those who enjoy this precious gift ought to be that it may be imparted to the whole race of mankind. Compare the number of those who have as yet received it with the number still remaining under the dominion of false Religions; and how small is the former! Does the policy of the Bill tend to lessen the disproportion? No; it at once discourages those who are strangers to the light of revelation from coming into the Region of it; and countenances by example the nations who continue in darkness, in shutting out those who might convey it to them. Instead of Levelling as far as possible, every obstacle to the victorious progress of Truth, the Bill with an ignoble and unchristian timidity would circumscribe it with a wall of defence against the encroachments of error.

13. Because attempts to enforce by legal sanctions, acts obnoxious to so great a proportion of Citizens, tend to enervate the laws in general, and to slacken the bands of Society. If it be difficult to execute any law which is not generally deemed necessary or salutary, what must be the case, where it is deemed invalid and dangerous? And what may be the effect of so striking an example of impotency in the Government, on its general authority?

14. Because a measure of such singular magnitude and delicacy ought not to be imposed, without the clearest evidence that it is called for by a majority of citizens, and no satisfactory method is yet proposed by which the voice of the majority in this case may be determined, or its influence secured. "The people of the respective counties are indeed requested to signify their opinion respecting the adoption of the Bill to the next Ses-

sion of Assembly." But the representation must be made equal, before the voice either of the Representatives or of the Counties will be that of the people. Our hope is that neither of the former will, after due consideration, espouse the dangerous principle of the Bill. Should the event disappoint us, it will still leave us in full confidence, that a fair appeal to the latter will reverse the sentence against our liberties.

15. Because finally, "the equal right of every citizen to the free exercise of his Religion according to the dictates of conscience" is held by the same tenure with all our other rights. If we recur to its origin, it is equally the gift of nature; if we weigh its importance, it cannot be less dear to us; if we consult the "Declaration of those rights which pertain to the good people of Virginia, as the basis and foundation of Government," it is enumerated with equal solemnity, or rather studied emphasis. Either then, we must say, that the Will of the Legislature is the only measure of their authority; and that in the plenitude of this authority, they may sweep away all our fundamental rights; or, that they are bound to leave this particular right untouched and sacred: Either we must say, that they may controul the freedom of the press, may abolish the Trial by Jury, may swallow up the Executive and Judiciary Powers of the State; nay that they may despoil us of our very right of suffrage, and erect themselves into an independent and hereditary Assembly or, we must say, that they have no authority to enact into law the Bill under consideration. We the Subscribers say, that the General Assembly of this Commonwealth have no such authority: And that no effort may be omitted on our part against so dangerous an usurpation, we oppose to it, this remonstrance; earnestly praying, as we are in duty bound, that the Supreme Lawgiver of the Universe, by illuminating those to whom it is addressed, may on the one hand, turn their Councils from every act which would affront his holy prerogative, or violate the trust committed to them: and on the other, guide them into every measure which may be worthy of his [blessing, may re]dound to their own praise, and may establish more firmly the liberties, the prosperity and the happiness of the Commonwealth.

Source

James Madison, "Memorial and Remonstrance against Religious Assessments, [ca. 20 June] 1785," *The Papers of James Madison*, vol. 8, *10 March 1784–28 March 1786*, ed. Robert A. Rutland and William M. E. Rachal. Chicago: University of Chicago Press, 1973, 295–306.

The Papers of James Madison, Founders Online, National Archives (http://founders.archives.gov/documents/Madison/01-08-02-0163 [last update: 2015-03-20]).

Further Reading

Kidd, Thomas S. *God of Liberty: A Religious History of the American Revolution*. New York: Basic, 2010.

Lambert, Frank. *The Founding Fathers and the Place of Religion in America.* Princeton: Princeton University Press, 2003.

THOMAS JEFFERSON, ACT FOR ESTABLISHING RELIGIOUS FREEDOM IN VIRGINIA (1786)

Long after his death, Thomas Jefferson's religious views remain elusive. In a time before television, the Internet, and investigative journalism, presidents did not always feel the obligation to state their faith commitments publicly. Existing evidence suggests, though, that Jefferson was an unorthodox Christian, if he could be classed as a Christian at all.

His Enlightenment views led Jefferson to deny much of the supernatural content of Christianity, most dramatically in the so-called Jefferson Bible, which he produced by literally cutting out selected passages from the Gospels to create his own version of scripture. In Jefferson's patchwork narrative, Jesus is an exemplary moral teacher, his miracles are excised, and he remains in the tomb without resurrection. Understandably, Jefferson never published this potentially scandalous revision. His Act for Establishing Religious Freedom, however, defeated Patrick Henry's proposal for supporting Christian teachers and became the law of Virginia.

Jefferson's audacious approach to challenging received traditions informed the Act for Establishing Religious Freedom (a clever play on the concept of religious "establishment"). Insisting that "Almighty God hath created the mind free" and that truth can be grasped through "free argument and debate," Jefferson championed a faith amenable to the dictates of reason. His law also insisted that the sphere of religious belief, while important, existed somewhat apart from the rights of political citizenship, an idea Jefferson amplified with the metaphor of a "wall of separation between Church & State" in his 1802 letter to the Danbury Baptists.

These assertions are full of ambiguities and contradictions, but they form one crucial foundation of American ideas about how religion and politics should operate. For his part, Jefferson considered the Act for Establishing Religious Freedom to be one of his three greatest achievements, along with the founding of the University of Virginia and the Declaration of Independence.

Thomas Jefferson, Act for Establishing
Religious Freedom in Virginia

I. WHEREAS Almighty God hath created the mind free; that all attempts to influence it by temporal punishments or burthens, or by civil incapacitations, tend only to beget habits of hypocrisy and meanness, and are a departure from the plan of the Holy author of our religion, who being Lord both of body and mind, yet chose not to propagate it by coercions on either, as was in his Almighty power to do; that the impious presumption of legislators and rulers, civil as well as ecclesiastical, who being themselves but fallible and uninspired men, have assumed dominion over the faith of others, setting up their own opinions and modes of thinking as the only true and infallible, and as such endeavouring to impose them on others, hath established and maintained false religions over the greatest part of the world, and through all time; that to compel a man to furnish contributions of money for the propagation of opinions which he disbelieves, is sinful and tyrannical; that even the forcing him to support this or that teacher of his own religious persuasion, is depriving him of the comfortable liberty of giving his contributions to the particular pastor, whose morals he would make his pattern, and whose powers he feels most persuasive to righteousness, and is withdrawing from the ministry those temporary rewards, which proceeding from an approbation of their personal conduct, are an additional incitement to earnest and unremitting labours for the instruction of mankind; that our civil rights have no dependence on our religious opinions, any more than our opinions in physics or geometry; that therefore the proscribing any citizen as unworthy the public confidence by laying upon him an incapacity of being called to offices of trust and emolument, unless he profess or renounce this or that religious opinion, is depriving him injuriously of those privileges and advantages to which in common with his fellow-citizens he has a natural right; that it tends only to corrupt the principles of that religion it is meant to encourage, by bribing with a monopoly of wor[l]dly honours and emoluments, those who will externally profess and conform to it; that though indeed these are criminal who do not withstand such temptation, yet neither are those innocent who lay the bait in their way; that to suffer the civil magistrate to intrude his powers into the field of opinion, and to restrain the profession or propagation of principles on supposition of their ill tendency, is a dangerous fallacy, which at once destroys all religious liberty, because he being of course judge of that tendency will make his opinions the rule of judgment; and approve or condemn the sentiments of others only as they shall square with or differ from his own; that it is time enough for the rightful purposes of civil government, for its officers to interfere when principles break out into overt acts against peace and good order; and finally, that truth is great and will prevail if left to herself, that she is the proper and sufficient antagonist to error, and has nothing to fear from the conflict, unless by human interposition disarmed of her natural weapons, free argument and debate, errors ceasing to be dangerous when it is permitted freely to contradict them:

II. *Be it enacted by the General Assembly,* That no man shall be compelled to frequent or support any religious worship, place, or ministry whatsoever, nor shall be enforced, restrained, molested, or burthened in his body or goods, nor shall otherwise suffer on account of his religious opinions or belief; but that all men shall be free to profess, and by argument to maintain, their opinion in matters of religion, and that the same shall in no wise diminish, enlarge, or affect their civil capacities.

III. And though we well know that this assembly elected by the people for the ordinary purposes of legislation only, have no power to restrain the acts of succeeding assemblies, constituted with powers equal to our own, and that therefore to declare this act to be irrevocable would be of no effect in law; yet we are free to declare, and do declare, that the rights hereby asserted are of the natural rights of mankind, and that if any act shall be hereafter passed to repeal the present, or to narrow its operation such act will be an infringement of natural right.

Source

Thomas Jefferson, Act for Establishing Religious Freedom in Virginia, [31 October] 1785, *The Papers of James Madison,* vol. 8, *10 March 1784–28 March 1786,* ed. Robert A. Rutland and William M. E. Rachal (Chicago: University of Chicago Press, 1973), 399–402.

Founders Online, National Archives (http://founders.archives.gov/documents/Madison/01-08-02-0206 [last update: 2015–03–20]).

Further Reading

Dreisbach, Daniel L. *Thomas Jefferson and the Wall of Separation between Church and State.* New York: New York University Press, 2002.

Gaustad, Edwin S. *Sworn on the Altar of God: A Religious Biography of Thomas Jefferson.* Grand Rapids, MI: Eerdmans, 1996.

Porterfield, Amanda. *Conceived in Doubt: Religion and Politics in the New American Nation.* Chicago: University of Chicago Press, 2012.

2

Slavery and the Civil War

A merican religion flourished in the decades between the Revolution and the Civil War. In particular, evangelical Christianity rose to a position of unprecedented cultural authority.
Although wide variations exist, evangelicals are generally defined by
four attributes: an emphasis on individual conversion; a focus on the
saving power of Jesus's death and Resurrection; an appeal to the Bible
as the ultimate religious authority; and an enthusiasm for witnessing
and activism. Evangelical beliefs and styles were shared by a number of Protestant denominations, most prominently the Methodists
and Baptists. The evangelical movement grew exponentially in these
years: the Methodists went from having virtually no American presence at the time of the Revolution to being the largest Protestant denomination by the end of the nineteenth century.

As evangelicalism expanded, political discourse increasingly adopted evangelical overtones. Nowhere was this more true than in the
conflict over American slavery, the focus of this section. Slavery became tied up with religion for several reasons. One was the "humanitarian revolution" between about 1750 and 1850 that produced, for
the first time, systematic condemnation of human bondage, including an American abolitionist movement that drew on Christian ethics
and imagery. Meanwhile, slaves and free blacks, like white Americans,
began to convert to evangelical Christianity in large numbers. This
shift presented a religious problem: when slaves practiced "supersti-
tious" African faiths, it was easy to dismiss their humanity, but what
obligations did masters have to their enslaved brothers and sisters in
Christ?

The conflict over slavery ultimately tempered the optimism of early evangelicalism and blighted the new nation's political hopes. The Civil War was precipitated less by religion as such than by southern slaveowners' attempts to expand the institution of slavery to new territories and by northerners' determination to resist this menacing "Slave Power." However, as the readings in this section show, proslavery and antislavery forces alike appealed to Christian doctrine to back up their positions. Religious division exposed deep rifts between northern and southern whites, with some of the most successful white Protestant denominations splitting along sectional lines: the Presbyterians in 1837, the Methodists in 1844, and the Baptists in 1845. When the Civil War began, Americans' faith commitments convinced them of the righteousness of their causes and justified unprecedented destruction. The violence of the war and its incomplete resolution of the question of African American freedom would haunt the nation long after the last shot was fired.

FREDERICK DOUGLASS, "LOVE OF GOD, LOVE OF MAN, LOVE OF COUNTRY" (1847)

Frederick Douglass (1818–1895) was a forceful critic of the acceptance of slavery by American Christianity and the American government. Born a slave in Maryland, Douglass escaped to the North in 1838 and became a leading abolitionist. In speeches and in a trio of autobiographies, the most famous of which was the *Narrative of the Life of Frederick Douglass*, he related his firsthand experience of slavery's horrors.

Although Douglass is a well-known historical figure, his interest in religion is seldom emphasized. Yet his condemnation of organized Christianity for its support of slavery, especially but not only in the South, was a common theme of his speaking and writing. "Of all slaveholders with whom I have ever met," he asserted in the *Narrative*, "religious slaveholders are the worst. I have ever found them the meanest and basest, the most cruel and cowardly." Douglass explained in detail the ways that slaveholders used religion to degrade and control their slaves. Still, he insisted that he was a Christian believer, and soon after he escaped slavery he joined a Methodist church.

This address to an antislavery audience emphasizes the differences that Douglass finds between proslavery and antislavery religion. He quotes extensively from eighteenth-century proslavery sermons by the

Anglican bishop Thomas Bacon, sermons that were recirculated by the Episcopal bishop of Virginia William Meade. Douglass therefore refers to them as Meade's words (the Butler and Stout volume referenced with this reading contains more discussion of this source material). Alongside the content of his address, one also catches some of the style of Douglass's performance, a glimpse into the oral culture of antebellum politics that, in the absence of recording technology, has mostly been lost. As for his analysis of the relationship of religion to racial equality, it would later be extended by other African American leaders, including W. E. B. Du Bois and Martin Luther King, Jr., documented in this volume.

Frederick Douglass, "Love of God, Love of Man, Love of Country"

I like radical measures, whether adopted by Abolitionists or slaveholders. I do not know but I like them better when adopted by the latter. Hence I look with pleasure upon the movements of Mr. Calhoun and his party. I rejoice at any movement in the slave States with reference to this system of Slavery. Any movement there will attract attention to the system—a system, as Junius once said to Lord Granby, "which can only pass without condemnation as it passes without observation." I am anxious to have it seen of all men: hence I am delighted to see any effort to prop up the system on the part of the slaveholders. It serves to bring up the subject before the people; and hasten the day of deliverance. It is meant otherwise. I am sorry that it is so. Yet the wrath of man may be made to praise God. He will confound the wisdom of the crafty, and bring to naught the counsels of the ungodly. The slaveholders are now marshalling their hosts for the propagation and extension of the institution—Abolitionists, on the other hand, are marshalling their forces not only against its propagation and extension, but against its very existence. Two large classes of the community, hitherto unassociated with the Abolitionists, have come up so far towards the right as to become opposed to the farther extension of the crime. I am glad to hear it. I like to gaze upon these two contending armies, for I believe it will hasten the dissolution of the present unholy Union, which has been justly stigmatized as "a covenant with death, an agreement with hell." I welcome the bolt, either from the North or the South, which shall shatter this Union; for under this Union lie the prostrate forms of three millions with whom I am identified. In consideration of their wrongs, of their sufferings, of their groans, I welcome the bolt, either from the celestial or from the infernal regions, which shall sever this Union in twain. Slaveholders are promoting it—Abolitionists are doing so. Let it come, and when it does, our land will rise up from an incubus;

her brightness shall reflect against the sky, and shall become the beacon light of liberty in the Western world. She shall then, indeed, become "the land of the free and the home of the brave."

For sixteen years, Wm. Lloyd Garrison and a noble army of the friends of emancipation have been labouring in season and out of season, amid smiles and frowns, sunshine and clouds, striving to establish the conviction through this land, that to hold and traffic in human flesh is a sin against God. They have been somewhat successful; but they have been in no wise so successful as they might have been, had the men and women at the North rallied around them as they had a right to hope from their profession. They have had to contend not only with skilful politicians, with a deeply prejudiced and pro-slavery community, but with eminent Divines, Doctors of Divinity, and Bishops. Instead of encouraging them as friends, they have acted as enemies. For many days did Garrison go the rounds of the city of Boston to ask of the ministers the poor privilege of entering their chapels and lifting up his voice for the dumb. But their doors were bolted, their gates barred, and their pulpits hermetically sealed. It was not till an infidel hall was thrown open, that the voice of dumb millions could be heard in Boston.

I take it that all who have heard at all on this subject, are well convinced that the stronghold of Slavery is in the pulpit. Say what we may of politicians and political parties, the power that holds the keys of the dungeon in which the bondman is confined, is the pulpit. It is that power which is dropping, dropping, constantly dropping on the ear of this people, creating and moulding the moral sentiment of the land. This they have sufficiently under their control that they can change it from the spirit of hatred to that of love to mankind. That they do it not, is evident from the results of their teaching. The men who wield the blood-clotted cow-skin come from our Sabbath schools in the Northern States. Who act as slave-drivers? The men who go forth from our own congregations here. Why, if the Gospel were truly preached among us, a man would as soon think of going into downright piracy as to offer himself as a slave-driver.

In Farmington, two sons of members of the Society of Friends are coolly proposing to go to the South and engage in the honourable office of slave-driving for a thousand dollars a year. People at the North talk coolly of uncles, cousins, and brothers, who are slaveholders, and of their coming to visit them. If the Gospel were truly preached here, you would as soon talk of having an uncle or brother a brothel keeper as a slaveholder; for I hold that every slaveholder, no matter how pure he may be, is a keeper of a house of ill-fame. Every kitchen is a brothel, from that of Dr. Fuller's to that of James K. Polk's. (Applause.) I presume I am addressing a virtuous audience—I presume I speak to virtuous females— and I ask you to consider this one feature of Slavery. Think of a million of females absolutely delivered up into the hands of tyrants, to do what they will with them—to dispose of their persons in any way they see fit. And so entirely are they at the disposal of their masters, that if they raise their hands against them, they may be put to death for daring to resist their infernal aggression.

We have been trying to make this thing appear sinful. We have not been able to do so yet. It is not admitted, and I hardly know how to argue against it. I confess that the time for argument seems almost gone by. What do the people want? Affirmation upon affirmation,—denunciation upon denunciation,—rebuke upon rebuke?

We have men in this land now advocating evangelical flogging. I hold in my hand a sermon recently published by Rev. Bishop Meade, of Virginia. Before I read that part in favour of evangelical flogging, let me read a few extracts from another part, relating to the duties of the slave. The sermon, by the way, was published with a view of its being read by *Christian* masters to their slaves. White black birds! (Laughter.)

(Mr. Douglass here assumed a most grotesque look, and with a canting tone of voice, read as follows:)

"Having thus shown you the chief duties you owe to your great Master in Heaven, I now come to lay before you the duties you owe to your masters and mistresses on earth. And for this you have one general rule that you ought always to carry in your minds, and that is, to *do all service for them, as if you did it for God himself.* Poor creatures! you little consider when you are idle, and neglectful of your master's business; when you steal, waste, and hurt any of their substance; when you are saucy and impudent; when you are telling them lies and deceiving them; or when you prove stubborn and sullen, and will not do the work you are set about, without stripes and vexation; you do not consider, I say, that what faults you are guilty of towards your masters and mistresses, are faults done against God himself, who hath set your masters and mistresses over you in his own stead, and expects that you will do for them just as you would do for him. And pray, do not think that I want to deceive you, when I tell you that your *masters and mistresses are God's overseers*; and that if you are faulty towards them, God himself will punish you severely for it."

This is some of the Southern religion. Do you not think you would "grow in grace and in the knowledge of the truth?"—(Applause.)

I come now to evangelical flogging. There is nothing said about flogging—that word is not used. It is called correction; and that word as it is understood at the North, is some sort of medicine. (Laughter.) Slavery has always sought to hide itself under different names. The mass of the people call it "our peculiar institution." There is no harm in that. Others call it (they are the more pious sort), "our Patriarchal institution." (Laughter.) Politicians have called it "our social system;" and people in social life have called it "our domestic institution." Abbot Lawrence has

recently discovered a new name for it—he calls it "unenlightened labour." (Laughter.) The Methodists in their last General Conference, have
invented a new name—"the impediment." (Laughter.) To give you some
idea of evangelical flogging, under the name of correction, there are laws
of this description,—"any white man killing a slave shall be punished as
though he shall have killed a white person, unless such a slave die under
moderate correction." It commences with a plain proposition.

"Now when correction is given you, you either deserve it, or you do
not deserve it."—(Laughter.)

That is very plain, almost as safe as that of a certain orator:—"Ladies
and Gentlemen, it is my opinion, my deliberate opinion, after a long consideration of the whole matter, that as a general thing, all other things
being equal, there are fewer persons to be found in towns sparsely popu-
lated, than in larger towns more thickly settled." (Laughter.) The Bishop
goes on to say—

"Whether you really deserve it or not," (one would think that would
make some difference), "it is your duty, and Almighty God requires that
you bear it patiently. You may perhaps think that this is a hard doctrine,"
(and it admits of little doubt), "but if you consider it right you must needs
think otherwise of it." (It is clear as mud. I suppose he is now going to
reason them into the propriety of being flogged evangelically.) "Suppose
you deserve correction; you cannot but see it is just and right you should
meet with it. Suppose you do not, or at least so much or so severe; you
perhaps have escaped a great many more, and are at last paid for all. Suppose you are quite innocent; is it not possible you may have done some
other bad thing which was never discovered, and Almighty God would
not let you escape without punishment one time or another? Ought you
not in such cases to give glory to Him?" (Glory!) (Much laughter.)

I am glad you have got to the point that you can laugh at the religion
of such fellows as this Doctor. There is nothing that will facilitate our
cause more than getting the people to laugh at that religion which brings
its influence to support traffic in human flesh. It has deceived us so long
that it has overawed us.

For a long time when I was a slave, I was led to think from hearing
such passages as "servants obey, &c." that if I dared to escape, the wrath
of God would follow me. All are willing to acknowledge my right to be
free; but after this acknowledgment, the good man goes to the Bible and
says, "After all I see some difficulty about this thing. You know, after the
deluge, there was Shem, Ham, and Japhet; and you know that Ham was
black and had a curse put upon him; and I know not but it would be
an attempt to thwart the purposes of Jehovah, if these men were set at
liberty." It is this kind of religion I wish to have you laugh at—it breaks
the charm there is about it. If I could have the men at this meeting who
hold such sentiments and could hold up the mirror to let them see them-

selves as others see them, we should soon make head[way] against this pro-slavery religion.

I dwell mostly upon the religious aspects, because I believe it is the religious people who are to be relied on in this Anti-Slavery movement. Do not misunderstand my railing—do not class me with those who despise religion—do not identify me with the infidel. I love the religion of Christianity—which cometh from above—which is pure, peaceable, gentle, easy to be entreated, full of good fruits, and without hypocrisy. I love that religion which sends its votaries to bind up the wounds of those who have fallen among thieves. By all the love I bear to such a Christianity as this, I hate that of the Priest and Levite, that with long-faced Phariseeism goes up to Jerusalem and worship[s], and leaves the bruised and wounded to die. I despise that religion that can carry Bibles to the heathen on the other side of the globe and withhold them from heathen on this side—which can talk about human rights yonder and traffic in human flesh here. I love that which makes its votaries do to others as they would that others should do to them. I hope to see a revival of it—thank God it is revived. I see revivals of it in the absence of the other sort of revivals. I believe it to be confessed now, that there has not been a sensible man converted after the old sort of way, in the last five years. Le Roy Sunderland, the mesmerizer, has explained all this away, so that Knapp and others who have converted men after that sort have failed.

There is another religion. It is that which takes off fetters instead of binding them on—that breaks every yoke—that lifts up the bowed down. The Anti-Slavery platform is based on this kind of religion. It spreads its table to the lame, the halt, and the blind. It goes down after a long neglected race. It passes, link by link till it finds the lowest link in humanity's chain—humanity's most degraded form in the most abject condition. It reaches down its arm and tells them to stand up. This is Anti-Slavery—this is Christianity. It is reviving gloriously among the various denominations. It is threatening to supercede those old forms of religion having all of the love of God and none of man in it. (Applause.)

I now leave this aspect of the subject and proceed to inquire into that which probably must be the inquiry of every honest mind present. I trust I do not misjudge the character of my audience when I say they are anxious to know in what way they are contributing to uphold Slavery.

The question may be answered in various ways. I leave the outworks of political parties and social arrangements, and come at once to the Constitution, to which I believe all present are devotedly attached—I will not say all, for I believe I know some, who, however they may be disposed to admire some of the beautiful truths set forth in that instrument, recognize its pro-slavery features, and are ready to form a republic in which there shall be neither tyrant nor slave. The Constitution I hold to be radically and essentially slaveholding, in that it gives the physical and numerical

power of the nation to keep the slave in his chains, by promising that
that power shall in any emergency be brought to bear upon the slave, to
crush him in obedience to his master. The language of the Constitution
is you shall be a slave or die. We know it is such, and knowing it we are
not disposed to have part nor lot with that Constitution. For my part I
had rather that my right hand should wither by my side than cast a ballot
under the Constitution of the United States.

Then, again, in the clause concerning fugitives—in this you are implicated. Your whole country is one vast hunting ground from Texas to
Maine.

Ours is a glorious land; and from across the Atlantic we welcome those
who are stricken by the storms of despotism. Yet the damning fact remains, there is not a rood of earth under the stars and the eagle on your
flag, where a man of my complexion can stand free. There is no mountain
so high, no plain so extensive, no spot so sacred, that it can secure to me
the right of liberty. Wherever waves the star-spangled banner there the
bondman may be arrested and hurried back to the jaws of Slavery. This
is your "land of the free," your "home of the brave." From Lexington,
from Ticonderoga, from Bunker Hill, where rises that grand shaft with
its cap stone in the clouds, ask, in the name of the first blood that spurted
in behalf of freedom, to protect the slave from the infernal clutches of his
master. That petition would be denied, and he bid go back to the tyrant.

I never knew what freedom was till I got beyond the limits of the
American eagle. When I first rested my head on a British Island, I felt that
the eagle might scream, but from its talons and beak I was free, at least
for a time. No slaveholder can clutch me on British soil. There I could
gaze the tyrant in the face and with the indignation of a tyrant in my
look, wither him before me. But republican, Christian America will aid
the tyrant in catching his victim.

I know this kind of talk is not agreeable to what are called patriots
Indeed some have called me a traitor. That profanely religious Journal
"The Olive Branch," edited by the Rev. Mr. Norris, recommended that
I be hung as a traitor. Two things are necessary to make a traitor. One
is, he shall have a country. (Laughter and applause.) I believe if I had a
country, I should be a patriot. I think I have all the feelings necessary—all
the moral material, to say nothing about the intellectual. I do not know
that I ever felt the emotion, but sometimes thought I had a glimpse of it.
When I have been delighted with the little brook that passes by the cottage in which I was born,—with the woods and the fertile fields, I felt a
sort of glow which I suspect resembles a little what they call patriotism.
I can look with some admiration on your wide lakes, your fertile fields,
your enterprise, your industry, your many lovely institutions. I can read
with pleasure your Constitution to establish justice, and secure the blessings of liberty to posterity. Those are precious sayings to my mind. But

when I remember that the blood of four sisters and one brother, is making fat the soil of Maryland and Virginia,—when I remember that an aged grandmother who has reared twelve children [for] the Southern market, and these one after anot[her a]s they arrived at the most interesting age, were torn from her bosom,—when I remember that when she became too much racked for toil, she was turned out by a professed Christian master to grope her way in the darkness of old age, literally to die with none to help her, and the institutions of this country sanctioning and sanctifying this crime, I have no words of eulogy, I have no patriotism. How can I love a country where the blood of my own blood, the flesh of my own flesh, is now toiling under the lash?—America's soil reddened by the stain from woman's shrinking flesh.

No, I make no pretension to patriotism. So long as my voice can be heard on this or the other side of the Atlantic, I will hold up America to the lightning scorn of moral indignation. In doing this, I shall feel myself discharging the duty of a true patriot; for he is a lover of his country who rebukes and does not excuse its sins. It is righteousness that exalteth a nation while sin is a reproach to any people.

But to the idea of what you at the North have to do with Slavery. You furnish the bulwark of protection, and promise to put the slaves in bondage. As the American Anti-Slavery Society says, "if you will go on branding, scourging, sundering family ties, trampling in the dust your down trodden victims, you must do it at your own peril." But if you say, "we of the North will render you no assistance: if you still continue to trample on the slave, you must take the consequences," I tell you the matter will soon be settled.

I have been taunted frequently with the want of valour: so has my race, because we have not risen upon our masters. It is adding insult to injury to say this. You belong to 17,000,000, with arms, with means of locomotion, with telegraphs. We are kept in ignorance—three millions to seventeen. You taunt us with not being able to rescue ourselves from your clutch. Shame on you! Stand aside—give us fair play—leave us with the tyrants, and then if we do not take care of ourselves, you may taunt us. I do not mean by this to advocate war and bloodshed. I am not a man of war. The time was when I was. I was then a slave: I had dreams, horrid dreams of freedom through a sea of blood. But when I heard of the Anti-Slavery movement, light broke in upon my dark mind. Bloody visions fled away, and I saw the star of liberty peering above the horizon. Hope then took the place of desperation, and I was led to repose in the arms of Slavery. I said, I would suffer rather than do any act of violence—rather than that the glorious day of liberty might be postponed.

Since the light of God's truth beamed upon my mind, I have become a friend of that religion which teaches us to pray for our enemies—which, instead of shooting balls into their hearts, loves them. I would not hurt a hair of a slaveholder's head. I will tell you what else I would not do. I would not stand around the slave with my bayonet pointed at his breast, in order to keep him in the power of the slaveholder.

I am aware that there are many who think the slaves are very well off, and that they are very well treated, as if it were possible that such a thing could be. A man happy in chains! Even the eagle loves liberty.

> "Go, let a cage, with grates of gold,
> And pearly roof, the eagle hold;
> Let dainty viands be his fare,
> And give the captive tenderest care;
> But say, in luxury's limits pent,
> Find you the king of birds *content*?
> No, oft he'll sound the startling shriek,
> And dash the grates with angry beak.
> Precarious freedom's far more dear,
> Than all the prison's pamp'ring cheer!
> He longs to see his eyrie's seat,
>   Some cliff on ocean's lonely shore,
> Whose old bare top the tempests beat,
> And round whose base the billows roar,
> When tossed by gales, they yawn like graves,—
> He longs for joy to skim those waves;
> Or rise through tempest-shrouded air,
> All thick and dark, with wild winds swelling,
> To brave the lightning's lurid glare,
> And talk with thunders in their dwelling."

As with the eagle, so with man. No amount of attention or finery, no dainty dishes can be a substitute for liberty. Slaveholders know this, and knowing it, they exclaim—"The South are surrounded by a dangerous population, degraded, stupid savages, and if they could but entertain the idea that immediate, unconditional death would not be their portion, they would rise at once and enact the St. Domingo tragedy. But they are held in subordination by the consciousness that the whole nation would rise and crush them." Thus they live in constant dread from day to day.

Friends, Slavery must be abolished, and that can only be done by enforcing the great principles of justice. Vainly you talk about voting it down. When you have cast your millions of ballots, you have not reached the evil. It has fastened its root deep into the heart of the nation, and nothing but God's truth and love can cleanse the land. We must change the moral sentiment. Hence we ask you to support the Anti-Slavery Society. It is not an organization to build up political parties, or churches, nor to pull them down, but to stamp the image of Anti-Slavery truth upon the community. Here we may all do something.

> "In the world's broad field of battle,
>   In the bivouac of life,
> Be not like dumb driven cattle—
>   Be a hero in the strife."

Source

Frederick Douglass, "Love of God, Love of Man, Love of Country: An Address Delivered in Syracuse, New York, on 24 September 1847," *National Anti-Slavery Standard*, October 28, 1847. In *The Frederick Douglass Papers*, ed. John W. Blassingame (New Haven: Yale University Press, 1979), 2:93–105.

Further Reading

Butler, Jon, and Harry S. Stout, eds. *Religion in American History: A Reader.* New York: Oxford University Press, 1998.

Shulman, George. *American Prophecy: Race and Redemption in American Political Culture.* Minneapolis: University of Minnesota Press, 2008.

Stauffer, John. *The Black Hearts of Men: Radical Abolitionists and the Transformation of Race.* Cambridge, MA: Harvard University Press, 2004.

GEORGE ARMSTRONG, *THE CHRISTIAN DOCTRINE OF SLAVERY* (1857)

In response to denunciations by abolitionists such as Frederick Douglass, defenders of slavery constructed an increasingly robust religious justification of it. George Armstrong (1813–1899), a scholar and longtime pastor at the First Presbyterian Church of Norfolk, Virginia, wrote one of the most elaborate and controversial vindications of the institution as a response to the antislavery writings of Albert Barnes, a northern Presbyterian pastor. As the provocative title *The Christian Doctrine of Slavery* suggests, Armstrong argued that the ownership of human property in the American South was not only permitted but endorsed by biblical teaching. The book's concluding chapter, reprinted here, is entitled "God's Work in God's Way" and stresses the mutual obligations of slaves and masters, noting in particular that slaveholders ought to share the Gospel with those they held in bondage.

When the Civil War came, Armstrong continued to defend the Southern cause. Early in the war, his victory sermon "The Good Hand of Our God upon Us; a Thanksgiving Sermon, Preached on the

Occasion of the Victory of Manassas" celebrated the apparent divine favor that had helped the Confederacy. After the war, he became a respected Presbyterian scholar, most notable for his theological opposition to the emerging theories of evolution.

George Armstrong, *The Christian Doctrine of Slavery*

Where God has appointed a *work* for his Church, he has generally appointed the *way* also in which that work is to be done. And where this is the case, the Church is as much bound to respect the one appointment as the other. Both the *work* of the Church and the *way* are often more distincly set forth in the life and ministry of Christ and his Apostles than in any positive precept. But in whatever manner the will of God is made known, that will is law to his Church.

In the case of a race of men in slavery, the *work* which God has appointed his Church—as we learn it, both from the example and the precepts of inspired men—is to labor to secure in them a Christian life on earth and meetness for his heavenly kingdom. The African slave, in our Southern States, may be deeply degraded; the debasing effects of generations of sin may, at first sight, seem to have almost obliterated his humanity, yet is he an immortal creature; one for whom God the Son died; one whom God the Spirit can re-fashion, so as to make him a worthy worshipper among God's people on earth, and a welcome worshipper among the ransomed in heaven; one whom God the Father waiteth to receive as a returning prodigal to his heart and to his home. And the commission of the Church, "go ye into *all the world* and preach the Gospel *to every creature*," sends her a messenger of glad tidings to him as truly as to men far above him in the scale of civilization. On this point there can be no difference of opinion among God's people, North or South, who intelligently take the word of God as their "only rule of faith and obedience." This is *the work* of God, assigned by him to his Church, in so far as the slave race among us is concerned.[1]

In what *way* is this work to be done? We answer, By preaching the same Gospel of God's grace alike to the master and the slave; and when there is credible evidence given that this Gospel has been received in faith, to admit them, master and slave, into the same Church—the Church of the Lord Jesus Christ, in which "there is neither bond nor free"—and to seat them at the same table of the Lord, that drinking of the same cup, and eating of the same loaf, they may witness to the world their communion in the body and blood of the same Saviour. And having received

---

1. "The fact is, that the great duty of the South is not emancipation, but improvement. The former is obligatory only as a means to an end, and therefore only under circumstances where it would promote that end."—*Hodge's Essays and Reviews*, p. 507.

them into the same Church, to teach them the duties belonging to their several "callings" out of the same Bible, and subject them to the discipline prescribed by the same law, the law of Christ. And this, the teaching of the Church, is to be addressed not to her members only, but to the world at large; and her discipline of her members is to be exercised not in secret, but before the world, that the light which God has given her may appear unto all men. This is just *the way* in which Christ and his Apostles dealt with slavery. The instructions they have given us in their life and in their writings prohibit any other.

In this way must the Church labor to make "good masters and good slaves," just as she labors to make "good husbands, good wives, good parents, good children, good rulers, good subjects." With the ultimate effect of this upon the civil and political condition of the slave the Church has nothing directly to do. If the ultimate effect of it be the emancipation of the slave—we say—in God's name, "let it come." "If it be of God, we *cannot*"—and we *would not* if we could—"overthrow it, lest haply we be found even to fight against God." If the ultimate effect be the perpetuation of slavery divested of its incidental evils—a slavery in which the master shall be required, by the laws of man as well as that of God, "to give unto the slave that which is just and equal," and the slave to render to the master a cheerful obedience and hearty service—we say, let slavery continue. It may be, that such a slavery, regulating the relations of capital and labor, though implying some deprivation of personal liberty, will prove a better defense of the poor against the oppression of the rich, than the too great freedom in which capital is placed in many of the free States of Europe at the present day. Something of this kind is what the masses of free laborers in France are clamoring for under the name of *"the right to labor."* Something of this kind would have protected the ejected tenantry of the Duke of Sutherland against the tyranny which drove them forth from the home of their childhood, and quenched the fire upon many a hearth-stone, and converted once cultivated fields into sheep-walks. It may be, that *Christian slavery* is God's solution of the problem about which the wisest statesmen of Europe confess themselves "at fault." "Bonds make free, be they but righteous bonds. Freedom enslaves, if it be an unrighteous freedom."[2]

To this way of dealing with slavery, thus clearly pointed out in God's word, does God in his providence "shut us up," for years to come. None but the sciolist in political philosophy can regard the problem of emancipation—even granting that this were the aim which the Christian citizen should have immediately in view—as a problem of easy solution. And thoughtful Christian men at the North, it has seemed to us, often lose

---

2. For an able examination of this point the reader is referred to *Slavery and the Remedy; or, Principles and Suggestions for a Remedial Code,* by Samuel Nott. Crocker and Brewster, publishers, Boston.

sight of the greatest difficulties in the case. It is comparatively an easy matter to devise a scheme of emancipation in which all the just rights and the well-being of the master shall be provided for. But how shall we, as God-fearing men, provide for the just rights and well-being of the emancipated slave? To leave the partially civilized slave race, in a state of freedom, in contact with a much more highly civilized race, as all history testifies, is inevitable destruction to the former. Their writ of enfranchisement is their death-warrant. To remove one hundredth part of the annual increase of the slave race to Liberia, year by year, would soon quench for ever that light of Christian civilization which a wise philanthropy has kindled upon the dark coast of Africa. How shall we provide for the well-being of the enfranchised slave? Here is the real difficulty in the problem of emancipation.

We mean to express no opinion respecting the feasibility of the future emancipation of the slave race among us. As we stated in the outset, our purpose is to introduce no question on which the Bible does not give us specific instruction. And we have referred to the question of emancipation—a question which it belongs to the State, and not the Church, to settle—simply that the reader may see how completely God's word and God's providence are "at one," in so far as the present duty of the Church is concerned. Is slavery to continue? We want the best of Christian masters and the best of Christian slaves, that it may prove a blessing to both the one and the other. Is ultimate emancipation before us? We want the best of Christian masters to devise and carry out the scheme by which it shall be effected, and the best of Christian slaves, that their emancipation may be an enfranchisement indeed. And this is just what the Bible plan of dealing with slavery aims at. The *future* may be hidden from view in "the clouds and darkness" with which God oft veils his purposes; but there is light—heaven's light—upon the *present*. And it is with the *present alone* we have immediately to do.

This is *one way* of dealing with slavery, and so firmly convinced are we that it is *God's way* for his Church that we cannot abandon it.

Another way proposed is—confounding the distinction between slavery itself and the incidental evils which attach to it in our country, and at the present day, under the guise of dealing with "AMERICAN SLAVERY;" in *the teaching* of the Church to denounce slave-holding as a SIN, as "evil, always evil, and only evil," (*Barnes' Notes*, 1 *Cor. VII.* 21); and in *the discipline* of the Church to treat it as an *"offence,"* and "detach the Church from it, as it is detached from piracy, intemperance, theft, licentiousness, and duelling," (*Church and State*, p. 193), and so labor directly to put an end to slavery throughout the world.[3]

3. That the reader may see how far Dr. B. would go, we give his own words:—"A Church, located in the midst of slavery, though all its members may be wholly unconnected with slavery, yet owes an important duty to society and to God in reference to the system, and its mission will not be accomplished

To all this we object—

FIRST.—There is a radical fallacy involved in the use which is made of the expression, "AMERICAN SLAVERY."

By American Slavery, Dr. Barnes means—and the same is true of all anti-slavery writers whose works we have seen—the aggregate of, 1. Slavery itself; and, 2. The incidental evils which attach to it in this country and at this day, considered as inseparable—an indivisible unit. This treatment of the subject is—

1. *Unphilosophical.* Nothing is more real than the distinction, as set forth in the writings of Paul. (See § 15.) The fact that Dr. B. can write about Jewish slavery, and Roman slavery, and American slavery, as different the one from the others, shows that there must be something common to them all, to which we give the common name, Slavery; and something peculiar to each, which we designate by the adjuncts Jewish, Roman, American. Dr. B. admits that Roman slavery, as encountered by the Apostles in their day, was far more cruel and oppressive than American slavery now is[4]—that is, that much of the incidental evil which once attached to slavery has disappeared. If much has already disappeared, why may not all that remains disappear in like manner? The change that has taken place, has been effected under the benign influence of Christianity. And just as certainly as we believe that Christianity is from God, and is destined to a final triumph in the world, just so certainly do we believe that slavery—if it is to continue to exist—must continue to be modified by it, until all its incidental evils disappear.

2. It is *unscriptural.* By this we mean, 1. It is an essentially different way of approaching the subject of slavery from that adopted by the Apostles. Paul never wrote a line respecting *Jewish* slavery—meaning thereby, slavery itself and the incidental evils which attached to it in his day and among the Jews—or *Roman* slavery; nor does he give the Churches any directions couched in any such language as this. He writes about *slavery,*

---

by securing merely *the sanctification of its members, or even by drawing within its fold multitudes of those who shall be saved. Its primary work as a Church* may have reference to an existing evil within its own geographical limits. The burden which is laid upon it may not be primarily *the conversion of the heathen,* or the diffusion of *Bibles* and *tracts* abroad. *The* work which God requires it to do, and for which *specifically* it has been planted there, may be to diffuse a definite moral influence in respect to an existing evil institution."—*Church and Slavery,* p. 21. To convert the Church of God into a kind of "omnibus," in which everything called a moral reform shall be free to ride on an equal footing with the Gospel, as Dr. B. does, (see *Church and Slavery,* pp. 159–164,) is bad enough; but thus actually to turn the Gospel out upon the *pave,* until a certain moral reform has been carried home, is at once the folly of fanaticism and the fanaticism of folly.

4. "It is proper to concede that the state of things was such that they (the Apostles) must have encountered it (slavery), and that it then had all the features of cruelty, oppression, and wrong, which can ever exist to make it repellant to any of the feelings of humanity, or revolting to the principles of a Christian. It is fair that the advocates of the system should have all the advantage which can be derived from the fact that the Apostles found it in its most odious forms, and in such circumstances as to make it proper that they should regard and treat it as an evil, if Christianity regards it as such at all."—*Scriptural Views of Slavery,* pp. 250, 251. Compare this with a quotation given a little further on.

which he treats as neither a sin nor an offence; and about *certain evils* attaching to slavery as he encountered it, which he treats as sinful, and requires the Church, in her own proper sphere, to labor to correct. 2. It ignores the very ground upon which the whole method of dealing with slavery prescribed in the Word of God, is predicated.

In his introduction to his "Scriptural Views of Slavery," Dr. Barnes justifies his dealing, as he does, with what he calls "American Slavery," upon the ground—

1. That slavery, as it exists in the United States, is slavery divested of all the incidental evils of which it is reasonable to suppose Christianity will ever divest it; and hence, that all which now belongs to it, ought to be considered as, for all practical purposes, essential to the system.[5]

This is certainly "American glorification"—"with a witness." For ourselves, we love our country; and we feel an honest, patriotic pride in her standing among the nations. But God forbid, that we should entertain the thought that her social institutions, either in law or in fact, shall never be brought more fully under the control of God's truth than they now are; that the wife shall never be better protected against the wrong often inflicted by the profligate husband; and the child against the cruelty of the drunken father; and all this, without destroying the essential character of the marital and parental relations as set forth in the Word of God; that our heart and our home relations shall never be more thoroughly Christian than they now are. And so, too, with respect to slavery. Had we heard such sentiments as those just quoted from Dr. B., as part of a Fourth-of-July oration of some beardless Sophomore, we could have comforted ourselves with the reflection—increasing years may give the young man wisdom. That we should read them from the pen of one who must have "gray hairs here and there upon him," we can account for only by calling to mind what Paul tells us of the effects of feeding on "unwholesome words."—1 *Tim: VI. 3.*

2. That what we have designated as God's way of dealing with slavery, is dealing with slavery *in the abstract,* and not as a *practical* matter.[6]

---

5. "If any system of slavery is sanctioned by the Bible, it may be presumed that that which exists in the United States is. This is a Christian land—a land, to a degree elsewhere unknown, under the influence of the Christian religion. It could hardly be hoped that a state of society could be found, in which slavery could be better developed, or where its developments would more accord with the principles of the Bible, than in our own land."—*Scriptural Views,* p. 14.

6. It is a subject of not unfrequent complaint, that, in the examination of this subject (slavery), the adversaries of the system endeavor to show that slavery *as it exists* in our country, is contrary to the Bible, instead of confining themselves to the naked question, whether slavery *in the abstract* is right or wrong. The very question—the only one that is of any *practical* importance to us—is, whether slavery as it exists in the United States is, or is not, in accordance with the principles and the spirit of Christianity. As an *abstract* matter, there might indeed be some interest attached to the inquiry whether slavery, as it existed in the Roman empire in the time of the Apostles, or in Europe in the Middle Ages, was in accordance with the spirit of the Christian religion.—*Scriptural Views,* pp. 10, 12.

What Dr. B.'s idea of dealing with an institution *in the abstract* is, we know not. We have always supposed that such dealing implied the abstraction—i.e., the taking away or neglecting for the time being—something, either essential or incidental, belonging to such institution. But, surely, we are not dealing with American slavery—slavery as it exists among us, in the abstract—in any such sense as this.

We take slavery, and the whole of slavery, just as it exists among us, and, after Paul's example, we separate it into—1. That which is *essential,* i.e., that which must continue if slavery continues; and, 2. That which is *incidental,* i.e., that which may disappear and slavery yet remain. Having done this, we then, *in discussion, deal with both parts.* We prove from the Word of God, that the *first* is not in violation of his law; and show, just as clearly, that much of the *second* is in violation of that law. And *in our practical dealing with it, as a Church, we deal with both parts.* The *first* we treat as not sinful, and require both the parties to conform to its obligations; much of the *second*—and just so much of it as is in violation of God's law—we prohibit, with all the authority given by Christ to his Church over her members, and in every proper way, we seek to remove from the world at large. If this is not dealing with slavery in its entirety, we ask, What is? If this is dealing with slavery *in the abstract,* we ask, What have we abstracted?

We remarked that there was "a radical fallacy involved in the use which is made of the expression, *American slavery,*" as used by Dr. B. and other writers of the same school. The reader will now see just what was meant by that remark.

The only meaning which can properly attach to the expression *American slavery,* is that of slavery as it exists in these United States of America. In this sense of the expression, we are dealing with American slavery, just as truly, and just as fully, and with far more of *practical* wisdom, we think, than Dr. B. is. The real difference between us is, that we distinguish between that which is essential and that which is incidental, as Paul did, and we deal with each as it deserves, as Paul did. Whilst Dr. B., neglecting this distinction, and thus, practically, treating all as essential, deals with it as an indivisible unit; and he does this under the guise of dealing with "American slavery," foisting upon that phrase; in addition to its proper meaning, the idea of the indivisible unity of the mass. To take such a course as this, when the issues in question are such as they are, is nothing more nor less than "a begging of the question."

SECOND.—We object to the course proposed by Dr. B. and others, for dealing with slavery, because it requires the Church to obtrude herself into the province of the State, and this, in direct violation of the ordinance of God. A course which has never been taken in times past, without disastrous consequences to the Church which did the wrong, as well as to the State which permitted the wrong to be done. Many a thing which it is right and proper, and even the duty of the Christian citizen, in this our free country, to do, the Church, as such, has no right to intermeddle with. It is, doubtless, the duty of the Christian citizen, for example, to use all proper means to inform himself respecting the qualifications of candidates for office, and having thus informed himself, to vote for the one whom he believes will best discharge the duties of the office. But will any Christian man, hence contend that it is right for the preacher, in the pulpit and on the Sabbath, to discuss the claims of rival candidates, and the Church, in her councils to direct her members how to vote? The Church and State has each its own appropriate sphere of operation assigned it of God, and neither can innocently intrude herself into the province of the other.

THIRD.—It leads to tampering with God's truth, and "wresting the Scripture," as Dr. B. has done in his Notes, by the application to them of principles and methods of interpretation, which destroy all certainty in human language. In order to make the Bible declare that slave-holding is a sin, when it plainly teaches just the contrary;[7] and to teach in the Church doctrines which we are forbidden to teach under the most solemn sanctions. (See § 12.) This course has led not a few, once fair and promising members of the Church, and even ministers, into open "blasphemy;" and Paul teaches us, that such is its natural tendency, (1 Tim. VI. 4.) We have no desire to walk in their way, or to meet their doom.

FOURTH.—It requires us to quit a method of dealing with slavery which has worked well in time past—all of real advantage to the slave that has ever been done by the Church has been done in this way—and to substitute for it a method which, to say the least of it, is a mere experiment, and an experiment which has wrought nothing but harm to the slave[8]

---

7. "As it appears to us too clear to admit of either denial or doubt, that the Scriptures do sanction slave-holding; that under the old dispensation it was expressly permitted by divine command, and under the New Testament is nowhere forbidden or denounced, but on the contrary, acknowledged to be consistent with the Christian character and profession, (that is, consistent with justice, mercy, holiness, love to God, and love to man;) to declare it to be a heinous crime is a direct impeachment of the Word of God." "When Southern Christians are told that they are guilty of a heinous crime, worse than piracy, robbery, or murder, because they hold slaves, when they know that Christ and his Apostles never denounced slave-holding as a crime, never called upon men to renounce it as a condition of admission into the Church, they are shocked and offended without being convinced. They are sure that their accusers cannot be wiser or better than their Divine Master, and their consciences are untouched by denunciations which they know if well founded, must affect not them only, but the authors of the religion of the Bible."—Hodge's Essays and Reviews, pp. 503, 484.

8. In illustration of this remark, we quote from Fletcher—"Thirty years ago, we occasionally had schools for negro children; nor was it uncommon for masters to send their favorite young slaves to these schools; nor did such acts excite attention or alarm, and, at the same time, any missionary had free access to that class of our population.

But when we found, with astonishment, that our country was flooded with abolition prints, deeply laden with the most abusive falsehoods, with the obvious design to excite rebellion among the slaves, and to spread assassination and bloodshed through the land; when we found these transient missionaries, mentally too insignificant to foresee the result of their conduct, or wholly careless of the consequences, preaching the same doctrines—these little schools, and the mouths of these missionaries, thus far—and we say this, after watching its operation during a ministry of twenty years, all of it, in God's providence, spent in a slave-holding state.

For all these reasons, we can never adopt this second *way* proposed. GOD'S WORK IN GOD'S WAY, the Church at the South, in common with some portions of the Church at the North also,[9] have inscribed upon their banner; and under that banner do we mean to fight the "Lord's battles," grace assisting us, until he who bid us gird on our armor shall give us leave to put it off. Churches of God may cut us off from their communion. They cannot break our union with Christ, "the Head." Ministers of the Gospel, from whom we have a right to expect better things, may revile us—we "fear God rather than man." "A conscience void of offence before God," is above all price. With this whole subject of slavery, we mean to deal just as Christ and his Apostles dealt—to preach what they preached—to labor as they labored—to govern the Church of God as they governed it—in Christian fellowship and brotherhood with God's people at the North, and in other lands, *if we* MAY:—in faithfulness to Christ, though in opposition to all the world, *if we* MUST.

Source

George D. Armstrong, *The Christian Doctrine of Slavery* (New York: Scribner, 1857), 131–48.

Further Reading

Irons, Charles. *The Origins of Proslavery Christianity: White and Black Evangelicals in Colonial and Antebellum Virginia.* Chapel Hill: University of North Carolina Press, 2008.

Tise, Larry. *Proslavery: A History of the Defense of Slavery in America, 1701–1840.* Athens: University of Georgia Press, 1987.

JULIA WARD HOWE,
"BATTLE HYMN OF THE REPUBLIC" (1862)

Literary and musical sources can sometimes reveal as much about American religion and politics as sermons, speeches, and court cases. The "Battle Hymn of the Republic" sheds light on how participants in the Civil War conceived of God's will and His work in the world. The song itself has a complicated history. It began as a tune sung at

---

were closed. And great was the cry. Dr. Wayland knows whereabout lies the wickedness of these our acts! Let him and his coadjutors well understand that these results, whether for the benefit or injury of the slave, have been brought about by the work of their hand."—*Studies on Slavery*, p. 41.

We could add much of similar character, from our own observation.

9. See the paper adopted by the General Assembly of the Presbyterian Church, O. S., in 1845. (*Assembly's Digest*, pp. 811–813.)

Methodist camp meetings, extolling the joy of salvation: "Say brothers, will you meet us? On Canaan's happy shore?" During the Civil War, new lyrics were added: "John Brown's body lies a-mouldering in the grave, His soul is marching on!" Though the "John Brown" in the song may have originally referred to an unknown Union soldier, the lines soon became associated with the radical abolitionist who raided Harpers Ferry in 1859.

"The John Brown Song" became popular while also causing discomfort among Union leaders, many of whom considered Brown a megalomaniacal fanatic and certainly not an inspiration for the Northern cause. Julia Ward Howe (1819–1910), an abolitionist and suffragist, solved the difficulty. She was inspired to write a poem by her 1861 trip to Washington, DC, where she saw at close range the preparations for war and its deadly results. Her verses, published in the *Atlantic Monthly* in 1862, eventually served as the Union anthem we know today.

"The Battle Hymn of the Republic" is so familiar that few notice its harrowing sanctification of warfare. In Howe's vision, the Lord is present in the fires of the soldiers' camps, Union guns write a "gospel," and the death of soldiers in war is equated with Christ's sacrifice on the cross for the sins of humanity. In the evangelical culture of Civil War America, this was highly compelling imagery.

The "Battle Hymn" has had a long afterlife. Theodore Roosevelt was a great admirer of it. The labor movement used the music for the union song "Solidarity Forever," and after World War I a pacifist wrote the justly forgotten "Peace Hymn of the World" ("Peace and friendliness forever, Good Will and Peace to men"). In 1965, Martin Luther King, Jr. recited Howe's poem at the climax of his speech following the Selma-to-Montgomery march, powerfully invoking the struggle for African American freedom one hundred years earlier.

Julia Ward Howe, "Battle Hymn of the Republic"

Mine eyes have seen the glory of the coming of the Lord:
He is trampling out the vintage where the grapes of wrath are stored;
He hath loosed the fateful lightnings of His terrible swift sword:
　　　His truth is marching on.
CHORUS—Glory, glory, hallelujah!
　　　Glory, glory, hallelujah!
　　　Glory, glory, hallelujah!
　　　Glory, glory, hallelujah!
　　　His truth is marching on.

I have seen Him in the watch-fires of a hundred circling camps;
They have builded Him an altar in the evening dews and damps:
I can read His righteous sentence by the dim and flaring lamps:
        His day is marching on.
  Chorus—Glory, glory, hallelujah, &c.
        His day is marching on.

I have read a fiery gospel writ in burnished rows of steel:
"As ye deal with my contemners, so with you my grace shall deal;
Let the Hero, born of woman, crush the serpent with his heel,
        Since God is marching on."
  Chorus—Glory, glory, hallelujah, &c.
        Since God is marching on.

He has sounded forth the trumpet that shall never call retreat:
He is sifting out the hearts of men before His judgment seat:
Oh, be swift, my soul, to answer Him! be jubilant my feet!
        Our God is marching on!
  Chorus—Glory, glory, hallelujah, &c.
        Our God is marching on!

In the beauty of the lilies Christ was born across the sea,
With a glory in His bosom that transfigures you and me;
As he died to make men holy, let us die to make men free,
        While God is marching on.
  Chorus—Glory, glory, hallelujah, &c.
        While God is marching on.

Source

Julia Ward Howe, "Battle Hymn of the Republic" (1862). Library of Congress, Rare Book and Special Collections Division. http://www.loc.gov/item/amss001991/

Further Reading

"The Battle Hymn of the Republic." *Performing Arts Encyclopedia*. Library of Congress. http://lcweb2.loc.gov/diglib/ihas/loc.natlib.ihas.200000003/default.html

Stauffer, John, and Benjamin Soskis. *The Battle Hymn of the Republic: A Biography of the Song That Marches On*. New York: Oxford University Press, 2013.

ABRAHAM LINCOLN,
SECOND INAUGURAL ADDRESS (1865)

Like Thomas Jefferson, Abraham Lincoln (1809–1865) is usually ranked as one of our greatest presidents. And as with Jefferson,

Lincoln's beliefs are difficult to fit into the prevalent religious currents
of his era. Living in an age of evangelical fervor, he never joined a
church. While Christian leaders North and South confidently claimed
divine sanction for their causes, Lincoln remained ambivalent. "I am
approached," he noted, "with the most opposite opinions and advice,
and that by religious men who are equally certain that they represent
the Divine will."

The presidential campaign of 1864 had shown the nation's widespread disagreements over the war. Although Lincoln was ultimately
reelected in a landslide, he had to fend off a challenge from within
his own party by John Frémont, who represented radical Republican
efforts to make racial equality a central goal of the war. Then he ran
against George McClellan, one of his former generals. By the time
Lincoln gave this speech, the Union appeared to be on the course to
victory, but the character of the postwar era was utterly uncertain.

The Second Inaugural Address reflects both the tumultuous political situation and Lincoln's own complex theology. By modern standards, the speech has a few peculiar features, besides its brevity. Sur-
prisingly, Lincoln says almost nothing about the progress of the war,
omitting discussion of military strategy and instead offering theological reflection, even suggesting that the bloodshed taking place may
be a form of divine judgment. Lincoln suggests that, while God rules
human affairs, His purposes remain somewhat beyond human comprehension. The Second Inaugural Address is considered one of the
most important speeches in American history, but few presidents since
Lincoln have dared to stray so far from the optimistic mood of our
usual public discourse. A month after his inauguration, Lincoln was
assassinated in Ford's Theatre, on April 14, 1865. It was Good Friday,
and so in death, as in life, Lincoln led Americans to believe that their
nation was a part of sacred history.

Abraham Lincoln, Second Inaugural Address

At this second appearing to take the oath of the presidential office,
there is less occasion for an extended address than there was at the
first. Then a statement, somewhat in detail, of a course to be pursued,
seemed fitting and proper. Now, at the expiration of four years, during
which public declarations have been constantly called forth on every
point and phase of the great contest which still absorbs the attention, and engrosses the energies of the nation, little that is new could
be presented. The progress of our arms, upon which all else chiefly

depends, is as well known to the public as to myself; and it is, I trust, reasonably satisfactory and encouraging to all. With high hope for the future, no prediction in regard to it is ventured.

On the occasion corresponding to this four years ago, all thoughts were anxiously directed to an impending civil-war. All dreaded it—all sought to avert it. While the inaugural address was being delivered from this place, devoted altogether to *saving* the Union without war, insurgent agents were in the city seeking to *destroy* it without war— seeking to dissol[v]e the Union, and divide effects, by negotiation. Both parties deprecated war; but one of them would *make* war rather than let the nation survive; and the other would *accept* war rather than let it perish. And the war came.

One eighth of the whole population were colored slaves, not distributed generally over the Union, but localized in the Southern part of it. These slaves constituted a peculiar and powerful interest. All knew that this interest was, somehow, the cause of the war. To strengthen, perpetuate, and extend this interest was the object for which the insurgents would rend the Union, even by war; while the government claimed no right to do more than to restrict the territorial enlargement of it. Neither party expected for the war, the magnitude, or the duration, which it has already attained. Neither anticipated that the *cause* of the conflict might cease with, or even before, the conflict itself should cease. Each looked for an easier triumph, and a result less fundamental and astounding. Both read the same Bible, and pray to the same God; and each invokes His aid against the other. It may seem strange that any men should dare to ask a just God's assistance in wringing their bread from the sweat of other men's faces; but let us judge not that we be not judged. The prayers of both could not be answered; that of neither has been answered fully. The Almighty has His own purposes. "Woe unto the world because of offences! for it must needs be that offences come; but woe to that man by whom the offence cometh!" If we shall suppose that American Slavery is one of those offences which, in the providence of God, must needs come, but which, having continued through His appointed time, He now wills to remove, and that He gives to both North and South, this terrible war, as the woe due to those by whom the offence came, shall we discern therein any departure from those divine attributes which the believers in a Living God always ascribe to Him? Fondly do we hope— fervently do we pray—that this mighty scourge of war may speedily pass away. Yet, if God wills that it continue, until all the wealth piled by the bond-man's two hundred and fifty years of unrequited toil shall be sunk, and until every drop of blood drawn with the lash, shall be paid by another drawn with the sword, as was said three thousand years ago, so still it must be said "the judgments of the Lord, are true and righteous altogether."

With malice toward none; with charity for all; with firmness in the right, as God gives us to see the right, let us strive on to finish the work we are in; to bind up the nation's wounds; to care for him who shall have borne the battle, and for his widow, and his orphan—to do all which may achieve and cherish a just, and a lasting peace, among ourselves, and with all nations.

Source

Abraham Lincoln, Second Inaugural Address, *Collected Works of Abraham Lincoln*, vol. 8 (New Brunswick: Rutgers University Press, 1953). http://quod.lib .umich.edu/l/lincoln/

Further Reading

Faust, Drew Gilpin. *This Republic of Suffering: Death and the American Civil War.* New York: Knopf, 2008.

Foner, Eric. *The Fiery Trial: Abraham Lincoln and American Slavery.* New York: Norton, 2010.

Szasz, Ferenc Morton, and Margaret Connell Szasz. *Lincoln and Religion.* Carbondale, IL: Southern Illinois University Press, 2014.

White, Ronald C., Jr. *Lincoln's Greatest Speech: The Second Inaugural.* New York: Simon and Schuster, 2002.

3

Modernizing America

I n the half-century after the Civil War, the United States became recognizably modern in several key ways. The end of slavery removed the major challenge to industrial capitalism as the reigning system of economic organization. Americans moved from the countryside to towns and cities, becoming by 1920 a predominantly urban society. That urbanization was also a consequence of mass immigration during this period, as millions of new arrivals made the nation far more diverse in ethnic and religious terms than it had ever been. In the intellectual sphere, the natural and social sciences gained increasing sophistication, particularly in the new research universities that were developing across the nation. The suffrage movement transformed political ideas about gender and citizenship, an achievement enshrined in the 1920 constitutional amendment granting women the vote. These changes, and many others, posed formidable challenges to religious authority. In fact, some of the most prominent intellectuals of this era predicted that religion itself, unable to contend with modern life, was entering a period of inexorable decline known as secularization.

Many of the most significant writers on religious politics in this period were not government officials (though they remained important) but reformers who sought to remake Americans' public life. Theologians of the Social Gospel argued that the teachings of Jesus demanded a political response to the poverty and inequality that capitalism produced. Feminists noted that the Bible was deployed to exclude them from leadership in both political and religious institutions. African Americans, violently denied the rights of citizenship after Reconstruction, formed alternative political communities in their churches. In short, the group struggles for power and the visions of a common good that make up politics in the broadest sense existed beyond the realms of legislative debates and presidential speeches.

These readings hint at some reasons why the United States in this era defied many of the assumptions of secularization theory. In Europe, where many of the most prominent theorists worked, religion did in fact enter a period of decline from which it has never recovered. Although religion lost some of its public authority in America as well, creative adaptations helped it survive and even thrive amid what the social critic Walter Lippmann called the "acids of modernity."

REYNOLDS V. UNITED STATES (1878)

Throughout its history, the Church of Jesus Christ of Latter-Day Saints has tested the limits of American religious toleration. In some ways, the Mormons (as LDS church members are usually called) had much in common with mainstream Christianity. After all, Mormons professed faith in God, Jesus Christ, and the Bible, they emphasized moral living and community obligations, and they undertook extensive evangelistic efforts. However, this homegrown American religion diverged sharply from older traditions in a few important ways. First, the Mormons' founder, Joseph Smith, claimed to have discovered a new sacred text, equal in importance to the Bible. The *Book of Mormon* purported to tell the story of ancient America and even recounted the visit of Jesus to the continent, leading Smith's opponents to denounce him as a blasphemer and a false prophet.

The other major marker of Mormon difference was the practice of polygamy, which began under Smith and continued under his successor Brigham Young. Polygamy, though not widespread among ordinary Mormons, was common and even expected for the leaders of the church. Young himself was exemplary in this regard, marrying at least sixteen wives and fathering fifty-seven children. Mormons defended the practice as God's will and stressed the serious commitments that polygamous men made to their plural wives and children.

Most Americans remained unconvinced. Politicians and Protestant reform organizations saw polygamy as an unspeakable perversion of proper family relations, comparing it to prostitution and slavery. During the 1870s and 1880s, the federal government passed new laws and stepped up enforcement to try to stamp out the practice and undercut the economic power of the LDS church in Utah. Facing this hostile climate, the Mormons put forward a test case involving Young's secretary George Reynolds, who had just married his second wife. The case ascended all the way to the Supreme Court, which ruled that polygamy was not a legitimate expression of religious freedom.

Among the case's many complexities, two themes are emphasized in this excerpt. The first is the ambiguous meaning of religious freedom and of religion itself. "The word 'religion' is nowhere defined in the Constitution," admits Chief Justice Morrison Waite, who then tries to craft a definition from other texts and from historical examples. The second emphasis is the centrality of the family to Americans' conceptions of religion and democracy. Although we often consider marriage to be a private matter, *Reynolds* shows how it became a matter of public interest. The political dimension of marriage would recur in debates over interracial marriage in the 1960s and over same-sex marriage in the twenty-first century, the latter a concern of John Shelby Spong later in this anthology.

Reynolds v. United States

MR. CHIEF JUSTICE WAITE delivered the opinion of the court.
[...]
On the trial, the plaintiff in error, the accused, proved that at the time of his alleged second marriage he was, and for many years before had been, a member of the Church of Jesus Christ of Latter-Day Saints, commonly called the Mormon Church, and a believer in its doctrines; that it was an accepted doctrine of that church "that it was the duty of male members of said church, circumstances permitting, to practise polygamy; . . . that this duty was enjoined by different books which the members of said church believed to be of divine origin, and among others the Holy Bible, and also that the members of the church believed that the practice of polygamy was directly enjoined upon the male members thereof by the Almighty God, in a revelation to Joseph Smith, the founder and prophet of said church; that the failing or refusing to practise polygamy by such male members of said church, when circumstances would admit, would be punished, and that the penalty for such failure and refusal would be damnation in the life to come." He also proved "that he had received permission from the recognized authorities in said church to enter into polygamous marriage"; . . . that Daniel H. Wells, one having authority in said church to perform the marriage ceremony, married the said defendant on or about the time the crime is alleged to have been committed, to some woman by the name of Schofield, and that such marriage ceremony was performed under and pursuant to the doctrines of said church."

Upon this proof he asked the court to instruct the jury that if they found from the evidence that he "was married as charged—if he was married—in pursuance of and in conformity with what he believed at

the time to be a religious duty, that the verdict must be 'not guilty.'" This
request was refused, and the court did charge "that there must have been
a criminal intent, but that if the defendant, under the influence of a religious belief that it was right,—under an inspiration, if you please, that it
was right,—deliberately married a second time, having a first wife living,
the want of consciousness of evil intent—the want of understanding on
his part that he was committing a crime—did not excuse him; but the law
inexorably in such case implies the criminal intent."

Upon this charge and refusal to charge the question is raised, whether
religious belief can be accepted as a justification of an overt act made
criminal by the law of the land. The inquiry is not as to the power of
Congress to prescribe criminal laws for the Territories, but as to the guilt
of one who knowingly violates a law which has been properly enacted, if
he entertains a religious belief that the law is wrong.

Congress cannot pass a law for the government of the Territories which
shall prohibit the free exercise of religion. The first amendment to the
Constitution expressly forbids such legislation. Religious freedom is guaranteed everywhere throughout the United States, so far as congressional
interference is concerned. The question to be determined is, whether the
law now under consideration comes within this prohibition.

The word "religion" is not defined in the Constitution. We must go
elsewhere, therefore, to ascertain its meaning, and nowhere more appropriately, we think, than to the history of the times in the midst of which
the provision was adopted. The precise point of the inquiry is, what is the
religious freedom which has been guaranteed.

Before the adoption of the Constitution, attempts were made in some
of the colonies and States to legislate not only in respect to the establishment of religion, but in respect to its doctrines and precepts as well. The
people were taxed, against their will, for the support of religion, and
sometimes for the support of particular sects to whose tenets they could
not and did not subscribe. Punishments were prescribed for a failure
to attend upon public worship, and sometimes for entertaining heretical opinions. The controversy upon this general subject was animated in
many of the States, but seemed at last to culminate in Virginia. In 1784,
the House of Delegates of that State having under consideration "a bill
establishing provision for teachers of the Christian religion," postponed it
until the next session, and directed that the bill should be published and
distributed, and that the people be requested "to signify their opinion
respecting the adoption of such a bill at the next session of assembly."

This brought out a determined opposition. Amongst others, Mr. Madison prepared a "Memorial and Remonstrance," which was widely circulated and signed, and in which he demonstrated "that religion, or the
duty we owe the Creator," was not within the cognizance of civil government. At the next session the proposed bill was not only defeated, but

another, "for establishing religious freedom," drafted by Mr. Jefferson, was passed. In the preamble of this act religious freedom is defined; and after a recital "that to suffer the civil magistrate to intrude his powers into the field of opinion, and to restrain the profession or propagation of principles on supposition of their ill tendency, is a dangerous fallacy which at once destroys all religious liberty," it is declared "that it is time enough for the rightful purposes of civil government for its officers to interfere when principles break out into overt acts against peace and good order." In these two sentences is found the true distinction between what properly belongs to the church and what to the State.

In a little more than a year after the passage of this statute the convention met which prepared the Constitution of the United States. Of this convention Mr. Jefferson was not a member, he being then absent as minister to France. As soon as he saw the draft of the Constitution proposed for adoption, he, in a letter to a friend, expressed his disappointment at the absence of an express declaration insuring the freedom of religion, but was willing to accept it as it was, trusting that the good sense and honest intentions of the people would bring about the necessary alterations. Five of the States, while adopting the Constitution, proposed amendments. Three—New Hampshire, New York, and Virginia—included in one form or another a declaration of religious freedom in the changes they desired to have made, as did also North Carolina, where the convention at first declined to ratify the Constitution until the proposed amendments were acted upon. Accordingly, at the first session of the first Congress the amendment now under consideration was proposed with others by Mr. Madison. It met the views of the advocates of religious freedom, and was adopted. Mr. Jefferson afterwards, in reply to an address to him by a committee of the Danbury Baptist Association, took occasion to say: "Believing with you that religion is a matter which lies solely between man and his God; that he owes account to none other for his faith or his worship; that the legislative powers of the government reach actions only, and not opinions,—I contemplate with sovereign reverence that act of the whole American people which declared that their legislature should 'make no law respecting an establishment of religion or prohibiting the free exercise thereof,' thus building a wall of separation between church and State. Adhering to this expression of the supreme will of the nation in behalf of the rights of conscience, I shall see with sincere satisfaction the progress of those sentiments which tend to restore man to all his natural rights, convinced he has no natural right in opposition to his social duties." Coming as this does from an acknowledged leader of the advocates of the measure, it may be accepted almost as an authoritative declaration of the scope and effect of the amendment thus secured. Congress was deprived of all legislative power over mere opinion, but was left free to reach actions which were in violation of social duties or subversive of good order.

Polygamy has always been odious among the northern and western nations of Europe, and, until the establishment of the Mormon Church, was
almost exclusively a feature of the life of Asiatic and of African people. At
common law, the second marriage was always void, and from the earliest history of England polygamy has been treated as an offence against
society. After the establishment of the ecclesiastical courts, and until the
time of James I., it was punished through the instrumentality of those
tribunals, not merely because ecclesiastical rights had been violated, but
because upon the separation of the ecclesiastical courts from the civil the
ecclesiastical were supposed to be the most appropriate for the trial of
matrimonial causes and offences against the rights of marriage, just as
they were for testamentary causes and the settlement of the estates of
deceased persons.

By the statute of 1 James I. (c. 11), the offence, if committed in England
or Wales, was made punishable in the civil courts, and the penalty was
death. As this statute was limited in its operation to England and Wales, it
was at a very early period re-enacted, generally with some modifications,
in all the colonies. In connection with the case we are now considering,
it is a significant fact that on the 8th of December, 1788, after the passage of the act establishing religious freedom, and after the convention of
Virginia had recommended as an amendment to the Constitution of the
United States the declaration in a bill of rights that "all men have an equal,
natural, and unalienable right to the free exercise of religion, according
to the dictates of conscience," the legislature of that State substantially
enacted the statute of James I., death penalty included, because, as recited
in the preamble, "it hath been doubted whether bigamy or poligamy be
punishable by the laws of this Commonwealth." From that day to this
we think it may safely be said there never has been a time in any State of
the Union when polygamy has not been an offence against society, cogni-
zable by the civil courts and punishable with more or less severity. In the
face of all this evidence, it is impossible to believe that the constitutional
guaranty of religious freedom was intended to prohibit legislation in respect to this most important feature of social life. Marriage, while from
its very nature a sacred obligation, is nevertheless, in most civilized nations, a civil contract, and usually regulated by law. Upon it society may
be said to be built, and out of its fruits spring social relations and social
obligations and duties, with which government is necessarily required to
deal. In fact, according as monogamous or polygamous marriages are allowed, do we find the principles on which the government of the people,
to a greater or less extent, rests. Professor Lieber says, polygamy leads to
the patriarchal principle, and which, when applied to large communities,
fetters the people in stationary despotism, while that principle cannot
long exist in connection with monogamy. Chancellor Kent observes that
this remark is equally striking and profound. An exceptional colony of

polygamists under an exceptional leadership may sometimes exist for a time without appearing to disturb the social condition of the people who surround it; but there cannot be a doubt that, unless restricted by some form of constitution, it is within the legitimate scope of the power of every civil government to determine whether polygamy or monogamy shall be the law of social life under its dominion.

In our opinion, the statute immediately under consideration is within the legislative power of Congress. It is constitutional and valid as prescribing a rule of action for all those residing in the Territories, and in places over which the United States have exclusive control. This being so, the only question which remains is, whether those who make polygamy a part of their religion are excepted from the operation of the statute. If they are, then those who do not make polygamy a part of their religious belief may be found guilty and punished, while those who do, must be acquitted and go free. This would be introducing a new element into criminal law. Laws are made for the government of actions, and while they cannot interfere with mere religious belief and opinions, they may with practices. Suppose one believed that human sacrifices were a necessary part of religious worship, would it be seriously contended that the civil government under which he lived could not interfere to prevent a sacrifice? Or if a wife religiously believed it was her duty to burn herself upon the funeral pile of her dead husband, would it be beyond the power of the civil government to prevent her carrying her belief into practice?

So here, as a law of the organization of society under the exclusive dominion of the United States, it is provided that plural marriages shall not be allowed. Can a man excuse his practices to the contrary because of his religious belief? To permit this would be to make the professed doctrines of religious belief superior to the law of the land, and in effect to permit every citizen to become a law unto himself. Government could exist only in name under such circumstances.

Source

Reynolds v. United States 98 U.S. 145 (1878).

Further Reading

Bowman, Matthew. *The Mormon People: The Making of an American Faith.* New York: Random House, 2012.

Flake, Kathleen. *The Politics of American Religious Identity: The Seating of Senator Reed Smoot, Mormon Apostle.* Chapel Hill: University of North Carolina Press, 2004.

Gordon, Sarah Barringer. *The Mormon Question: Polygamy and Constitutional Conflict in Nineteenth-Century America.* Chapel Hill: University of North Carolina Press, 2002.

PITTSBURGH PLATFORM OF
REFORM JUDAISM (1885)

In the late nineteenth century, American Jews engaged in wide-ranging consideration of the meaning of their faith. Many of the debates centered on the question of modernity: Should Judaism be part of American progress, or a bulwark against it? Christians were asking similar questions, but Jews' outlooks were shaped especially by their minority status in the United States. While the nation looked to them at times like a pluralistic "Promised Land," it also manifested a Christian culture that often included overt anti-Semitism. Disagreements within Judaism stemmed as well from differing national origins, as large numbers of Jews from many different countries entered the United States with their own distinctive traditions.

In this context, the branch of Judaism known as Reform articulated a religious worldview that was self-consciously in dialogue with the modern world. Coming together near Pittsburgh in 1885, a group of Reform rabbis led by Isaac Mayer Wise put together a document crystallizing this new perspective. Wise had long been a proponent of Jewish modernization and Americanization; his earlier prayer book *Minhag Amerika* had sought to unite American Jews of all nationalities around an updated liturgy.

The "Pittsburgh Platform" that resulted from the conference constitutes a ringing defense of liberal religion, what Wise called a "Declaration of Independence." The authors define a version of Judaism that is compatible with science and reason, dynamic in its adaptation to modernity, and focused on social justice more than ritual practice. Orthodox Judaism, the other major wing of the religion in the United States, denied these tenets. Orthodox believers, for instance, insisted on observing Jewish dietary laws, whereas Reform Jews jettisoned such laws as vestiges of a less enlightened age. These fissures beneath the surface of the Pittsburgh Platform ensured that Wise's vision of a unified American Judaism would be impossible.

Pittsburgh Platform of Reform Judaism

In view of the wide divergence of opinion, of conflicting ideas in Judaism to-day, we, as representatives of Reform Judaism in America, in continuation of the work begun at Philadelphia, in 1869, unite upon the following principles:

First. We recognize in every religion an attempt to grasp the Infinite, and in every mode, source or book of revelation, held sacred in any religious system, the consciousness of the indwelling of God in man. We hold that Judaism presents the highest conception of the God-idea as taught in our Holy Scriptures and developed and spiritualized by the Jewish teachers, in accordance with the moral and philosophical progress of their respective ages. We maintain that Judaism preserved and defended, midst continual struggles and trials and under enforced isolation, this God-idea as the central religious truth for the human race.

Second. We recognize in the Bible the record of the consecration of the Jewish people to its mission as priest of the one God, and value it as the most potent instrument of religious and moral instruction. We hold that the modern discoveries of scientific researches in the domains of nature and history are not antagonistic to the doctrines of Judaism, the Bible reflecting the primitive ideas of its own age, and at times clothing its conception of Divine Providence and justice dealing with man in miraculous narratives.

Third. We recognize in the Mosaic legislation a system of training the Jewish people for its mission during its national life in Palestine, and today we accept as binding only the moral laws, and maintain only such ceremonies as elevate and sanctify our lives, but reject all such as are not adapted to the views and habits of modern civilization.

Fourth. We hold that all such Mosaic and rabbinical laws as regulate diet, priestly purity and dress originated in ages and under the influence of ideas altogether foreign to our present mental and spiritual state. They fail to impress the modern Jew with a spirit of priestly holiness; their observance in our days is apt rather to obstruct than to further modern spiritual elevation.

Fifth. We recognize in the modern era of universal culture of heart and intellect the approaching of the realization of Israel's great Messianic hope for the establishment of the kingdom of truth, justice and peace among all men. We consider ourselves no longer a nation, but a religious community, and, therefore, expect neither a return to Palestine, nor a sacrificial worship under the sons of Aaron, nor the restoration of any of the laws concerning the Jewish state.

Sixth. We recognize in Judaism a progressive religion, ever striving to be in accord with the postulates of reason. We are convinced of the utmost necessity of preserving the historical identity with our great past. Christianity and Islam being daughter religions of Judaism, we appreciate their providential mission to aid in the spreading of monotheistic and moral truth. We acknowledge that the spirit of broad humanity of our age is our ally in the fulfillment of our mission, and, therefore, we extend the hand of fellowship to all who cooperate with us in the establishment of the reign of truth and righteousness among men.

Seventh. We reassert the doctrine of Judaism that the soul of man is immortal, grounding this belief on the divine nature of the human spirit, which forever finds bliss in righteousness and misery in wickedness. We reject, as ideas not rooted in Judaism, the beliefs both in bodily resurrection and in Gehenna and Eden (Hell and Paradise) as abodes for everlasting punishment and reward.

Eighth. In full accordance with the spirit of Mosaic legislation, which strives to regulate the relation between the rich and poor, we deem it our duty to participate in the great task of modern times, to solve, on the basis of justice and righteousness, the problems presented by the contrasts and evils of the present organization of society.

Source

Pittsburgh Platform (1885), reprinted in Michael A. Meyer, *Response to Modernity: A History of the Reform Movement in Judaism* (New York: Oxford University Press, 1988), 387–88.

Further Reading

Sarna, Jonathan D. *American Judaism: A History.* New Haven: Yale University Press, 2004.

Walter, Jacob, ed. *The Changing World of Reform Judaism: The Pittsburgh Platform in Retrospect.* Pittsburgh: Rodef Shalom Congregation, 1985.

FRANCES WILLARD, *WOMAN IN THE PULPIT* (1888)

American religion has been shaped by a consistent gender hierarchy. In almost all religious groups, the majority of members have been women, while men have occupied most of the official positions of authority. Communities of faith have thus reinforced broader gender inequality in American life, but also sometimes offered women opportunities to assert more egalitarian ideals.

Frances Willard (1839–1898) challenged the gender constraints of American Christianity even as she worked within them. Willard, a Methodist, became one of the most famous women of her era as president of the Woman's Christian Temperance Union (WCTU), a post she held from 1879 until her death in 1898. In an age when women were denied the right to vote and otherwise treated as second-class citizens, she achieved extraordinary success as a leader and organizer, traveling around the country and overseas to promote the cause of temperance. Much ridiculed today, the campaign against alcohol was a powerful reform movement that combined religious fervor with new scientific approaches to public health. The motto of the WCTU, "Home Protection," suggested its domestic gender ideology, yet that ideology led Willard to support a range of reforms ranging from women's suffrage to the eight-hour day. Late in life she even described herself as a Christian socialist.

In this excerpt from her book *Woman in the Pulpit*, Willard confronts the incongruous fact that even an accomplished public speaker such as herself would be barred from giving a sermon in a Christian church simply because of her sex. With few exceptions, women were prohibited, formally or informally, from becoming ministers in Christian denominations; only in the middle of the twentieth century did practices begin to shift substantially. Here Willard argues the case for female clergy, at once drawing on and pushing against prevailing notions of gender difference.

Frances Willard, *Woman in the Pulpit*

Christ, not Paul, is the source of all churchly authority and power. What do we find him saying? How did he deal with women? In the presence of the multitude, he drew from Martha the same testimony that he required of his Apostles, and she publicly replied, almost in Peter's very words, "Yea, Lord, I believe that thou art the Christ, the Son of God, which should come into the world." He declared his commission to the woman at the well of Samaria, with an emphasis and a particularity hardly equalled in any of his public addresses, and her embassy was abundantly rewarded. What pastor would not rejoice to hear such words as these: "Now we believe, not because of thy saying, for we have heard him ourselves, and know that this is indeed the Christ, the Saviour of the world."

It is objected that he called no woman to be an apostle. Granted, but he himself said that he chose one man who had a devil; is this a precedent? One is half inclined to think so, when one reads the long record of priestly intolerance, its culmination being the ostracism of Christ's most faithful followers from their right to proclaim the risen Lord, who gave to Mary the first commission to declare his resurrection. True, he did not designate women as his followers; they came without a call; from their sex he had his human origin; with the immeasurable dignities of his incarnation and his birth, only God and woman were concerned; no utterance of his marks woman as ineligible to any position in the church he came to found; but his gracious words and deeds, his impartation of his purposes and plans to women, his stern reproofs to men who did them wrong, his chosen companionships, and the tenor of his whole life and teaching, all point out precisely the opposite conclusion. Indeed, Luke explicitly declares (viii. 1, 2, 3) that, as "he went throughout every city and village, preaching and showing the glad tidings of the Kingdom of God," "the twelve were with him, *and certain women*," among whom were "Joanna, the wife of Chuza, Herod's steward, and Susanna, and many others, which ministered unto him of their substance."

What a spectacle must that have been for the "Scribes and Pharisees, hypocrites." What loss of caste came to those fearless women, who, breaking away from the customs of society and traditions of religion, dared to follow the greatest of Iconoclasts from city to village with a publicity and a persistence nothing less than outrageous to the conservatives of that day.

Verily, Devotion, thy name is Woman!

> "Not she with trait'rous kiss her Saviour stung;
> Not she denied him with unholy tongue;
> She, while apostles shrank, could danger brave,
> Last at his cross, and earliest at his grave."

Christ's commission only is authoritative. To whom did he give it after his resurrection, until which time the new dispensation was not fairly ushered in? If we are to accept specific statements, rather than the drift and spirit of the inspired book, as conclusive of a question involving half the human race, let us, then, here take our stand on our Lord's final words and deeds. It is stated (Luke xxiv. 33) that the two disciples to whom Christ appeared on the way to Emmaus "returned to Jerusalem, and found the eleven gathered together, and *them that were with them*, saying, 'The Lord is risen, indeed, and hath appeared to Simon.'" Be it understood that women used this language, the women "which came with him from Galilee." It was "them that were with them" (*i. e.*, with the eleven), who were saying, "The Lord is risen indeed."

While they were thus assembled and talking of the wonderful experience of that day, Jesus appeared again, saying, "Peace be unto you." Let us turn to John xx. 19–23, where we have an account of this same appearance of Christ to his disciples, for it says explicitly (after stating that Mary Magdalene came and told the disciples that she had seen the Lord), "Then the same day at evening . . . Jesus stood in the midst and saith unto them, Peace be unto you; as my Father hath sent me even so send I you. And when he had said this, he breathed on them and saith unto them, Receive ye the Holy Ghost; whosesoever sins ye remit they are remitted unto them, and whosesoever sins ye retain they are retained." These, then, are his words spoken to the eleven and "*them* that were with them." He then "opened their understanding that they might understand the Scriptures," and declared that "repentance and remission of sins should be preached in his name among all nations, beginning at Jerusalem," and declared, "*ye are witnesses* of these things. And behold, I send the promise of my Father

upon you, but tarry ye in Jerusalem until ye be endued with power from
on high. And he led them out as far as to Bethany, and he lifted up his
hands, and blessed them. And it came to pass, while he blessed them, he
was parted from them, and carried up into heaven. And they worshipped
him, and returned to Jerusalem with great joy."

Does any reasonable person suppose that His mother was not there, or
that the other Marys were not? or the great company of women that had
ministered to Him? But we are not left in doubt. Turn to Acts i. 13–14.
After stating Christ's command that they should not depart from Jerusalem, but wait for the promise of the Father, "For ye shall be baptized
with the Holy Ghost not many days hence," after which "Ye shall be witnesses unto me unto the uttermost parts of the earth;" and after giving
a brief account of the Resurrection, this passage occurs: "Then returned
they unto Jerusalem, and when they were come in, they went up into an
upper room where abode both Peter and James and John . . . these all
continued with one accord in prayer and supplication *with the women,*
and Mary, the mother of Jesus, and with his brethren. And when the day
of Pentecost was fully come, they were *all* with one accord in one place.
. . . And they were *all* filled with the Holy Ghost and began to speak with
other tongues as the Spirit gave them utterance." Then Peter said: "This is
that which was spoken by the prophet Joel, I will pour out my Spirit upon
all flesh, and your sons and *your daughters* shall prophesy, and on my
servants and on my *handmaids* I will pour out my Spirit, and *they shall
prophesy.*" Paul proves that prophesying may be preaching when he says
(1 Cor. xiv. 3): "But he that prophesieth speaketh unto men to edification
and exhortation and comfort." Well said Gamaliel of this new dispensation: "If this counsel or this work be of men, it will come to naught; but
if it be of God, ye cannot overthrow it, lest haply ye be found to fight
against God."

Let not conservative ecclesiastical leaders try to steady the Lord's ark;
let them not bind what God hath loosed: let them not retain the bondage
he hath remitted, lest haply they be found to fight against God!

"We want the earth," is the world-old motto of men. They have had
their desire, and we behold the white male dynasty reigning undisputed
until our own day; lording it over every heritage, and constituting the
only unquestioned "apostolic succession." Only one thing can end the
dire enchantment we are under, and that is to know the truth, for truth
alone makes free. And the truth of God, a thousand times repeated by
the voice of history, science, and every-day experience, resounds louder
to-day than in all preceding ages: "It is not good for man to be alone!"
Suppose it be admitted that the dual-natured founder of Christianity, in
whose character the force that smote the money-changers of the temple
was commingled with the love that yearned to gather Jerusalem as a hen
gathers "her chickens under her wings," chose as his apostles the only

ones who in that barbarous age would be tolerated in preaching it. Be it remembered that Protestantism recognizes the apostles as having had no successors. Hence, any argument built on man's primacy as related to them and the manner of their choosing falls to the ground. It is curious, considering certain exegetical literalism, that their method of choosing by lot should not have been insisted upon as a part of the divine order!

In the revolt from Roman license, the clergy early declared woman a delusion and a snare, banished her from the company of men who aspired to holiness, and, by introducing the denaturalizing heresy of a celibate clergy, made it impossible for the doctrine of God's eternal fatherhood to be so understood by the preacher that it should become vital in the hearer's heart. It is *men* who have defrauded manhood and womanhood, in the persons of priest and monk and nun, of the right to the sanctities of home; men who have invented hierarchies, enthroned a fisherman as God's vice-gerent, lighted inquisitorial fires, and made the Prince of peace a mighty man of war. It is men who have taken the simple, loving, tender Gospel of the New Testament, so suited to be the proclamation of a woman's lips, and translated it in terms of sacerdotalism, dogma, and martyrdom. It is men who have given us the dead letter rather than the living Gospel. The mother-heart of God will never be known to the world until translated into terms of speech by mother-hearted women. Law and love will never balance in the realm of grace until a woman's hand shall hold the scales.

Men preach a creed; women will declare a life. Men deal in formulas, women in facts. Men have always tithed mint and rue and cummin in their exegesis and their ecclesiasticism, while the world's heart has cried out for compassion, forgiveness, and sympathy. Men's preaching has left heads committed to a catechism, and left hearts hard as nether millstones. The Greek bishop who said, "My creed is faultless, with my life you have nothing to do," condensed into a sentence two thousand years of priestly dogma. Men reason in the abstract, women in the concrete. A syllogism symbolizes one, a rule of life the other. In saying this I wish distinctly to disclaim any attack upon the clergy, any slighting allusion to the highest and holiest of callings; I am speaking only of the intolerant sacerdotal element that has handicapped the church from the earliest ages even until now, and which has been more severely criticised by the best element in the church than by any words that I have penned.

Religion is an affair of the heart. The world is hungry for the comfort of Christ's Gospel, and thirsty for its every-day beatitudes of that holiness which alone constitutes happiness. Men have lost faith in themselves and each other. Boodlerism and "corners" on the market, greed of gain, passion for power, desire for drink, impurity of life, the complicity of the church, Protestant as well as Papal, with the liquor traffic, the preference of a partisan to a conscientious ballot, have combined to make the men of this generation faithless toward one another. The masses of the people have forsaken God's house, and solace themselves in the saloons or with the Sunday newspaper. But the masses will go to hear women when they speak, and every woman who leads a life of weekday holiness, and has the Gospel in her looks, however plain her face and dress may be, has round her head the sweet Madonna's halo, in the eyes of every man who sees her, and she speaks to him with the sacred cadence of his own mother's voice. The devil knew what he was doing when he exhausted sophistry to keep woman down and silent. He knew that "the only consecrated place on earth is where God's Spirit is," and that a Christian woman's heart enshrines that holy Guest more surely than many a "consecrated" pulpit.

Men have been preaching well-nigh two thousand years, and the large majority of the converts have been women. Suppose now that women should share the preaching power, might it not be reasonably expected that a majority of the converts under their administration would be men? Indeed, how else are the latter to have a fair chance at the Gospel? The question is asked in all seriousness, and if its practical answer shall be the equipping of women for the pulpit, it may be reasonably claimed that men's hopes of heaven will be immeasurably increased. Hence, one who urges the taking-off of the arbitrary ruling which now excludes woman from a choice portion of her kingdom may well claim to have manifested especial considerateness toward the interests of men.

The entrance of woman upon the ministerial vocation will give to humanity just twice the probability of strengthening and comforting speech, for women have at least as much sympathy, reverence, and spirituality as men, and they have at least equal felicity of manner and of utterance. Why, then, should the pulpit be shorn of half its power?

To the exegesis of the cloister we oppose that of common life. To the Orientalism that is passing off the stage, we oppose modern Christianity. In our day, the ministers of a great church[1] have struck the word "obey" out of the marriage service, have made women eligible to nearly every rank except the ecclesiastic, and are withheld from raising her to the ministerial office only by the influence of a few leaders, who are insecurely seated on the safety-valve of that mighty engine, Progress. In our day, all churches, except the hierarchical Presbyterian, Episcopal, and Roman Catholic, have made women eligible as members of their councils, leaders in their Sunday-school systems, in several cases have set them apart to the ministry, and in almost all have opened their pulpits to them; even the slow-moving Presbyterian having done this quite generally in later years, and the Episcopal, in several instances, granting women "where to stand" in its chapels, outside the charmed arc of its chancel-rail.

1. The Methodist Episcopal, with two millions of members.

Whoever quotes to the intelligent and devout women of the American church to-day the specific instructions given by Paul to the illiterate and immoral women of Corinth does so at the expense of sound judgment, not to say scholarship. An exegesis so strained and so outworn is on a par with that which would pronounce the Saviour of the world "a glutton and a wine-bibber," because the Pharisees, when he came eating and drinking, declared him to be such.

The lifeless prayer-meetings, from which women's voices are excluded, are largely given over to perfunctory, official prayers, and the churches that still quote "He shall rule over thee" as a Gospel precept are deserted by the great humanity that beats its life along the stony streets. "Behold, your house is left unto you desolate" is the requiem of empty pews that would be full if men and women stood side by side at the church, as they are now fast learning to do at the home altars. For the "man of the house" to do all the praying is to deprive the children of one of life's most sacred ministries—that of their mother's voice in prayer and in the giving of thanks for daily food. Observation in a great variety of homes convinces me that this joint leadership in household worship is being largely introduced. Probably the extreme of masculine prerogative in this regard was illustrated in an Eastern town some years ago, when a boy of twelve was called in from his play to say grace over the lunch prepared between meals for his young lady cousin, a guest newly arrived. The incident is perfectly authentic, and the act was entirely consistent and devout, upon the theory of man's divinely constituted primacy in matters spiritual.

"Behold, I make all things new" was the joyful declaration of woman's great Deliverer. "He hath sent me to heal the broken-hearted, to preach deliverance to the captives, and recovering of sight to the blind, to set at liberty them that are bruised." Above all other beings these words must refer to woman, who, without Christ, lies prostrate under society's pitiless and crushing pyramid. Whether they perceive it or not, it is chiefly ecclesiasticism and not Christianity that Robert Ingersoll and Elizabeth Cady Stanton have been fighting; it is the burdens grievous to be borne that men have laid upon weak shoulders, but which they themselves would not touch with one of their fingers. Christ knew that this would be; he had to place the treasure of his Gospel in the earthen vessels of selfish human hearts. But that treasure is like the leaven that a woman took and hid in three measures of meal until the whole was leavened.

"Behold, I make all things new;" "the letter killeth, the spirit giveth life." These are his words, who spake not as man speaketh; and how the letter killeth to-day, let the sectarianism, the sacerdotalism, and the woman-silencing of the church bear witness. The time has come when those men in high places, "dressed in a little brief authority" within the church of Christ, who seek to shut women out of the pastorate, cannot do so with impunity. To-day they are taking on themselves a responsibility in the presence of which they ought to tremble. To an earnest, intelligent, and devout element among their brethren they seem to be absolutely frustrating the grace of God. They cannot fail to see how many ministers neither draw men to the Gospel feast, nor go out into the highways and hedges seeking them. They cannot fail to see that, although the novelty of women's speaking has worn off, the people rally to hear them as to hear no others, save the most celebrated men of the pulpit and platform; and that especially is it true that "the common people hear them gladly." The plea, urged by some theologians with all the cogency of physiological illustration, that woman is born to one vocation, and one alone, is negatived by her magnificent success as a teacher, a philanthropist, and a physician, by which means she takes the part of foster-mother to myriads of children orphaned or worse than motherless. Their fear that incompetent women may become pastors and preachers should be put to flight by the survival of the church, in spite of centuries of the grossest incompetency in mind and profligacy in life, of men set apart by the laying-on of hands. Their anxiety lest too many women should crowd in is met by the method of choosing a pastor, in which both clergy and people must unite to attest the fitness and acceptability of every candidate.

Formerly the voices of women were held to render them incapable of public speech, but it has been discovered that what these voices lack in sonority they supply in clearness, and when women singers outrank all others, and women lecturers are speaking daily to assemblies numbering from one to ten thousand, this objection vanishes.[2] Lack of special preparation is but a temporary barrier.

[. . .]

But some men say it will disrupt the home. As well might they talk of driving back the tides of the sea. The mother-heart will never change. Woman enters the arena of literature, art, business, what you will, becomes a teacher, a physician, a philanthropist, but she is a woman first of all, and cannot deny herself. In all these great vocations she has still been "true to the kindred points of heaven and home;" and everybody knows that, beyond almost any other, the minister is one who lives at home. The firesides of the people are his week-day sanctuary, the pulpit is near his own door, and its publicity is so guarded by the people's reverence and sympathy as to make it of all others the place least inharmomous with woman's character and work.

---

2. It is probably no more "natural" to women to have feeble voices than it is for them to have long hair. The Greek priests of the East, not being allowed to cut their hair, wear it braided in long cues, even as our forefathers wore theirs. "Nature" has been saddled with the disabilities of women to an extent that must make the thoughtful ones among them smile. The truth is clearly enough proved from the analogies of Creation's lower orders that this gracious and impartial dame has given woman but a single disability, viz: she can never be a father; and this she has offset by man's single disability, he can never be a mother. Ignorance, prejudice, and tyranny have put upon her all the rest, and these are wearing off with encouraging rapidity.

[. . .]

There is hardly an objector who does not say, "I would be willing to hear Mrs. or Miss Blank preach, but then they are exceptions; if we open the flood-gates, we cannot tell what may happen." But have you ever opened the flood-gates to men? and certainly your dread of the unseemly behavior of Christian women (the most modest and conservative of human beings!) will lead you to greatly increased caution when their cases are being passed upon. The dominant sex has proved itself able to keep women-incapables out of the medical and the teachers' professions, and surely it will stand on guard with double diligence lest they invade the place where are declared the holy oracles. The whole difficulty is one of the imagination and vanishes when individualized, as it would necessarily be in practice, by the separate scrutiny of Conference and Synod upon each separate case.

"Oh, it must come, and let it come, since come it must, but not in our day." Why not in yours, my brother? The day in which it comes will be the most glorious one since Christ started the church based on his resurrection, by commissioning Mary to bear the gladdest tidings this dying world has ever heard: "Behold, he is risen!"

The time is hastening, the world grows smaller; we can compass it a thousand-fold more readily than could any previous generation. Within five years, so we are told by leading railroad authorities, we shall be able to go around the globe in forty days, and to go accompanied by all the security and comfort of our scientific and luxurious civilization. Women can do this just as readily as men. Then, let us send them forth full-panoplied; let us sound in their gentle ears the "Take thou authority" of the church's highest tribunal, that untrammelled and free they may lift up the standard of Christ's cross on every shore, and fulfil that wonderful and blessed prophecy (Ps. lxviii. 11, R.V.): "The Lord giveth the word. The women that publish the tidings are a great host."

Source

Frances Willard, *Woman in the Pulpit* (Boston: D. Lothrop, 1888), 40–55, 58–60.

Further Reading

Braude, Ann. "Women's History *Is* American Religious History." In *Retelling U.S. Religious History,* ed. Thomas A. Tweed. Berkeley: University of California Press, 1997.

Foster, Gaines M. *Moral Reconstruction: Christian Lobbyists and the Federal Legislation of Morality, 1865–1920.* Chapel Hill: University of North Carolina Press, 2002.

Tyrrell, Ian R. *Woman's World/Woman's Empire: The Woman's Christian Temperance Union in International Perspective, 1880–1930.* Chapel Hill: University of North Carolina Press, 1991.

——

ELIZABETH CADY STANTON,
THE WOMAN'S BIBLE (1895)

American unbelief has received much recent attention, but it boasts a long history. The freethinkers of the late nineteenth century undertook a robust public attack on organized religion, drawing especially on the rise of natural science to challenge biblical ideas about the origin of the universe and the nature of humanity. At the same time, this strain of criticism inveighed against religion's complicity in bigotry and violence, as in Mark Twain's satire of proslavery Christianity throughout his 1884 novel *The Adventures of Huckleberry Finn*.

Elizabeth Cady Stanton (1815–1902), one of the founders of the modern women's movement, promulgated a distinctively feminist version of freethought. A signer of the famous 1848 Declaration of Sentiments at Seneca Falls, New York, she promoted the cause of gender equality for over a half-century after that. Although she enjoyed many successes, she also came to notice that her opposition drew strength from religious justifications of male supremacy in the home and in various public realms. While other suffragists professed Christianity, or at least tolerated it, Stanton became one of its most outspoken antagonists.

Late in her life, Stanton assembled a team of female authors to produce a feminist commentary on the Christian scriptures. The *Woman's Bible* was released in two parts, the first in 1895 and the second three years later. In the introduction to the book supplied here, Stanton lays out her argument that Christianity has been bad for women, condemning the oppressive power of the Bible both as a religious text and as a source of secular authority.

Many of Stanton's feminist colleagues were outraged by her project. Some considered it sacrilege, while others feared that it would be politically disastrous for the suffrage movement. Nonetheless, the *Woman's Bible* was influential among freethinkers at the time and later feminist theologians such as Elisabeth Schüssler-Fiorenza.

Elizabeth Cady Stanton, *The Woman's Bible*

From the inauguration of the movement for woman's emancipation the Bible has been used to hold her in the "divinely ordained sphere," prescribed in the Old and New Testaments.

The canon and civil law; church and state; priests and legislators; all political parties and religious denominations have alike taught that woman was made after man, of man, and for man, an inferior being, subject to man. Creeds, codes, Scriptures and statutes, are all based on this idea. The fashions, forms, ceremonies and customs of society, church ordinances and discipline all grow out of this idea.

Of the old English common law, responsible for woman's civil and political status, Lord Brougham said, "it is a disgrace to the civilization and Christianity of the Nineteenth Century." Of the canon law, which is responsible for woman's status in the church, Charles Kingsley said, "this will never be a good world for women until the last remnant of the canon law is swept from the face of the earth."

The Bible teaches that woman brought sin and death into the world, that she precipitated the fall of the race, that she was arraigned before the judgment seat of Heaven, tried, condemned and sentenced. Marriage for her was to be a condition of bondage, maternity a period of suffering and anguish, and in silence and subjection, she was to play the role of a dependent on man's bounty for all her material wants, and for all the information she might desire on the vital questions of the hour, she was commanded to ask her husband at home. Here is the Bible position of woman briefly summed up.

Those who have the divine insight to translate, transpose and transfigure this mournful object of pity into an exalted, dignified personage, worthy our worship as the mother of the race, are to be congratulated as having a share of the occult mystic power of the eastern Mahatmas.

The plain English to the ordinary mind admits of no such liberal interpretation. The unvarnished texts speak for themselves. The canon law, church ordinances and Scriptures, are homogeneous, and all reflect the same spirit and sentiments.

These familiar texts are quoted by clergymen in their pulpits, by statesmen in the halls of legislation, by lawyers in the courts, and are echoed by the press of all civilized nations, and accepted by woman herself as "The Word of God." So perverted is the religious element in her nature, that with faith and works she is the chief support of the church and clergy; the very powers that make her emancipation impossible. When, in the early part of the Nineteenth Century, women began to protest against their civil and political degradation, they were referred to the Bible for an answer. When they protested against their unequal position in the church, they were referred to the Bible for an answer.

This led to a general and critical study of the Scriptures. Some, having made a fetish of these books and believing them to be the veritable "Word of God," with liberal translations, interpretations, allegories and symbols, glossed over the most objectionable features of the various books and clung to them as divinely inspired. Others, seeing the family resemblance between the Mosaic code, the canon law, and the old English common law, came to the conclusion that all alike emanated from the same source; wholly human in their origin and inspired by the natural love of domination in the historians. Others, bewildered with their doubts and fears, came to no conclusion. While their clergymen told them on the one hand, that they owed all the blessings and freedom they enjoyed to the Bible, on the other, they said it clearly marked out their circumscribed sphere of action: that the demands for political and civil rights were irreligious, dangerous to the stability of the home, the state and the church. Clerical appeals were circulated from time to time, conjuring members of their churches to take no part in the anti-slavery or woman suffrage movements, as they were infidel in their tendencies, undermining the very foundations of society. No wonder the majority of women stood still, and with bowed heads, accepted the situation.

Listening to the varied opinions of women, I have long thought it would be interesting and profitable to get them clearly stated in book form. To this end six years ago I proposed to a committee of women to issue a Woman's Bible, that we might have women's commentaries on women's position in the Old and New Testaments. It was agreed on by several leading women in England and America and the work was begun, but from various causes it has been delayed, until now the idea is received with renewed enthusiasm, and a large committee has been formed, and we hope to complete the work within a year.

Those who have undertaken the labor are desirous to have some Hebrew and Greek scholars, versed in Biblical criticism, to gild our pages with their learning. Several distinguished women have been urged to do so, but they are afraid that their high reputation and scholarly attainments might be compromised by taking part in an enterprise that for a time may prove very unpopular. Hence we may not be able to get help from that class.

Others fear that they might compromise their evangelical faith by affiliating with those of more liberal views, who do not regard the Bible as the "Word of God," but like any other book, to be judged by its merits. If the Bible teaches the equality of Woman, why does the church refuse to ordain women to preach the gospel, to fill the offices of deacons and elders, and to administer the Sacraments, or to admit them as delegates to the Synods, General Assemblies and Conferences of the different denominations? They have never yet invited a woman to join one of their Revising Committees, nor tried to mitigate the sentence pronounced on her by changing one count in the indictment served on her in Paradise.

The large number of letters received, highly appreciative of the undertaking, is very encouraging to those who have inaugurated the movement, and indicate a growing self-respect and self-assertion in the women of this generation. But we have the usual array of objectors to meet and answer. One correspondent conjures us to suspend the work, as it is "ridiculous" for "women to attempt the revision of the Scriptures." I wonder if any man wrote to the late revising committee of Divines to stop their work on the ground that it was ridiculous for men to revise the Bible. Why is it more ridiculous for women to protest against her present status in the Old and New Testament, in the ordinances and discipline of the church, than in the statutes and constitution of the state? Why is it more ridiculous to arraign ecclesiastics for their false teaching and acts of injustice to women, than members of Congress and the House of Commons? Why is it more audacious to review Moses than Blackstone, the Jewish code of laws, than the English system of jurisprudence? Women have compelled their legislators in every state in this Union to so modify their statutes for women that the old common law is now almost a dead letter. Why not compel Bishops and Revising Committees to modify their creeds and dogmas? Forty years ago it seemed as ridiculous to timid, time-serving and retrograde folk for women to demand an expurgated edition of the laws, as it now does to demand an expurgated edition of the Liturgies and the Scriptures. Come, come, my conservative friend, wipe the dew off your spectacles, and see that the world is moving. Whatever your views may be as to the importance of the proposed work, your political and social degradation are but an outgrowth of your status in the Bible. When you express your aversion, based on a blind feeling of reverence in which reason has no control, to the revision of the Scriptures, you do but echo Cowper, who, when asked to read Paine's "Rights of Man," exclaimed "No man shall convince me that I am improperly governed while I feel the contrary."

Others say it is not politic to rouse religious opposition.

This much-lauded policy is but another word for cowardice. How can woman's position be changed from that of a subordinate to an equal, without opposition, without the broadest discussion of all the questions involved in her present degradation? For so far-reaching and momentous a reform as her complete independence, an entire revolution in all existing institutions is inevitable.

Let us remember that all reforms are interdependent, and that whatever is done to establish one principle on a solid basis, strengthens all. Reformers who are always compromising, have not yet grasped the idea that truth is the only safe ground to stand upon. The object of an individual life is not to carry one fragmentary measure in human progress, but to utter the highest truth clearly seen in all directions, and thus to round out and perfect a well balanced character. Was not the sum of influence exerted by John Stuart Mill on political, religious and social questions far greater than that of any statesman or reformer who has sedulously limited his sympathies and activities to carrying one specific measure? We have many women abundantly endowed with capabilities to understand and revise what men have thus far written. But they are all suffering from inherited ideas of their inferiority; they do not perceive it, yet such is the true explanation of their solicitude, lest they should seem to be too self-asserting.

Again there are some who write us that our work is a useless expenditure of force over a book that has lost its hold on the human mind. Most intelligent women, they say, regard it simply as the history of a rude people in a barbarous age, and have no more reverence for the Scriptures than any other work. So long as tens of thousands of Bibles are printed every year, and circulated over the whole habitable globe, and the masses in all English-speaking nations revere it as the word of God, it is vain to belittle its influence. The sentimental feelings we all have for those things we were educated to believe sacred, do not readily yield to pure reason. I distinctly remember the shudder that passed over me on seeing a mother take our family Bible to make a high seat for her child at table. It seemed such a desecration. I was tempted to protest against its use for such a purpose, and this, too, long after my reason had repudiated its divine authority.

To women still believing in the plenary inspiration of the Scriptures, we say give us by all means your exegesis in the light of the higher criticism learned men are now making, and illumine the Woman's Bible, with your inspiration.

Bible historians claim special inspiration for the Old and New Testaments containing most contradictory records of the same events, of miracles opposed to all known laws, of customs that degrade the female sex of all human and animal life, stated in most questionable language that could not be read in a promiscuous assembly, and call all this "The Word of God."

The only points in which I differ from all ecclesiastical teaching is that I do not believe that any man ever saw or talked with God, I do not believe that God inspired the Mosaic code, or told the historians what they say he did about woman, for all the religions on the face of the earth degrade her, and so long as woman accepts the position that they assign her, her emancipation is impossible. Whatever the Bible may be made to do in Hebrew or Greek, in plain English it does not exalt and dignify woman. My standpoint for criticism is the revised edition of 1888. I will so far honor the revising committee of wise men who have given us the best exegesis they can according to their ability, although Disraeli said the last one before he died, contained 150,000 blunders in the Hebrew, and 7,000 in the Greek.

But the verbal criticism in regard to woman's position amounts to little. The spirit is the same in all periods and languages, hostile to her as an equal.

There are some general principles in the holy books of all religions that teach love, charity, liberty, justice and equality for all the human family, there are many grand and beautiful passages, the golden rule has been echoed and re-echoed around the world. There are lofty examples of good and true men and women, all worthy our acceptance and imitation whose lustre cannot be dimmed by the false sentiments and vicious characters bound up in the same volume. The Bible cannot be accepted or rejected as a whole, its teachings are varied and its lessons differ widely from each other. In criticising the peccadilloes of Sarah, Rebecca and Rachel, we would not shadow the virtues of Deborah, Huldah and Vashti. In criticising the Mosaic code, we would not question the wisdom of the golden rule and the fifth Commandment. Again the church claims special consecration for its cathedrals and priesthood, parts of these aristocratic churches are too holy for women to enter, boys were early introduced into the choirs for this reason, woman singing in an obscure corner closely veiled. A few of the more democratic denominations accord women some privileges, but invidious discriminations of sex are found in all religious organizations, and the most bitter outspoken enemies of woman are found among clergymen and bishops of the Protestant religion.

The canon law, the Scriptures, the creeds and codes and church discipline of the leading religions bear the impress of fallible man, and not of our ideal great first cause, "the Spirit of all Good," that set the universe of matter and mind in motion, and by immutable law holds the land, the sea, the planets, revolving round the great centre of light and heat, each in its own elliptic, with millions of stars in harmony all singing together, the glory of creation forever and ever.

Source

Elizabeth Cady Stanton, *The Woman's Bible*, part 1 (New York: European Publishing, 1895), 5–13.

Further Reading

Jacoby, Susan. *Freethinkers: A History of American Secularism.* New York: Metropolitan, 2004.

Kern, Kathi. *Mrs. Stanton's Bible.* Ithaca: Cornell University Press, 2001.

Schüssler-Fiorenza, Elisabeth. *In Memory of Her: A Feminist Theological Reconstruction of Christian Origins.* New York: Crossroad, 1983.

W. E. B. DU BOIS,
"OF THE FAITH OF THE FATHERS" (1903)

The end of slavery offered great political promise to African Americans, yet that promise withered with the demise of Reconstruction. By the 1880s, a new regime of white supremacy was taking hold in the South and to some extent throughout the nation. An increasingly strict system of segregation sought to keep whites and blacks separate in work, leisure, transportation, education, and worship. Legal authority, most notably the Supreme Court's *Plessy v. Ferguson* "separate but equal" ruling, and extralegal violence enforced this color line, leading many historians to label the decades around the turn of the century the "nadir" of race relations.

Still, African Americans evinced extraordinary creativity amid these harsh constraints, not least in their religious lives. Black churches were one of their most important sites of autonomy in this period, functioning as spiritual centers while also providing charity, employment, entertainment, and the news of the day, all sheltered from the gaze of hostile whites. By the early twentieth century, northern churches served as welcoming centers for the streams of migrants fleeing the Jim Crow South.

The most important African American intellectual of this era was W. E. B. Du Bois (1868–1963). Raised in Massachusetts and educated at Harvard, Du Bois's long career had an astonishing breadth; he was a sociologist, editor, novelist, educator, political organizer, and much else. One thing he did not do was affiliate himself with any organized religious group. Though scholars debate whether Du Bois should be understood as a Christian modernist, a dissenting "American prophet," or a freethinking secularist, all agree that he was an astute observer of African American religion, appreciating its power while also criticizing what he saw as its limitations in advancing the cause of African American freedom. In this piece, first published in 1900 and later included as a chapter in his 1903 classic *The Souls of Black Folk*, Du Bois recognizes that, under Jim Crow, black churches have become nothing less than "governments of men." Eventually, the civil rights movement would tap into the resources of those institutions to bring about a transformation of race in America.

W. E. B. Du Bois, "Of the Faith of the Fathers"

Dim face of Beauty haunting all the world,
    Fair face of Beauty all too fair to see,
Where the lost stars adown the heavens are hurled,—

    There, there alone for thee

    May white peace be.

Beauty, sad face of Beauty, Mystery, Wonder,
    What are these dreams to foolish babbling men
Who cry with little noises 'neath the thunder

Of Ages ground to sand,

To a little sand.

—Fiona MacLeod

It was out in the country, far from home, far from my foster home, on a dark Sunday night. The road wandered from our rambling log-house up the stony bed of a creek, past wheat and corn, until we could hear dimly across the fields a rhythmic cadence of song,—soft, thrilling, powerful, that swelled and died sorrowfully in our ears. I was a country school-teacher then, fresh from the East, and had never seen a Southern Negro revival. To be sure, we in Berkshire were not perhaps as stiff and formal as they in Suffolk of olden time; yet we were very quiet and subdued, and I know not what would have happened those clear Sabbath mornings had some one punctuated the sermon with a wild scream, or interrupted the long prayer with a loud Amen! And so most striking to me, as I approached the village and the little plain church perched aloft, was the air of intense excitement that possessed that mass of black folk. A sort of suppressed terror hung in the air and seemed to seize us,—a pythian madness, a demoniac possession, that lent terrible reality to song and word. The black and massive form of the preacher swayed and quivered as the words crowded to his lips and flew at us in singular eloquence. The people moaned and fluttered, and then the gaunt-cheeked brown woman beside me suddenly leaped straight into the air and shrieked like a lost soul, while round about came wail and groan and outcry, and a scene of human passion such as I had never conceived before.

Those who have not thus witnessed the frenzy of a Negro revival in the untouched backwoods of the South can but dimly realize the religious feeling of the slave; as described, such scenes appear grotesque and funny, but as seen they are awful. Three things characterized this religion of the slave,—the Preacher, the Music, and the Frenzy. The Preacher is the most unique personality developed by the Negro on American soil. A leader, a politician, an orator, a "boss," an intriguer, an idealist,—all these he is, and ever, too, the centre of a group of men, now twenty, now a thousand in number. The combination of a certain adroitness with deep-seated earnestness, of tact with consummate ability, gave him his preeminence, and helps him maintain it. The type, of course, varies according to time and place, from the West Indies in the sixteenth century to New England in the nineteenth, and from the Mississippi bottoms to cities like New Orleans or New York.

The Music of Negro religion is that plaintive rhythmic melody, with its touching minor cadences, which, despite caricature and defilement, still remains the most original and beautiful expression of human life and longing yet born on American soil. Sprung from the African forests, where its counterpart can still be heard, it was adapted, changed, and intensified by the tragic soul-life of the slave, until, under the stress of law and whip, it became the one true expression of a people's sorrow, despair, and hope.

Finally the Frenzy of "Shouting," when the Spirit of the Lord passed by, and, seizing the devotee, made him mad with supernatural joy, was the last essential of Negro religion and the one more devoutly believed in than all the rest. It varied in expression from the silent rapt countenance or the low murmur and moan to the mad abandon of physical fervor,— the stamping, shrieking, and shouting, the rushing to and fro and wild waving of arms, the weeping and laughing, the vision and the trance. All this is nothing new in the world, but old as religion, as Delphi and Endor. And so firm a hold did it have on the Negro, that many generations firmly believed that without this visible manifestation of the God there could be no true communion with the Invisible.

These were the characteristics of Negro religious life as developed up to the time of Emancipation. Since under the peculiar circumstances of the black man's environment they were the one expression of his higher life, they are of deep interest to the student of his development, both socially and psychologically. Numerous are the attractive lines of inquiry that here group themselves. What did slavery mean to the African savage? What was his attitude toward the World and Life? What seemed to him good and evil,—God and Devil? Whither went his longings and strivings, and wherefore were his heart-burnings and disappointments? Answers to such questions can come only from a study of Negro religion as a development, through its gradual changes from the heathenism of the Gold Coast to the institutional Negro church of Chicago.

Moreover, the religious growth of millions of men, even though they be slaves, cannot be without potent influence upon their contemporaries. The Methodists and Baptists of America owe much of their condition to the silent but potent influence of their millions of Negro converts. Especially is this noticeable in the South, where theology and religious philosophy are on this account a long way behind the North, and where the religion of the poor whites is a plain copy of Negro thought and methods. The mass of "gospel" hymns which has swept through American churches and well-nigh ruined our sense of song consists largely of debased imitations of Negro melodies made by ears that caught the jingle but not the music, the body but not the soul, of the Jubilee songs. It is thus clear that the study of Negro religion is not only a vital part of the history of the Negro in America, but no uninteresting part of American history.

The Negro church of to-day is the social centre of Negro life in the United States, and the most characteristic expression of African character. Take a typical church in a small Virginia town: it is the "First Baptist"—

a roomy brick edifice seating five hundred or more persons, tastefully fin-
ished in Georgia pine, with a carpet, a small organ, and stained-glass windows. Underneath is a large assembly room with benches. This building
is the central club-house of a community of a thousand or more Negroes.
Various organizations meet here,—the church proper, the Sunday-school,
two or three insurance societies, women's societies, secret societies, and
mass meetings of various kinds. Entertainments, suppers, and lectures are
held beside the five or six regular weekly religious services. Considerable
sums of money are collected and expended here, employment is found
for the idle, strangers are introduced, news is disseminated and charity
distributed. At the same time this social, intellectual, and economic centre
is a religious centre of great power. Depravity, Sin, Redemption, Heaven,
Hell, and Damnation are preached twice a Sunday after the crops are laid
by; and few indeed of the community have the hardihood to withstand
conversion. Back of this more formal religion, the Church often stands
as a real conserver of morals, a strengthener of family life, and the final
authority on what is Good and Right.

Thus one can see in the Negro church to-day, reproduced in microcosm,
all the great world from which the Negro is cut off by color-prejudice and
social condition. In the great city churches the same tendency is noticeable and in many respects emphasized. A great church like the Bethel of
Philadelphia has over eleven hundred members, an edifice seating fifteen
hundred persons and valued at one hundred thousand dollars, an annual
budget of five thousand dollars, and a government consisting of a pastor
with several assisting local preachers, an executive and legislative board,
financial boards and tax collectors; general church meetings for making
laws; sub-divided groups led by class leaders, a company of militia, and
twenty-four auxiliary societies. The activity of a church like this is immense and far-reaching, and the bishops who preside over these organizations throughout the land are among the most powerful Negro rulers
in the world.

Such churches are really governments of men, and consequently a little
investigation reveals the curious fact that, in the South, at least, practically every American Negro is a church member. Some, to be sure, are
not regularly enrolled, and a few do not habitually attend services; but,
practically, a proscribed people must have a social centre, and that centre
for this people is the Negro church. The census of 1890 showed nearly
twenty-four thousand Negro churches in the country, with a total enrolled membership of over two and a half millions, or ten actual church
members to every twenty-eight persons, and in some Southern States one
in every two persons. Besides these there is the large number who, while
not enrolled as members, attend and take part in many of the activities
of the church. There is an organized Negro church for every sixty black
families in the nation, and in some States for every forty families, own-

ing, on an average, a thousand dollars' worth of property each, or nearly twenty-six million dollars in all.

Such, then, is the large development of the Negro church since Emancipation. The question now is, What have been the successive steps of this social history and what are the present tendencies? First, we must realize that no such institution as the Negro church could rear itself without definite historical foundations. These foundations we can find if we remember that the social history of the Negro did not start in America. He was brought from a definite social environment,—the polygamous clan life under the headship of the chief and the potent influence of the priest. His religion was nature-worship, with profound belief in invisible surrounding influences, good and bad, and his worship was through incantation and sacrifice. The first rude change in this life was the slave ship and the West Indian sugar-fields. The plantation organization replaced the clan and tribe, and the white master replaced the chief with far greater and more despotic powers. Forced and long-continued toil became the rule of life, the old ties of blood relationship and kinship disappeared, and instead of the family appeared a new polygamy and polyandry, which, in some cases, almost reached promiscuity. It was a terrific social revolution, and yet some traces were retained of the former group life, and the chief remaining institution was the Priest or Medicine-man. He early appeared on the plantation and found his function as the healer of the sick, the interpreter of the Unknown, the comforter of the sorrowing, the supernatural avenger of wrong, and the one who rudely but picturesquely expressed the longing, disappointment, and resentment of a stolen and oppressed people. Thus, as bard, physician, judge, and priest, within the narrow limits allowed by the slave system, rose the Negro preacher, and under him the first church was not at first by any means Christian nor definitely organized; rather it was an adaptation and mingling of heathen rites among the members of each plantation, and roughly designated as Voodooism. Association with the masters, missionary effort and motives of expediency gave these rites an early veneer of Christianity, and after the lapse of many generations the Negro church became Christian.

Two characteristic things must be noticed in regard to the church. First, it became almost entirely Baptist and Methodist in faith; secondly, as a social institution it antedated by many decades the monogamic Negro home. From the very circumstances of its beginning, the church was confined to the plantation, and consisted primarily of a series of disconnected units; although, later on, some freedom of movement was allowed, still this geographical limitation was always important and was one cause of the spread of the decentralized and democratic Baptist faith among the slaves. At the same time, the visible rite of baptism appealed strongly to their mystic temperament. To-day the Baptist Church is still largest in membership among Negroes, and has a million and a half communicants.

Next in popularity came the churches organized in connection with the white neighboring churches, chiefly Baptist and Methodist, with a few Episcopalian and others. The Methodists still form the second greatest denomination, with nearly a million members. The faith of these two leading denominations was more suited to the slave church from the prominence they gave to religious feeling and fervor. The Negro membership in other denominations has always been small and relatively unimportant, although the Episcopalians and Presbyterians are gaining among the more intelligent classes to-day, and the Catholic Church is making headway in certain sections. After Emancipation, and still earlier in the North, the Negro churches largely severed such affiliations as they had had with the white churches, either by choice or by compulsion. The Baptist churches became independent, but the Methodists were compelled early to unite for purposes of episcopal government. This gave rise to the great African Methodist Church, the greatest Negro organization in the world, to the Zion Church and the Colored Methodist, and to the black conferences and churches in this and other denominations.

The second fact noted, namely, that the Negro church antedates the Negro home, leads to an explanation of much that is paradoxical in this communistic institution and in the morals of its members. But especially it leads us to regard this institution as peculiarly the expression of the inner ethical life of a people in a sense seldom true elsewhere. Let us turn, then, from the outer physical development of the church to the more important inner ethical life of the people who compose it. The Negro has already been pointed out many times as a religious animal,—a being of that deep emotional nature which turns instinctively toward the supernatural. Endowed with a rich tropical imagination and a keen, delicate appreciation of Nature, the transplanted African lived in a world animate with gods and devils, elves and witches; full of strange influences,—of Good to be implored, of Evil to be propitiated. Slavery, then, was to him the dark triumph of Evil over him. All the hateful powers of the Underworld were striving against him, and a spirit of revolt and revenge filled his heart. He called up all the resources of heathenism to aid,—exorcism and witch-craft, the mysterious Obi worship with its barbarious rites, spells, and blood-sacrifice even, now and then, of human victims. Weird midnight orgies and mystic conjurations were invoked, the witch-woman and the voodoo-priest became the centre of Negro group life, and that vein of vague superstition which characterizes the unlettered Negro even to-day was deepened and strengthened.

In spite, however, of such success as that of the fierce Maroons, the Danish blacks, and others, the spirit of revolt gradually died away under the untiring energy and superior strength of the slave masters. By the middle of the eighteenth century the black slave had sunk, with hushed murmurs, to his place at the bottom of a new economic system, and was unconsciously ripe for a new philosophy of life. Nothing suited his condition then better than the doctrines of passive submission embodied in the newly learned Christianity. Slave masters early realized this, and cheerfully aided religious propaganda within certain bounds. The long system of repression and degradation of the Negro tended to emphasize the elements of his character which made him a valuable chattel: courtesy became humility, moral strength degenerated into submission, and the exquisite native appreciation of the beautiful became an infinite capacity for dumb suffering. The Negro, losing the joy of this world, eagerly seized upon the offered conceptions of the next; the avenging Spirit of the Lord enjoining patience in this world, under sorrow and tribulation until the Great Day when He should lead His dark children home,—this became his comforting dream. His preacher repeated the prophecy, and his bards sang,—

> "Children, we all shall be free
> When the Lord shall appear!"

This deep religious fatalism, painted so beautifully in "Uncle Tom," came soon to breed, as all fatalistic faiths will, the sensualist side by side with the martyr. Under the lax moral life of the plantation, where marriage was a farce, laziness a virtue, and property a theft, a religion of resignation and submission degenerated easily, in less strenuous minds, into a philosophy of indulgence and crime. Many of the worst characteristics of the Negro masses of to-day had their seed in this period of the slave's ethical growth. Here it was that the Home was ruined under the very shadow of the Church, white and black; here habits of shiftlessness took root, and sullen hopelessness replaced hopeful strife.

With the beginning of the abolition movement and the gradual growth of a class of free Negroes came a change. We often neglect the influence of the freedman before the war, because of the paucity of his numbers and the small weight he had in the history of the nation. But we must not forget that his chief influence was internal,—was exerted on the black world; and that there he was the ethical and social leader. Huddled as he was in a few centres like Philadelphia, New York, and New Orleans, the masses of the freedmen sank into poverty and listlessness; but not all of them. The free Negro leader early arose and his chief characteristic was intense earnestness and deep feeling on the slavery question. Freedom became to him a real thing and not a dream. His religion became darker and more intense, and into his ethics crept a note of revenge, into his songs a day of reckoning close at hand. The "Coming of the Lord" swept this side of Death, and came to be a thing to be hoped for in this day. Through fugitive slaves and irrepressible discussion this desire for freedom seized the black millions still in bondage, and became their one ideal of life. The black bards caught new notes, and sometimes even dared to sing,—

"O Freedom, O Freedom, O Freedom over me!
Before I'll be a slave
I'll be buried in my grave,
And go home to my Lord
And be free."

For fifty years Negro religion thus transformed itself and identified itself with the dream of Abolition, until that which was a radical fad in the white North and an anarchistic plot in the white South had become a religion to the black world. Thus, when Emancipation finally came, it seemed to the freedman a literal Coming of the Lord. His fervid imagination was stirred as never before, by the tramp of armies, the blood and dust of battle, and the wail and whirl of social upheaval. He stood dumb and motionless before the whirlwind: what had he to do with it? Was it not the Lord's doing, and marvellous in his eyes? Joyed and bewildered with what came, he stood awaiting new wonders till the inevitable Age of Reaction swept over the nation and brought the crisis of to-day.

It is difficult to explain clearly the present critical stage of Negro religion. First, we must remember that living as the blacks do in close contact with a great modern nation, and sharing, although imperfectly, the soul-life of that nation, they must necessarily be affected more or less directly by all the religious and ethical forces that are to-day moving the United States. These questions and movements are, however, overshadowed and dwarfed by the (to them) all-important question of their civil, political, and economic status. They must perpetually discuss the "Negro Problem,"—must live, move, and have their being in it, and interpret all else in its light or darkness. With this come, too, peculiar problems of their inner life,—of the status of women, the maintenance of Home, the training of children, the accumulation of wealth, and the prevention of crime. All this must mean a time of intense ethical ferment, of religious heart-searching and intellectual unrest. From the double life every American Negro must live, as a Negro and as an American, as swept on by the current of the nineteenth while yet struggling in the eddies of the fifteenth century,—from this must arise a painful self-consciousness, an almost morbid sense of personality and a moral hesitancy which is fatal to self-confidence. The worlds within and without the Veil of Color are changing, and changing rapidly, but not at the same rate, not in the same way; and this must produce a peculiar wrenching of the soul, a peculiar sense of doubt and bewilderment. Such a double life, with double thoughts, double duties, and double social classes, must give rise to double words and double ideals, and tempt the mind to pretence or revolt, to hypocrisy or radicalism.

In some such doubtful words and phrases can one perhaps most clearly picture the peculiar ethical paradox that faces the Negro of to-day and is tingeing and changing his religious life. Feeling that his rights and his dearest ideals are being trampled upon, that the public conscience is ever more deaf to his righteous appeal, and that all the reactionary forces of prejudice, greed, and revenge are daily gaining new strength and fresh allies, the Negro faces no enviable dilemma. Conscious of his impotence, and pessimistic, he often becomes bitter and vindictive; and his religion, instead of a worship, is a complaint and a curse, a wail rather than a hope, a sneer rather than a faith. On the other hand, another type of mind, shrewder and keener and more tortuous too, sees in the very strength of the anti-Negro movement its patent weaknesses, and with Jesuitic casuistry is deterred by no ethical considerations in the endeavor to turn this weakness to the black man's strength. Thus we have two great and hardly reconcilable streams of thought and ethical strivings; the danger of the one lies in anarchy, that of the other in hypocrisy. The one type of Negro stands almost ready to curse God and die, and the other is too often found a traitor to right and a coward before force; the one is wedded to ideals remote, whimsical, perhaps impossible of realization; the other forgets that life is more than meat and the body more than raiment. But, after all, is not this simply the writhing of the age translated into black,—the triumph of the Lie which today, with its false culture, faces the hideousness of the anarchist assassin?

To-day the two groups of Negroes, the one in the North, the other in the South, represent these divergent ethical tendencies, the first tending toward radicalism, the other toward hypocritical compromise. It is no idle regret with which the white South mourns the loss of the old-time Negro,—the frank, honest, simple old servant who stood for the earlier religious age of submission and humility. With all his laziness and lack of many elements of true manhood, he was at least open-hearted, faithful, and sincere. To-day he is gone, but who is to blame for his going? Is it not those very persons who mourn for him? Is it not the tendency, born of Reconstruction and Reaction, to found a society on lawlessness and deception, to tamper with the moral fibre of a naturally honest and straightforward people until the whites threaten to become ungovernable tyrants and the blacks criminals and hypocrites? Deception is the natural defence of the weak against the strong, and the South used it for many years against its conquerors; to-day it must be prepared to see its black proletariat turn that same two-edged weapon against itself. And how natural this is! The death of Denmark Vesey and Nat Turner proved long since to the Negro the present hopelessness of physical defence. Political defence is becoming less and less available, and economic defence is still only partially effective. But there is a patent defence at hand,—the defence of deception and flattery, of cajoling and lying. It is the same defence which peasants of the Middle Age used and which left its stamp on their character for centuries. To-day the young Negro of the South who would

succeed cannot be frank and outspoken, honest and self-assertive, but
rather he is daily tempted to be silent and wary, politic and sly; he must
flatter and be pleasant, endure petty insults with a smile, shut his eyes to
wrong; in too many cases he sees positive personal advantage in deception and lying. His real thoughts, his real aspirations, must be guarded in
whispers; he must not criticise, he must not complain. Patience, humility,
and adroitness must, in these growing black youth, replace impulse, man-
liness, and courage. With this sacrifice there is an economic opening, and
perhaps peace and some prosperity. Without this there is riot, migration,
or crime. Nor is this situation peculiar to the Southern United States, is it
not rather the only method by which undeveloped races have gained the
right to share modern culture? The price of culture is a Lie.

On the other hand, in the North the tendency is to emphasize the radicalism of the Negro. Driven from his birthright in the South by a situation
at which every fibre of his more outspoken and assertive nature revolts,
he finds himself in a land where he can scarcely earn a decent living amid
the harsh competition and the color discrimination. At the same time,
through schools and periodicals, discussions and lectures, he is intellectually quickened and awakened. The soul, long pent up and dwarfed, suddenly expands in new-found freedom. What wonder that every tendency
is to excess,—radical complaint, radical remedies, bitter denunciation or
angry silence. Some sink, some rise. The criminal and the sensualist leave
the church for the gambling-hell and the brothel, and fill the slums of
Chicago and Baltimore; the better classes segregate themselves from the
group-life of both white and black, and form an aristocracy, cultured
but pessimistic, whose bitter criticism stings while it points out no way
of escape. They despise the submission and subserviency of the Southern
Negroes, but offer no other means by which a poor and oppressed minority can exist side by side with its masters. Feeling deeply and keenly the
tendencies and opportunities of the age in which they live, their souls are
bitter at the fate which drops the Veil between; and the very fact that this
bitterness is natural and justifiable only serves to intensify it and make it
more maddening.

Between the two extreme types of ethical attitude which I have thus
sought to make clear wavers the mass of the millions of Negroes, North
and South; and their religious life and activity partake of this social conflict within their ranks. Their churches are differentiating,—now into
groups of cold, fashionable devotees, in no way distinguishable from
similar white groups save in color of skin; now into large social and business institutions catering to the desire for information and amusement
of their members, warily avoiding unpleasant questions both within and
without the black world, and preaching in effect if not in word: Dum
vivimus, vivamus.

But back of this still broods silently the deep religious feeling of the
real Negro heart, the stirring, unguided might of powerful human souls

who have lost the guiding star of the past and seek in the great night a new religious ideal. Some day the Awakening will come, when the pent-up vigor of ten million souls shall sweep irresistibly toward the Goal, out of the Valley of the Shadow of Death, where all that makes life worth living—Liberty, Justice, and Right—is marked "For White People Only."

Source

W. E. B. (William Edward Burghardt) Du Bois, "Of the Faith of the Fathers," in *The Souls of Black Folk* (Chicago: A. C. McClurg, 1903), 189–206.

Further Reading

Blum, Edward J. *W. E. B. Du Bois: American Prophet*. Philadelphia: University of Pennsylvania Press, 2007.

Dorrien, Gary. *The New Abolition: W. E. B. Du Bois and the Black Social Gospel*. New Haven: Yale University Press, 2015.

Lewis, David Levering. *W. E. B. Du Bois: Biography of a Race, 1868–1919*. New York: H. Holt, 1993.

Luker, Ralph. *The Social Gospel in Black and White: American Racial Reform, 1885–1912*. Chapel Hill: University of North Carolina Press, 1991.

WALTER RAUSCHENBUSCH,
CHRISTIANITY AND THE SOCIAL CRISIS (1907)

In the late nineteenth and early twentieth centuries, the forces of in-dustrialization, urbanization, and immigration broke apart traditional communities and produced new forms of misery and deprivation. Some liberal Protestant reformers, trying to imagine how Christianity could address the resulting "social crisis," developed a theology that came to be known as the Social Gospel. Going beyond the widespread notion that followers of Jesus should do good works, the Social Gos-pel taught that justice in this world was at the very center of religion, at least as important as the personal salvation that evangelicals had historically preached. Christians had a responsibility to try to bring about, or at least work toward, the Kingdom of God on earth.

Walter Rauschenbusch (1861–1918) was the leading theologian of the Social Gospel. As a pastor to German Americans in the working-class area of New York City known as Hell's Kitchen, Rauschenbusch came face-to-face with the problems of the modern industrial city. Later, as a professor at Rochester Seminary, he wrote a series of books that laid out his vision for a modernized, politically relevant Chris-tianity. While Rauschenbusch was criticized by pro-business interests, many liberal Protestants supported his work.

Christianity and the Social Crisis, excerpted here, is Rauschenbusch's most famous statement of Social Gospel principles, reinterpreting

Christian theology and church history with a focus on the earthly dimension of the Kingdom of God. Martin Luther King, Jr. cited *Christianity and the Social Crisis* as one of his most important influences, and Rauschenbusch's ideas have shaped the thinking of many other leaders of the religious left.

Walter Rauschenbusch, *Christianity and the Social Crisis*

Western civilization is passing through a social revolution unparalleled in history for scope and power. Its coming was inevitable. The religious, political, and intellectual revolutions of the past five centuries, which together created the modern world, necessarily had to culminate in an economic and social revolution such as is now upon us.

By universal consent, this social crisis is the overshadowing problem of our generation. The industrial and commercial life of the advanced nations are in the throes of it. In politics all issues and methods are undergoing upheaval and re-alignment as the social movement advances. In the world of thought all the young and serious minds are absorbed in the solution of the social problems. Even literature and art point like compass-needles to this magnetic pole of all our thought.

The social revolution has been slow in reaching our country. We have been exempt, not because we had solved the problems, but because we had not yet confronted them. We have now arrived, and all the characteristic conditions of American life will henceforth combine to make the social struggle here more intense than anywhere else. The vastness and the free sweep of our concentrated wealth on the one side, the independence, intelligence, moral vigor, and political power of the common people on the other side, promise a long-drawn grapple of contesting forces which may well make the heart of every American patriot sink within him.

It is realized by friend and foe that religion can play, and must play, a momentous part in this irrepressible conflict.

The Church, the organized expression of the religious life of the past, is one of the most potent institutions and forces in Western civilization. Its favor and moral influence are wooed by all parties. It cannot help throwing its immense weight on one side or the other. If it tries not to act, it thereby acts; and in any case its choice will be decisive for its own future.

Apart from the organized Church, the religious spirit is a factor of incalculable power in the making of history. In the idealistic spirits that lead and in the masses that follow, the religious spirit always intensifies thought, enlarges hope, unfetters daring, evokes the willingness to sacrifice, and gives coherence in the fight. Under the warm breath of religious faith, all social institutions become plastic. The religious spirit removes mountains and tramples on impossibilities. Unless the economic and intellectual factors are strongly reënforced by religious enthusiasm, the whole social movement may prove abortive, and the New Era may die before it comes to birth.

It follows that the relation between Christianity and the social crisis is one of the most pressing questions for all intelligent men who realize the power of religion, and most of all for the religious leaders of the people who give direction to the forces of religion.

[. . .]

THE KINGDOM OF GOD AND THE ETHICS OF JESUS

All the teaching of Jesus and all his thinking centred about the hope of the kingdom of God. His moral teachings get their real meaning only when viewed from that centre. He was not a Greek philosopher or Hindu pundit teaching the individual the way of emancipation from the world and its passions, but a Hebrew prophet preparing men for the righteous social order. The goodness which he sought to create in men was always the goodness that would enable them to live rightly with their fellow-men and to constitute a true social life.

All human goodness must be social goodness. Man is fundamentally gregarious and his morality consists in being a good member of his community. A man is moral when he is social; he is immoral when he is anti-social. The highest type of goodness is that which puts freely at the service of the community all that a man is and can. The highest type of badness is that which uses up the wealth and happiness and virtue of the community to please self. All this ought to go without saying, but in fact religious ethics in the past has largely spent its force in detaching men from their community, from marriage and property, from interest in political and social tasks.

The fundamental virtue in the ethics of Jesus was love, because love is the society-making quality. Human life originates in love. It is love that holds together the basal human organization, the family. The physical expression of all love and friendship is the desire to get together and be together. Love creates fellowship. In the measure in which love increases in any social organism, it will hold together without coercion. If physical coercion is constantly necessary, it is proof that the social organization has not evoked the power of human affection and fraternity.

Hence when Jesus prepared men for the nobler social order of the kingdom of God, he tried to energize the faculty and habits of love and to stimulate the dormant faculty of devotion to the common good. Love with Jesus was not a flickering and wayward emotion, but the highest and most steadfast energy of a will bent on creating fellowship.

The force of that unitive will is best seen where fellowship is in danger of disruption. If a man has offended us, that fact is not to break up our fraternity, but we must forgive and forgive and forgive, and always stand ready to repair the torn tissues of fellowship. If we remember that we have offended and our brother is now alienated from us, we are to drop everything, though it be the sacrifice we are just offering in the temple, and go and re-create fellowship. If a man hates us or persecutes and reviles us, we must refuse to let fraternity be ruined, and must woo him back with love and blessings. If he smites us in the face, we must turn the other cheek instead of doubling the barrier by returning the blow. These are not hard and fast laws or detached rules of conduct. If they are used as such, they become unworkable and ridiculous. They are simply the most emphatic expressions of the determination that the fraternal relation which binds men together must not be ruptured. If a child can be saved from its unsocial self-will only by spanking it, parental love will have to apply that medicine. If a rough young fellow will be a happier member of society for being knocked down, we must knock him down and then sit down beside him and make a social man of him. The law of love transcends all other laws. It does not stop where they stop, and occasionally it may cut right across their beaten tracks. When Mary of Bethany broke the alabaster jar of ointment, the disciples voiced the ordinary law of conduct: it was wasteful luxury; the money might have fed the poor. Jesus took her side. While the disciples were thinking of the positions they were to get when their master became king, her feminine intuition had seen the storm-cloud lowering over his head and had heard the mute cry for sympathy in his soul, and had given him the best she had in the abandonment of love. "This is a beautiful deed that she has done." The instinct of love had been a truer guide of conduct than all machine-made rules of charity.

Jesus was very sociable. He was always falling into conversation with people, sometimes in calm disregard of the laws of propriety. When his disciples returned to him at the well of Samaria, they were surprised to find him talking with a woman! Society had agreed to ostracize certain classes, for instance the tax-collectors. Jesus refused to recognize such a partial negation of human society. He accepted their invitations to dinner and invited himself to their houses, thereby incurring the sneer of the respectable as a friend of publicans and a glutton and wine-drinker. He wanted men to live as neighbors and brothers and he set the example. Social meals are often referred to in the gospels and furnished him the illustrations for much of his teaching. His meals with his disciples had been so important a matter in their life that they continued them after his death. His manner in breaking the bread for them all had been so characteristic that they recognized him by it after his resurrection. One of the two great ritual acts in the Church grew out of his last social meal with his friends. If we have ever felt how it brings men together to put their feet under the same table, we shall realize that in these elements of Christ's life a new communal sociability was working its way and creating a happy human society, and Jesus refused to surrender so great an attainment to the ordinary laws of fasting.

Pride disrupts society. Love equalizes. Humility freely takes its place as a simple member of the community. When Jesus found the disciples disputing about their rank in the kingdom, he rebuked their divisive spirit of pride by setting a little child among them as their model; for an unspoiled child is the most social creature, swift to make friends, happy in play with others, lonely without human love. When Jesus overheard the disciples quarrelling about the chief places at the last meal, he gave them a striking object lesson in the subordination of self to the service of the community, by washing their dusty sandalled feet.

All these acts and sayings receive their real meaning when we think of them in connection with the kingdom of God, the ideal human society to be established. Instead of a society resting on coercion, exploitation, and inequality, Jesus desired to found a society resting on love, service, and equality. These new principles were so much the essence of his character and of his view of life, that he lived them out spontaneously and taught them in everything that he touched in his conversations or public addresses. God is a father; men are neighbors and brothers; let them act accordingly. Let them love, and then life will be true and good. Let them seek the kingdom, and all things would follow. Under no circumstance let them suffer fellowship to be permanently disrupted. If an individual or a class was outside of fraternal relations, he set himself to heal the breach. The kingdom of God is the true human society; the ethics of Jesus taught the true social conduct which would create the true society. This would be Christ's test for any custom, law, or institution: does it draw men together or divide them?

[. . .]

THE CHRISTIAN CONCEPTION OF LIFE AND PROPERTY

The spiritual force of Christianity should be turned against the materialism and mammonism of our industrial and social order.

If a man sacrifices his human dignity and self-respect to increase his income, or stunts his intellectual growth and his human affections to swell his bank account, he is to that extent serving mammon and denying God. Likewise if he uses up and injures the life of his fellow-men to make money for himself, he serves mammon and denies God. But our industrial order does both. It makes property the end, and man the means to produce it.

Man is treated as a *thing* to produce more things. Men are hired as hands and not as men. They are paid only enough to maintain their working capacity and not enough to develop their manhood. When their working force is exhausted, they are flung aside without consideration of their human needs. Jesus asked, "Is not a man more than a sheep?" Our industry says "No." It is careful of its live stock and machinery, and careless of its human working force. It keeps its electrical engines immaculate in burnished cleanliness and lets its human dynamos sicken in dirt. In the 15th Assembly District in New York City, between 10th and 11th avenues, 1321 families in 1896 had three bath tubs between them. Our industrial establishments are institutions for the creation of dividends, and not for the fostering of human life. In all our public life the question of profit is put first. Pastor Stöcker, in a speech on child and female labor in the German Reichstag, said: "We have put the question the wrong way. We have asked: How much child and female labor does industry need in order to flourish to pay dividends, and to sell goods abroad? Whereas we ought to have asked: How ought industry to be organized in order to protect and foster the family, the human individual, and the Christian life?" That simple reversal of the question marks the difference between the Christian conception of life and property and the mammonistic.

"Life is more than food and raiment." More, too, than the apparatus which makes food and raiment. What is all the machinery of our industrial organization worth if it does not make human life healthful and happy? But is it doing that? Men are first of all men, folks, members of our human family. To view them first of all as labor force is civilized barbarism. It is the attitude of the exploiter. Yet unconsciously we have all been taught to take that attitude and talk of men as if they were horse-powers or volts. Our commercialism has tainted our sense of fundamental human verities and values. We measure our national prosperity by pig-iron and steel instead of by the welfare of the people. In city affairs the property owners have more influence than the family owners. For instance, the pall of coal smoke hanging over our industrial cities is injurious to the eyes; it predisposes to diseases of the respiratory organs; it depresses the joy of living; it multiplies the labor of housewives in cleaning and washing. But it continues because it would impose expense on business to install smoke consumers or pay skilled stokers. If an agitation is begun to abolish the smoke nuisance, the telling argument is not that it inflicts injury on the mass of human life, but that the smoke "hurts business," and that it really "pays" to consume the wasted carbon. In political life one can constantly see the cause of human life pleading long and vainly for redress, like the widow before the unjust judge. Then suddenly comes the bass voice of Property, and all men stand with hat in hand.

Our scientific political economy has long been an oracle of the false god. It has taught us to approach economic questions from the point of view of goods and not of man. It tells us how wealth is produced and divided and consumed by man, and not how man's life and development can best be fostered by material wealth. It is significant that the discussion of "Consumption" of wealth has been most neglected in political economy; yet that is humanly the most important of all. Theology must become christocentric; political economy must become anthropocentric. Man is Christianized when he puts God before self; political economy will be Christianized when it puts man before wealth. Socialistic political economy does that. It is materialistic in its theory of human life and history, but it is humane in its aims, and to that extent is closer to Christianity than the orthodox science has been.

It is the function of religion to teach the individual to value his soul more than his body, and his moral integrity more than his income. In the same way it is the function of religion to teach society to value human life more than property, and to value property only in so far as it forms the material basis for the higher development of human life. When life and property are in apparent collision, life must take precedence. This is not only Christian but prudent. When commercialism in its headlong greed deteriorates the mass of human life, it defeats its own covetousness by killing the goose that lays the golden egg. Humanity is that goose—in more senses than one. It takes faith in the moral law to believe that this penny-wise craft is really suicidal folly, and to assert that wealth which uses up the people paves the way to beggary. Religious men have been cowed by the prevailing materialism and arrogant selfishness of our business world. They should have the courage of religious faith and assert that "man liveth not by bread alone," but by doing the will of God, and that the life of a nation "consisteth not in the abundance of things" which it produces, but in the way men live justly with one another and humbly with their God.

[. . .]

Source

Walter Rauschenbusch, *Christianity and the Social Crisis* (1907; New York: Macmillan, 1920), xi–xii, 67–71, 369–72.

Further Reading

Dorrien, Gary. *The Making of American Liberal Theology: Idealism, Realism, and Modernity, 1900–1950.* Louisville: Westminster John Knox Press, 2003.

Evans, Christopher. *The Kingdom Is Always But Coming: A Life of Walter Rauschenbusch.* Grand Rapids, MI: Eerdmans, 2004.

WILLIAM JENNINGS BRYAN, "MR. BRYAN'S LAST SPEECH" (1925)

Although he lost each of the three presidential elections in which he ran, William Jennings Bryan (1860–1925) was one of the most important politicians of his era. Known as the "Great Commoner," Bryan became the leading champion of Populism, a movement that sought to defend the "producing classes," particularly farmers, against the ravages of industrial capitalism. The current division of political ideology into left and right wings does not work very well to clarify Bryan's politics: he advocated policies that would seem liberal today, such as increased government intervention in the economy and a commitment to international peacemaking. At other times, he sounded like a conservative, supporting Prohibition and, as in the reading here, attacking the theory of evolution. All of his views, though, sprang from his conviction that the Bible ought to be a guide to economics, politics, and social life.

In the last decade of his life, Bryan's writing and speaking turned increasingly to religious themes. His last public undertaking was to assist the prosecution in the 1925 trial of Dayton, Tennessee, teacher John Scopes. The so-called monkey trial was a test case challenging Tennessee's anti-evolution law, but it quickly gained national attention for the way it symbolized the popular idea of a conflict between religion and science. Scopes was represented by Clarence Darrow, the most famous lawyer in America and a harsh critic of organized religion. Though the defendant was found guilty of teaching evolution, Darrow and the newly prominent mass media, led by journalist H. L. Mencken, made the anti-evolution forces look like uneducated, intolerant fools.

Bryan was, however, no fool. He never got to read the closing statement excerpted here (he died shortly after the trial ended), but it serves as a fascinating window onto the politics of religion and science in a modernizing nation. While criticizing the theory of evolution, it weaves in its author's longstanding concerns about the relationship of majority rule to professional expertise, the imperative of social reform, and the broader relationship between religious and scientific knowledge. Though many accounts of the Scopes trial have judged it yet another loss for Bryan, the concerns he raised have continued to trouble Americans throughout the twentieth century and into the twenty-first.

William Jennings Bryan, "Mr. Bryan's Last Speech"

Let us now separate the issues from the misrepresentations, intentional or unintentional, that have obscured both the letter and the purpose of the law. This is not an interference with freedom of conscience. A teacher can think as he pleases and worship God as he likes, or refuse to worship God at all. He can believe in the Bible or discard it; he can accept Christ or reject Him. This law places no obligations or restraints upon him. And so with freedom of speech; he can, so long as he acts as an individual, say anything he likes on any subject. This law does not violate any rights guaranteed by any constitution to any individual. It deals with the defendant, not as an individual, but as an employee, an official or public servant, paid by the State, and therefore under instructions from the State.

The right of the State to control the public schools is affirmed in the recent decision in the Oregon case, which declares that the State can direct what shall be taught and also forbid the teaching of anything "manifestly inimical to the public welfare." The above decision goes even farther and declares that the parent not only has the right to guard the religious welfare of the child, but is in duty bound to guard it. That decision fits this case exactly. The State had a right to pass this law, and the law represents the determination of the parents to guard the religious welfare of their children.

It need hardly be added that this law did not have its origin in bigotry. It is not trying to force any form of religion on anybody. The majority is not trying to establish a religion or to teach it—it is trying to protect itself from the effort of an insolent minority to force irreligion upon the children under the guise of teaching science. What right has a little irresponsible oligarchy of self-styled "intellectuals" to demand control of the schools of the United States, in which twenty-five millions of children are being educated at an annual expense of nearly two billions of dollars?

Christians must, in every State of the Union, build their own colleges in which to teach Christianity; it is only simple justice that atheists, agnostics and unbelievers should build their own colleges if they want to teach their own religious views or attack the religious views of others.

The statute is brief and free from ambiguity. It prohibits the teaching, in the public schools, of "any theory that denies the story of Divine creation as taught in the Bible," and teaches, "instead, that man descended from a lower order of animals." The first sentence sets forth the purpose of those who passed the law. They forbid the teaching of any evolutionary theory that disputes the Bible record of man's creation and, to make sure that there shall be no misunderstanding, they place their own interpretation on their language and specifically forbid the teaching of any theory that makes man a descendant of any lower form of life.

The evidence shows that defendant taught, in his own language as well as from a book outlining the theory, that man descended from lower forms of life. Howard Morgan's testimony gives us a definition of evolution that will become known throughout the world as this case is discussed. Howard, a fourteen-year-old boy, has translated the words of the teacher and the text-book into language that even a child can understand. As he recollects it, the defendant said, "A little germ of one cell organism was formed in the sea; this kept evolving until it got to be a pretty good-sized animal, then came on to be a land animal, and it kept evolving, and from this was man." There is no room for difference of opinion here, and there is no need of expert testimony. Here are the facts, corroborated by another student, Harry Shelton, and admitted to be true by counsel for defense. Mr. White, Superintendent of Schools, testified to the use of Hunter's Civic Biology, and to the fact that the defendant not only admitted teaching evolution, but declared that he could not teach it without violating the law. Mr. Robinson, the chairman of the School Board, corroborated the testimony of Superintendent White in regard to the defendant's admissions and declaration. These are the facts; they are sufficient and undisputed. A verdict of guilty must follow.

But the importance of this case requires more. The facts and arguments presented to you must not only convince you of the justice of conviction in this case but, while not necessary, to a verdict of guilty, they should convince you of the righteousness of the purpose of the people of the State in the enactment of this law. The State must speak through you to the outside world and repel the aspersions cast by the counsel for the defense upon the intelligence and the enlightenment of the citizens of Tennessee. The people of this State have a high appreciation of the value of education. The State Constitution testifies to that in its demand that education shall be fostered and that science and literature shall be cherished. The continuing and increasing appropriations for public instruction furnish abundant proof that Tennessee places a just estimate upon the learning that is secured in its schools.

Religion is not hostile to learning; Christianity has been the greatest patron learning has ever had. But Christians know that "the fear of the Lord is the beginning of wisdom" now just as it has been in the past, and they therefore oppose the teaching of guesses that encourage godlessness among the students.

Neither does Tennessee undervalue the service rendered by science. The Christian men and women of Tennessee know how deeply mankind is indebted to science for benefits conferred by the discovery of the laws of nature and by the designing of machinery for the utilization of these laws. Give science a fact and it is not only invincible, but it is of incalculable service to man. If one is entitled to draw from society in proportion to the service that he renders to society, who is able to estimate the reward earned by those who have given to us the use of steam, the use of electricity, and enabled us to utilize the weight of water that flows down the mountainside? Who will estimate the value of the service rendered by those who invented the phonograph, the telephone, and the radio? Or, to come more closely to our home life, how shall we recompense those who gave us the sewing machine, the harvester, the threshing machine, the tractor, the automobile, and the method now employed in making artificial ice? The department for medicine also opens an unlimited field for invaluable service. Typhoid and yellow fever are not feared as they once were. Diphtheria and pneumonia have been robbed of some of their terrors, and a high place on the scroll of fame still awaits the discoverer of remedies for arthritis, cancer, tuberculosis and other dread diseases to which mankind is heir.

Christianity welcomes truth from whatever source it comes, and is not afraid that any real truth from any source can interfere with the divine truth that comes by inspiration from God Himself. It is not scientific truth to which Christians object, for true science is classified knowledge, and nothing therefore can be scientific unless it is true.

Evolution is not truth; it is merely an hypothesis—it is millions of guesses strung together. It had not been proven in the days of Darwin; he expressed astonishment that with two or three million species it had been impossible to trace any species to any other species. It had not been proven in the days of Huxley, and it has not been proven up to today. It is less than four years ago that Prof. Bateson came all the way from London to Canada to tell the American scientists that every effort to trace one species to another had failed—every one. He said he still had faith in evolution but had doubts about the origin of species. But of what value is evolution if it cannot explain the origin of species? While many scientists accept evolution as if it were a fact, they all admit, when questioned, that no explanation has been found as to how one species developed into another.

Darwin suggested two laws, sexual selection and natural selection. Sexual selection has been laughed out of the class room, and natural selection is being abandoned, and no new explanation is satisfactory even to scientists. Some of the more rash advocates of evolution are wont to say that evolution is as firmly established as the law of gravitation or the Copernican theory. The absurdity of such a claim is apparent when we remember that anyone can prove the law of gravitation by throwing a weight into the air, and that anyone can prove the roundness of the earth by going around it, while no one can prove evolution to be true in any way whatever.

Chemistry is an insurmountable obstacle in the path of evolution. It is one of the greatest of the sciences; it separates the atoms—isolates them and walks about them, so to speak. If there were in nature a progressive force, an eternal urge, Chemistry would find it. But it is not there. All of the ninety-two original elements are separate and distinct; they combine in fixed and permanent proportions. Water is H_2O, as it has been from the beginning. It was here before life appeared and has never changed; neither can it be shown that any thing else has materially changed.

There is no more reason to believe that man descended from some inferior animal than there is to believe that a stately mansion has descended from a small cottage. Resemblances are not proof—they simply put us on inquiry. As one fact, such as the absence of the accused from the scene of the murder, outweighs all the resemblances that a thousand witnesses could swear to, so the inability of science to trace any one of the millions of species to another species, outweighs all the resemblances upon which evolutionists rely to establish man's blood relationship with the brutes.

But while the wisest scientists cannot prove a pushing power, such as evolution is supposed to be, there is a *lifting* power that any child can understand. The plant lifts the mineral up into a higher world, and the animal lifts the plant up into a world still higher. So, it has been reasoned by analogy, man rises, not by a power within him, but only when drawn upward by a higher power. There is a spiritual gravitation that draws all souls toward heaven, just as surely as there is a physical force that draws all matter on the surface of the earth towards the earth's center. Christ is our drawing power; He said, "I, if I be lifted up from the earth, will draw all men unto me," and His promise is being fulfilled daily all over the world.

It must be remembered that the law under consideration in this case does not prohibit the teaching of evolution up to the line that separates man from the lower forms of animal life. The law might well have gone farther than it does and prohibit the teaching of evolution in lower forms of life; the law is a very conservative statement of the people's opposition to an anti-Biblical hypothesis. The defendant was not content to teach what the law permitted; he, for reasons of his own, persisted in teaching that which was forbidden for reasons entirely satisfactory to the law-makers.

Most of the people who believe in evolution do not know what evolution means. One of the science books taught in the Dayton High School has a chapter on "The Evolution of Machinery." This is a very common misuse of the term. People speak of the evolution of the telephone, the automobile, and the musical instrument. But these are merely illustrations of man's power to deal intelligently with inanimate matter; there is no growth from within in the development of machinery.

Equally improper is the use of the word "evolution" to describe the growth of a plant from a seed, the growth of a chicken from an egg, or the development of any form of animal life from a single cell. All these give us a circle, not a change from one species to another.

Evolution—the evolution involved in this case, and the only evolution that is a matter of controversy anywhere—is the evolution taught by defendant, set forth in the books now prohibited by the new State law, and illustrated in the diagram printed on page 194 of Hunter's Civic Biology. The author estimates the number of species in the animal kingdom at five hundred and eighteen thousand, nine hundred. These are divided into eighteen classes, and each class is indicated on the diagram by a circle, proportionate in size to the number of species in each class and attached by a stem to the trunk of the tree. It begins with protozoa and ends with the mammals. Passing over the classes with which the average man is unfamiliar, let me call your attention to a few of the larger and better known groups. The insects are numbered at three hundred and sixty thousand, over two-thirds of the total number of species in the animal world. The fishes are numbered at thirteen thousand, the amphibians at fourteen hundred, the reptiles at thirty-five hundred, and the birds are thirteen thousand, while thirty-five hundred mammals are crowded together in a little circle that is barely higher than the bird circle. *No circle is reserved for man alone.* He is, according to the diagram, shut up in the little circle entitled "Mammals," with thirty-four hundred and ninety-nine other species of mammals. Does it not seem a little unfair not to distinguish between man and lower forms of life? What shall we say of the intelligence, not to say religion, of those who are so particular to distinguish between fishes and reptiles and birds; but put a man with an immortal soul in the same circle with the wolf, the hyena and the skunk? What must be the impression made upon children by such a degradation of man?

In the preface of this book, the author explains that it is for children, and adds that "the boy or girl of average ability upon admission to the secondary school is not a thinking individual." Whatever may be said in favor of teaching evolution to adults, it surely is not proper to teach it to children who are not yet able to think.

The evolutionist does not undertake to tell us how protozoa, moved by interior and resident forces, sent life up through all the various species, and cannot prove that there was actually any such compelling power at all. And yet, the school children are asked to accept their guesses and build a philosophy of life upon them. If it were not so serious a matter, one might be tempted to speculate upon the various degrees of relationship that, according to evolutionists, exist between man and other forms of life. It might require some very nice calculation to determine at what degree of relationship the killing of a relative ceases to be murder and the eating of one's kin ceases to be cannibalism.

But it is not a laughing matter when one considers that evolution not only offers no suggestions as to a Creator but tends to put the creative act so far away as to cast doubt upon creation itself. And, while it is shaking faith in God as a beginning, it is also creating doubt as to a heaven at the end of life. Evolutionists do not feel that it is incumbent upon them to show how life began or at what point in their long-drawn-out scheme of changing species man became endowed with hope and promise of immortal life. God may be a matter of indifference to the evolutionists, and a life beyond may have no charm for them, but the mass of mankind will continue to worship their Creator and continue to find comfort in the promise of their Saviour that He has gone to prepare a place for them. Christ has made of death a narrow, star-lit strip between the companionship of yesterday and the reunion of tomorrow; evolution strikes out the stars and deepens the gloom that enshrouds the tomb.

If the results of evolution were unimportant, one might require less proof in support of the hypothesis, but before accepting a new philosophy of life, built upon a materialistic foundation, we have reason to demand something more than guesses; "we may well suppose" is not a sufficient substitute for "Thus saith the Lord."

If you, your honor, and you, gentlemen of the jury, would have an understanding of the sentiment that lies back of the statute against the teaching of evolution, please consider the facts that I shall now present to you. First, as to the animals to which evolutionists would have us trace our ancestry. The following is Darwin's family tree, as you will find it set forth on pages 180–181 of his "Descent of Man":

"The most ancient progenitors in the kingdom of Vertrebrata, at which we are able to obtain an obscure glance, apparently consisted of a group of marine animals, resembling the larvae of existing ascidians. These animals probably gave rise to a group of fishes, as lowly organized as the lancelot; and from these the Ganoids, and other fishes like the Lepidosiren, must have been developed. From such fish a very small advance would carry us on to the amphibians. We have seen that birds and reptiles were once intimately connected together; and the Monotremata now connect mammals with reptiles in a slight degree. But no one can at present say by what line of descent the three higher and related classes, namely, mammals, birds, and reptiles, were derived from the two lower vertebrate classes, namely, amphibians and fishes. In the classes of mammals the steps are not difficult to conceive which led from the ancient Monotremata to the ancient Marsupials; and from these to the early progenitors of the placental mammals. We may thus ascend to the Lemuridae; and the interval is not very wide from these to the Simiadae. The Simiadae then branched off into two great stems, the New World and Old World monkeys; and from the latter, at a remote period, Man, the wonder and glory of the Universe, proceeded. Thus we have given to man a pedigree of prodigious length, but not, it may be said, of noble quality." (Ed. 1874, Hurst.)

Note the words implying uncertainty; "obscure glance," "apparently," "resembling," "must have been," "slight degree," and "conceive."

Darwin, on page 171 of the same book, tries to locate his first man—that is, the first man to come down out of the trees—in Africa. After leaving man in company with gorillas and chimpanzees, he says, "But it is useless to speculate on this subject." If he had only thought of this earlier, the world might have been spared much of the speculation that his brute hypothesis has excited.

On page 79 Darwin gives some fanciful reasons for believing that man is more likely to have descended from the chimpanzee than from the gorilla. His speculations are an excellent illustration of the effect that the evolutionary hypothesis has in cultivating the imagination. Professor J. Arthur Thomson says that the "idea of evolution is the most potent thought economizing formula the world has yet known." It is more than that; it dispenses with thinking entirely and relies on the imagination.

On page 141 Darwin attempts to trace the mind of man back to the mind of lower animals. On pages 113 and 114 he endeavors to trace man's moral nature back to the animals. It is all animal, animal, animal, with never a thought of God or of religion.

Our first indictment against evolution is that it disputes the truth of the Bible account of man's creation and shakes faith in the Bible as the Word of God. This indictment we prove by comparing the processes described as evolutionary with the text of Genesis. It not only contradicts the Mosaic record as to the beginning of human life, but it disputes the Bible doctrine of reproduction according to kind—the greatest scientific principle known.

Our second indictment is that the evolutionary hypothesis, carried to its logical conclusion, disputes every vital truth of the Bible. Its tendency, natural, if not inevitable, is to lead those who really accept it, first to agnosticism and then to atheism. Evolutionists attack the truth of the Bible, not openly at first, but by using weazel-words like "poetical," "symbolical" and "allegorical" to suck the meaning out the inspired record of man's creation.

We call as our first witness Charles Darwin. He began life a Christian. On page 39, Vol. I of the Life and Letters of Charles Darwin, by his son, Francis Darwin, he says, speaking of the period from 1828 to 1831, "I did not then in the least doubt the strict and literal truth of every word in the Bible." On page 412 of Vol. II of the same publication, he says, "When I was collecting facts for 'The Origin' my belief in what is called a personal God was as firm as that of Dr. Pusey himself." It may be a surprise to your honor and to you, gentlemen of the jury, as it was to me, to learn that Darwin spent three years at Cambridge *studying for the ministry.*

This was Darwin as a young man, before he came under the influence of the doctrine that man came from a lower order of animals. The change wrought in his religious views will be found in a letter written to a German youth in 1879, and printed on page 277 of Vol I of the Life and Letters above referred to. The letter begins: "I am much engaged, an old man, and out of health, and I cannot spare time to answer your questions fully,—nor indeed can they be answered. Science has nothing to do with Christ, except in so far as the habit of scientific research makes a man cautious in admitting evidence. For myself, I do not believe that there ever has been any revelation. As for a future life, every man must judge for himself between conflicting vague probabilities."

Note that "science has nothing to do with Christ, except in so far as the habit of scientific research makes a man cautious in admitting evidence." Stated plainly, that simply means that "the habit of scientific research" makes one cautious in accepting the only evidence that we have of Christ's existence, mission, teachings, crucifixion, and resurrection, namely the evidence found in the Bible. To make this interpretation of his words the only possible one, he adds, "For myself, I do not believe that there ever has been any revelation." In rejecting the Bible as a revelation from God, he rejects the Bible's conception of God and he rejects also the supernatural Christ of whom the Bible, and the Bible alone, tells. And, it will be observed, he refuses to express any opinion as to a future life.

Now let us follow with his son's exposition of his father's views as they are given in extracts from a biography written in 1876. Here is Darwin's language as quoted by his son:

"During these two years (October, 1838, to January, 1839) I was led to think much about religion. Whilst on board the Beagle I was quite orthodox and I remember being heartily laughed at by several of the officers (though themselves orthodox) for quoting the Bible as an unanswerable authority on some point of morality. When thus reflecting, I felt compelled to look for a First Cause, having an intelligent mind in some degree analogous to man; and I deserved to be called an atheist. This conclusion was strong in my mind about the time, as far as I can remember, when I wrote the 'Origin of Species'; it is since that time that it has very gradually, with many fluctuations, become weaker. But then arises the doubt, can the mind of man, which has, as I fully believe, been developed from a mind as low as that possessed by the lowest animals, be trusted when it draws such grand conclusions?

"I cannot pretend to throw the least light on such abstruse problems. The mystery of the beginning of all things is insoluble by us; and I for one must be content to remain an Agnostic."

When Darwin entered upon his scientific career he was "quite orthodox and quoted the Bible as an unanswerable authority on some point of morality." Even when he wrote "The Origin of Species," the thought of "a First Cause, having an intelligent mind in some degree analogous to man" was strong in his mind. It was *after* that time that "very gradually, with many fluctuations," his belief in God became weaker. He traces this decline for us and concludes by telling us that he cannot pretend to throw the least light on such abstruse problems—the religious problems above referred to. Then comes the flat statement that he "must be content to remain an Agnostic"; and to make clear what he means by the word, agnostic, he says that "the mystery of the beginning of all things is insoluble by us"—not by him alone, but by everybody. Here we have the effect of evolution upon its most distinguished exponent; it led from an orthodox Christian, believing every word of the Bible and in a personal God, down and down and down to helpless and hopeless agnosticism.

But there is one sentence upon which I reserved comment—it throws light upon his downward pathway. "Then arises the doubt, can the mind of man which has, as I fully believe, been developed from a mind as low as that possessed by the lowest animals, be trusted when it draws such grand conclusions?"

Here is the explanation; he drags man down to the brute level, and then, judging man by brute standards, he questions whether man's mind can be trusted to deal with God and immortality!

How can any teacher tell his students that evolution *does not tend* to destroy his religious faith? How can an honest teacher *conceal* from his students the effect of evolution upon Darwin himself? And is it not stranger still that preachers who advocate evolution never speak of Darwin's loss of faith, due to his belief in evolution? The parents of Tennessee have reason enough to fear the effect of evolution on the minds of their children. Belief in evolution cannot bring to those who hold such a belief any compensation for the loss of faith in God, trust in the Bible, and belief in the supernatural character of Christ. It is belief in evolution that has caused so many scientists and so many Christians to reject the miracles of the Bible, and then give up, one after another, every vital truth of Christianity. They finally cease to pray and sunder the tie that binds them to their Heavenly Father.

The miracle should not be a stumbling block to any one. It raises but three questions: 1st. *Could* God perform a miracle? Yes, the God who created the universe can do anything He wants to with it. He can temporarily suspend any law that He has made or He may employ higher laws that we do not understand. 2nd. *Would* God perform a miracle? To answer that question in the negative one would have to know more about God's plans and purposes than a finite mind can know, and yet some are so wedded to evolution that they deny that God *would* perform a miracle merely because a miracle is inconsistent with evolution.

If we believe that God *can* perform a miracle and *might* desire to do so, we are prepared to consider with open mind the third question, namely, *Did* God perform the miracles recorded in the Bible? The same evidence that establishes the authority of the Bible establishes the truth of the record of miracles performed.

Now let me read to the honorable court and to you, gentlemen of the jury, one of the most pathetic confessions that has come to my notice. George John Romanes, a distinguished biologist, sometimes called the successor of Darwin, was prominent enough to be given extended space in both the Encyclopedia Britannica and Encyclopedia Americana. Like Darwin, he was reared in the orthodox faith, and like Darwin, was led away from it by evolution (see "Thoughts on Religion," page 180). For twenty-five years he could not pray. Soon after he became an agnostic, he wrote a book entitled, "A Candid Examination of Theism," publishing it under the assumed name, "Physicus." In this book (see page 29, "Thoughts on Religion"), he says:

"And forasmuch as I am far from being able to agree with those who affirm that the twilight doctrine of the 'New Faith' is a desirable substitute for the waning splendor of 'the old,' I am not ashamed to confess that with this virtual negation of God the universe to me has lost its soul of loveliness; and although from henceforth the precept to 'work while it is day' will doubtless but gain an intensified force from the terribly intensified meaning of the words that 'the night cometh when no man can work,' yet when at times I think, as think at times I must, of the appalling contrast between the hallowed glory of that creed which once was mine, and the lonely mystery of existence as now I find it,—at such times I shall ever feel it impossible to avoid the sharpest pang of which my nature is susceptible."

Do these evolutionists stop to think of the crime they commit when they take faith out of the hearts of men and women and lead them out into a starless night? What pleasure can they find in robbing a human being of "the hallowed glory of that creed" that Romanes once cherished, and in substituting "the lonely mystery of existence" as he found it? Can the fathers and mothers of Tennessee be blamed for trying to protect their children from such a tragedy?

If anyone has been led to complain of the severity of the punishment that hangs over the defendant, let him compare this crime and its mild punishment with the crimes for which a greater punishment is prescribed. What is the taking of a few dollars from one in day or night in comparison with the crime of leading one away from God and away from Christ?

Shakespeare regards the robbing one of his good name as much more grave than the stealing of his purse. But we have a higher authority than Shakespeare to invoke in this connection. He who spake as never man spake, thus describes the crimes that are committed against the young. "It is impossible but that offences will come: but woe unto him through whom they come. It were better for him that a millstone were hanged about his neck, and he cast into the sea, than that he should offend one of these little ones."

Christ did not overdraw the picture. Who is able to set a price upon the life of a child—a child into whom a mother has poured her life and for whom a father has labored? What may a noble life mean to the child itself, to the parents, and to the world?

And, it must be remembered, that we can measure the effect on only that part of life which is spent on earth; we have no way of calculating the effect on that infinite circle of life of which existence here is but a small arc. The soul is immortal and religion deals with the soul; the logical effect of the evolutionary hypothesis is to undermine religion and thus affect the soul. I recently received a list of questions that were to be discussed in a prominent Eastern school for women. The second question in the list read, "Is religion an obsolescent function that should be allowed to atrophy quietly, without arousing the passionate prejudice of outworn superstition?" The *real* attack of evolution, it will be seen, is not upon *orthodox* Christianity, or even upon *Christianity*, but upon *religion*—the most basic fact in man's existence and the most practical thing in life.

But I have some more evidence of the effect of evolution upon the life of those who accept it and try to harmonize their thought with it.

James H. Leuba, a Professor of Psychology at Bryn Mawr College, Pennsylvania, published a few years ago, a book entitled "Belief in God and Immortality." In this book he relates how he secured the opinions of scientists as to the existence of a personal God and a personal immortality. He used a volume entitled "American Men of Science," which, he says, included the names of "practically every American who may properly be called a scientist." There were fifty-five hundred names in the book. He selected one thousand names as representative of the fifty-five hundred, and addressed them personally. Most of them, he said, were teachers in schools of higher learning. The names were kept confidential. Upon the answers received, he asserts that over *half* of them *doubt* or *deny* the existence of a personal God and a personal immortality, and he asserts that *unbelief increases* in proportion to prominence, the percentage of unbelief being greatest among the most prominent. Among biologists, believers in a personal God numbered less than thirty-one per cent, while believers in a personal immortality numbered only thirty-seven per cent.

He also questioned the students in nine colleges of high rank and from one thousand answers received, ninety-seven per cent of which were from students between eighteen and twenty, he found that unbelief increased from fifteen per cent in the Freshman class up to forty to forty-five per cent among the men who graduated. On page 280 of this book, we read, "The students' statistics show that young people enter college, possessed of the beliefs still accepted, more or less perfunctorily, in the average home of the land, and gradually abandon the cardinal Christian beliefs." This change from belief to unbelief he attributes to the influence of the persons "of high culture under whom they studied."

The people of Tennessee have been patient enough; they acted none too soon. How can they expect to protect society, and even the church, from the deadening influence of agnosticism and atheism if they permit the teachers employed by taxation to poison the minds of the youth with this destructive doctrine? And remember, that the law has not heretofore required the writing of the word "poison" on poisonous doctrines. The bodies of our people are so valuable that druggists and physicians must be careful to properly label all poisons; why not be as careful to protect the spiritual life of our people from the poisons that kill the soul?

There is a test that is sometimes used to ascertain whether one suspected of mental infirmity is really insane. He is put into a tank of water and told to dip the tank dry while a stream of water flows into the tank. If he has not sense enough to turn off the stream, he is adjudged insane. Can parents justify themselves if, knowing the effect of belief in evolution, they permit irreligious teachers to inject skepticism and infidelity into the minds of their children?

[. . .]

Our third indictment against evolution is that it diverts attention from pressing problems of great importance to trifling speculation. While one evolutionist is trying to imagine what happened in the dim past, another is trying to pry open the door of the distant future. One recently grew eloquent over ancient worms, and another predicted that seventy-five thousand years hence everyone will be bald and toothless. Both those who endeavor to clothe our remote ancestors with hair and those who endeavor to remove the hair from the heads of our remote descendants ignore the present with its imperative demands. The science of "How to Live" is the most important of all the sciences. It is *desirable* to know the physical sciences, but it is *necessary* to know how to live. Christians desire that their children shall be taught all the sciences, but they do not want them to lose sight of the Rock of Ages while they study the age of the rocks; neither do they desire them to become so absorbed in measuring the distance between the stars that they will forget Him who holds the stars in His hand.

While not more than two per cent of our population are college graduates, these, because of enlarged powers, need a "Heavenly Vision" even more than those less learned, both for their own restraint and to assure society that their enlarged powers will be used for the benefit of society and not against the public welfare.

Evolution is deadening the spiritual life of a multitude of students. Christians do not desire less education, but they desire that religion shall be entwined with learning so that our boys and girls will return from college with their hearts aflame with love of God and love of fellow-men, and prepared to lead in the altruistic work that the world so sorely needs. The cry in the business world, in the industrial world, in the professional world, in the political world—even in the religious world—is for consecrated talents—for ability plus a passion for service.

Our fourth indictment against the evolutionary hypothesis is that, by paralyzing the hope of reform, it discourages those who labor for the improvement of man's condition. Every upward-looking man or woman seeks to lift the level upon which mankind stands, and they trust that they will see beneficient changes during the brief span of their own lives. Evolution chills their enthusiasm by substituting aeons for years. It obscures all beginnings in the mists of endless ages. It is represented as a cold and heartless process, beginning with time and ending in eternity, and acting so slowly that even the rocks cannot preserve a record of the imaginary changes through which it is credited with having carried an original germ of life that appeared sometime from somewhere. Its only program for man is scientific breeding, a system under which a few supposedly superior intellects, self-appointed, would direct the mating and the movements of the mass of mankind—an impossible system! Evolution, disputing the miracle, and ignoring the spiritual in life, has no place for the regeneration of the individual. It recognizes no cry of repentance and scoffs at the doctrine that one can be born again.

It is thus the intolerant and unrelenting enemy of the only process that can redeem society through the redemption of the individual. An evolutionist would never write such a story as The Prodigal Son; it contradicts the whole theory of evolution. The two sons inherited from the same parents and, through their parents, from the same ancestors, proximate and remote. And these sons were reared at the same fireside and were surrounded by the same environment during all the days of their youth; and yet they were different. If Mr. Darrow is correct in the theory applied to Loeb, namely, that his crime was due either to inheritance or to environment, how will he explain the difference between the elder brother and the wayward son? The evolutionist may understand from observation, if not by experience, even though he cannot explain, why one of these boys was guilty of every immorality, squandered the money that the father had laboriously earned, and brought disgrace upon the family name; but his theory does not explain why a wicked young man underwent a change of heart, confessed his sin, and begged for forgiveness. And because the evolutionists cannot understand this fact, one of the most important in the human life, he cannot understand the infinite love of the Heavenly Father who stands ready to welcome home any repentant sinner, no matter how far he has wandered, how often he has fallen, or how deep he has sunk in sin.

Your honor has quoted from a wonderful poem written by a great Tennessee poet, Walter Malone. I venture to quote another stanza which puts into exquisite language the new opportunity which a merciful God gives to every one who will turn from sin to righteousness.

> "Though deep in mire, wring not your hands and weep;
>   I lend my arm to all who say, 'I can.'
> No shame-faced outcast ever sank so deep
>   But he might rise and be again a man."

There are no lines like these in all that evolutionists have ever written. Darwin says that science has nothing to do with the Christ who taught the spirit embodied in the words of Walter Malone, and yet this spirit is the only hope of human progress. A heart can be changed in the twinkling of an eye and a change in the life follows a change in the heart. If one heart can be changed, it is possible that many hearts can be changed, and if many hearts can be changed it is possible that all hearts can be changed—that a world can be born in a day. It is this fact that inspires all who labor for man's betterment. It is because Christians believe in individual regeneration and in the regeneration of society through the regeneration of individuals that they pray, "Thy kingdom come, Thy will be done in earth as it is in heaven." Evolution makes a mockery of the Lord's Prayer!

To interpret the words to mean that the improvement desired must come slowly through unfolding ages,—a process with which each generation could have little to do—is to defer hope, and hope deferred maketh the heart sick.

Our fifth indictment of the evolutionary hypothesis is that, if taken seriously and made the basis of a philosophy of life, it would eliminate love and carry man back to a struggle of tooth and claw. The Christians who have allowed themselves to be deceived into believing that evolution is a beneficent, or even a rational process, have been associating with those who either do not understand its implications or dare not avow their knowledge of these implications. Let me give you some authority on this subject. I will begin with Darwin, the high priest of evolution, to whom all evolutionists bow.

On pages 149 and 150, in "The Descent of Man," already referred to, he says:

"With savages, the weak in body or mind are soon eliminated; and those that survive commonly exhibit a vigorous state of health. We civilized men, on the other hand, do our utmost to check the process of elimination; we build asylums for the imbecile, the maimed, and the sick; we institute poor laws; and our medical men exert their utmost skill to save the life of everyone to the last moment. There is reason to believe that vaccination has preserved thousands who from a weak constitution would formerly have succumbed to smallpox. Thus the weak members of civilized society propagate their kind. No one who has attended to the breeding of domestic animals will doubt that this must be highly injurious to the race of man. It is surprising how soon a want of care, or care wrongly directed, leads, to the degeneration of a domestic race; but, excepting in the case of man himself, hardly anyone is so ignorant as to allow his worst animals to breed.

"The aid which we feel impelled to give to the helpless is mainly an incidental result of the instinct of sympathy, which was originally acquired as part of the social instincts, but subsequently rendered, in the manner previously indicated, more tender and more widely diffused. How could we check our sympathy, even at the urging of hard reason, without deterioration in the noblest part of our nature. . . . We must therefore bear the undoubtedly bad effects of the weak surviving and propagating their kind."

Darwin reveals the barbarous sentiment that runs through evolution and dwarfs the moral nature of those who become obsessed with it. Let us analyze the quotation just given. Darwin speaks with approval of the savage custom of eliminating the weak so that only the strong will survive and complains that "we civilized men do our utmost to check the process of elimination." How inhuman such a doctrine as this! He thinks it injurious to "build asylums for the imbecile, the maimed, and the sick," or to care for the poor. Even the medical men come in for criticism because they "exert their utmost skill to save the life of everyone to the last moment." And then note his hostility to *vaccination* because it has "preserved thousands who, from a weak constitution would, but for vaccination, have succumbed to smallpox"! All of the sympathetic activities of civilized society are condemned because they enable "the weak members to propagate their kind." Then he drags mankind down to the level of the brute and compares the freedom given to man unfavorably with the restraint that we put on barnyard beasts.

The second paragraph of the above quotation shows that his kindly heart rebelled against the cruelty of his own doctrine. He says that we "feel *impelled* to give to the helpless," although he traces it to a sympathy which he thinks is developed by evolution; he even admits that we could not check this sympathy "even at the urging of hard reason, without deterioration of the noblest part of our nature." "*We must therefore bear*" what he regards as "the undoubtedly *bad effects* of the weak surviving and propagating their kind." Could any doctrine be more destructive of civilization? And what a commentary on evolution! He wants us to believe that evolution develops a human sympathy that finally becomes so tender that it repudiates the law that created it and thus invites a return to a level where the extinguishing of pity and sympathy will permit the brutal instincts to again do their progressive (?) work.

[. . .]

Can any Christian remain indifferent? Science needs religion to direct its energies and to inspire with lofty purpose those who employ the forces that are unloosed by science. Evolution is at war with religion because religion is supernatural; it is, therefore, the relentless foe of Christianity, which is a revealed religion.

Let us, then, hear the conclusion of the whole matter. Science is a magnificent material force, but it is not a teacher of morals. It can perfect machinery, but it adds no moral restraints to protect society from the misuse of the machine. It can also build gigantic intellectual ships, but it constructs no moral rudders for the control of storm-tossed human vessels. It not only fails to supply the spiritual element needed but some of its unproven hypotheses rob the ship of its *compass* and thus endanger its cargo.

In war, science has proven itself an evil genius; it has made war more terrible than it ever was before. Man used to be content to slaughter his fellowmen on a single plain—the earth's surface. Science has taught him to go down into the water and shoot up from below, and to go up into the clouds and shoot down from above, thus making the battlefield three times as bloody as it was before; but science does *not* teach brotherly love. Science has made war so hellish that civilization was about to commit suicide; and now we are told that newly discovered instruments of destruction will make the cruelties of the late war seem trivial in comparison with the cruelties of wars that may come in the future. If civilization is to be saved from the wreckage threatened by intelligence not consecrated by love, it must be saved by the moral code of the meek and lowly Nazarene. His teachings, and His teachings alone, can solve the problems that vex the heart and perplex the world.

The world needs a Saviour more than it ever did before, and there is only one "Name under heaven given among men whereby we must be saved." It is this Name that evolution degrades, for, carried to its logical conclusion, it robs Christ of the glory of a virgin birth, of the majesty of His deity and mission, and of the triumph of His resurrection. It also disputes the doctrine of the atonement.

It is for the jury to determine whether this attack upon the Christian religion shall be permitted in the public schools of Tennessee by teachers employed by the State and paid out of the public treasury. This case is no longer local; the defendant ceases to play an important part. The case has assumed the proportions of a battle-royal between unbelief that attempts to speak through so-called science and the defenders of the Christian faith, speaking through the Legislators of Tennessee. It is again a choice between God and Baal; it is also a renewal of the issue in Pilate's court. In that historic trial—the greatest in history—force, impersonated by Pilate, occupied the throne. Behind it was the Roman government, mistress of the world, and behind the Roman Government were the legions of Rome. Before Pilate, stood Christ, the Apostle of Love. Force triumphed; they nailed Him to the tree and those who stood around mocked and jeered and said, "He is dead." But from that day the power of Caesar waned and the power of Christ increased. In a few centuries the Roman government was gone and its legions forgotten; while the crucified and risen Lord has become the greatest fact in history and the growing figure of all time.

Again force and love meet face to face, and the question, "What shall I do with Jesus?" must be answered. A bloody, brutal doctrine—Evolution—demands, as the rabble did nineteen hundred years ago, that He be crucified. That cannot be the answer of this jury representing a Christian State and sworn to uphold the laws of Tennessee. Your answer will be heard throughout the world; it is eagerly awaited by a praying multitude. If the law is nullified, there will be rejoicing wherever God is repudiated, the Saviour scoffed at and the Bible ridiculed. Every unbeliever of every kind and degree will be happy. If, on the other hand, the law is upheld and the religion of the school children protected, millions of Christians will call you blessed and, with hearts full of gratitude to God, will sing again that grand old song of triumph:

"Faith of our fathers, living still,
In spite of dungeon, fire and sword;
O how our hearts beat high with joy
Whene'er we hear that glorious word—
Faith of our fathers—holy faith;
We will be true to thee till death!"

Source

William Jennings Bryan and Mary Baird Bryan, *The Memoirs of William Jennings Bryan* (Chicago: John C. Winston, 1925), 530–43, 547–51, 554–56.

Further Reading

Kazin, Michael. *A Godly Hero: The Life of William Jennings Bryan.* New York: Knopf, 2006.

Larson, Edward J. *Summer for the Gods: The Scopes Trial and America's Continuing Debate over Science and Religion.* Cambridge, MA: Harvard University Press, 1997.

Levine, Lawrence W. *Defender of the Faith: William Jennings Bryan: The Last Decade, 1915–1925.* New York: Oxford University Press, 1965.

4

Faith, Freedom, and the Meaning
of Citizenship

Americans often remember the Second World War as a golden
age and the participants in that conflict as members of the
"Greatest Generation." Back then, the story goes, a sense of
national unity and purpose provided the strength to achieve a heroic
victory. Most of all, the war is invoked as a moment of moral clarity, in which American virtue and the evil of the enemy were beyond
question.

For historians, this memory is misleading. Although Americans performed many heroic acts, and although Adolf Hitler was unquestion-
ably evil, the global crisis was not a time when everything was clear.
Instead, it raised the most difficult questions about how a democracy
ought to wage a modern war. In particular, Americans confronted the
conundrum of when a nation built on the inalienable rights of "life,
liberty, and the pursuit of happiness" might ask its citizens to kill and
be killed overseas. National unity, meanwhile, became not an assumption but a continuing argument: what did it mean to be American and
how much difference could be tolerated?

Religion became deeply implicated in these debates over the morality of violence and the limits of dissent. World War II is seldom
described as a holy war, but religious ethics and identities became
central to the way it was waged and understood. The Nazis explicitly
described their project as a defense of Germany's Christian culture
against Jewish influence, leading many American liberals to adopt the
term "Judeo-Christian" to talk about their own nation's heritage in
a more inclusive way. On the home front, pacifists sparred with pro-
interventionist "realists" over the true meaning of Christian peace,
love, and justice, a disagreement represented here by Reinhold Nie-

buhr and Dorothy Day. Meanwhile, Jehovah's Witnesses steadfastly maintained that true religion was absolutely incompatible with modern nationalism, bringing down harsh reprisals from their neighbors who assumed that God and country went together.

These unresolved tensions surrounding war and tolerance would linger into the postwar period. Not long after 1945, the nation found itself engaged in a rivalry with the Soviet Union that became known as the Cold War. That struggle, too, lent itself to religious interpretations; indeed, many Americans believed that the fundamental division in the Cold War was between their own faith and the Soviets' atheism. For better and for worse, the massive campaigns against Nazism and Communism have shaped the country's political and ethical reasoning about every subsequent geopolitical conflict.

REINHOLD NIEBUHR,
"WHY THE CHRISTIAN CHURCH
IS NOT PACIFIST" (1940)

Reinhold Niebuhr (1892–1971), the most influential American theologian of the twentieth century, was a liberal Protestant who nonetheless criticized religious and political liberalism for holding optimistic views of human nature and ignoring the power of sin and evil in the world. Niebuhr belonged to a generation that lived through two world wars— the most destructive events ever produced by human beings—and then witnessed the rise of the Cold War, which threatened to destroy civilization in a nuclear Armageddon. He tried to understand what Christian politics might mean amid such unfathomable catastrophes.

Niebuhr's long career took a number of intellectual twists and turns. Like many progressives, he supported intervention by the United States in the First World War, putting his hope in Woodrow Wilson's idea of a "war to end all wars." The results left him disillusioned, and he soon joined the peace movement, becoming a leader in the pacifist Fellowship of Reconciliation. By the 1930s, though, pacifism, too, seemed inadequate. Niebuhr's 1932 book *Moral Man and Immoral Society* emphasized the selfishness that drove economic and political conflicts, but the book also chastised pacifists and other reformers for naively believing that moral progress could eliminate conflict entirely. Such "idealists" failed to recognize that force was sometimes necessary in the service of a just cause. In the Depression decade, Niebuhr, then a socialist, suggested that economic power for the working class might be such a cause.

Niebuhr came to believe that the fight against Nazism, too, was important enough to justify the evil of war. In "Why the Christian Church Is Not Pacifist," he argues against the "law of love" as an adequate guide to practical politics. Because we live in a sinful world, he explains, our actions will never be as loving as we might wish, yet the cost of inaction might be even worse. This view was deeply compelling to liberals who tried to balance the lofty imperative of justice with the sordid realities of power politics.

By the time of the Cold War, Niebuhr had distanced himself from his earlier radicalism and ascended to the highest foreign policy circles in Washington. His writing continues to influence politicians and theorists across the political spectrum; most recently, Barack Obama has cited him as a major force in his own thinking about the ethical use of power.

Reinhold Niebuhr, "Why the Christian Church Is Not Pacifist"

I

Whenever the actual historical situation sharpens the issue, the debate whether the Christian Church is, or ought to be, pacifist is carried on with fresh vigor both inside and outside the Christian community. Those who are not pacifists seek to prove that pacifism is a heresy; while the pacifists contend, or at least imply, that the Church's failure to espouse pacifism unanimously can only be interpreted as apostasy, and must be attributed to its lack of courage or to its want of faith.

There may be an advantage in stating the thesis, with which we enter this debate, immediately. The thesis is, that the failure of the Church to espouse pacifism is not apostasy, but is derived from an understanding of the Christian Gospel which refuses simply to equate the Gospel with the "law of love." Christianity is not simply a new law, namely, the law of love. The finality of Christianity cannot be proved by analyses which seek to reveal that the law of love is stated more unambiguously and perfectly in the life and teachings of Christ than anywhere else. Christianity is a religion which measures the total dimension of human existence not only in terms of the final norm of human conduct, which is expressed in the law of love, but also in terms of the fact of sin. It recognizes that the same man who can become his true self only by striving infinitely for self-realization beyond himself is also inevitably involved in the sin of infinitely making his partial and narrow self the true end of existence. It believes, in other words, that though Christ is the true norm (the "second Adam") for every man, every man is also in some sense a crucifier of Christ.

The good news of the gospel is not the law that we ought to love one another. The good news of the gospel is that there is a resource of divine mercy which is able to overcome a contradiction within our own souls, which we cannot ourselves overcome. This contradiction is that, though we know we ought to love our neighbor as ourself, there is a "law in our members which wars against the law that is in our mind," so that, in fact, we love ourselves more than our neighbor.

The grace of God which is revealed in Christ is regarded by Christian faith as, on the one hand, an actual "power of righteousness" which heals the contradiction within our hearts. In that sense Christ defines the actual possibilities of human existence. On the other hand, this grace is conceived as "justification," as pardon rather than power, as the forgiveness of God, which is vouchsafed to man despite the fact that he never achieves the full measure of Christ. In that sense Christ is the "impossible possibility." Loyalty to him means realization in intention, but does not actually mean the full realization of the measure of Christ. In this doctrine of forgiveness and justification, Christianity measures the full seriousness of sin as a permanent factor in human history. Naturally, the doctrine has no meaning for modern secular civilization, nor for the secularized and moralistic versions of Christianity. They cannot understand the doctrine precisely because they believe there is some fairly simple way out of the sinfulness of human history.

It is rather remarkable that so many modern Christians should believe that Christianity is primarily a "challenge" to man to obey the law of Christ; whereas it is, as a matter of fact, a religion which deals realistically with the problem presented by the violation of this law. Far from believing that the ills of the world could be set right "if only" men obeyed the law of Christ, it has always regarded the problem of achieving justice in a sinful world as a very difficult task. In the profounder versions of the Christian faith the very utopian illusions, which are currently equated with Christianity, have been rigorously disavowed.

Nevertheless, it is not possible to regard pacifism simply as a heresy. In one of its aspects modern Christian pacifism is simply a version of Christian perfectionism. It expresses a genuine impulse in the heart of Christianity, the impulse to take the law of Christ seriously and not to allow the political strategies, which the sinful character of man makes necessary, to become final norms. In its profounder forms this Christian perfectionism did not proceed from a simple faith that the "law of love" could be regarded as an alternative to the political strategies by which the world achieves a precarious justice. These strategies invariably involve the balancing of power with power; and they never completely escape the peril of tyranny on the one hand, and the peril of anarchy and warfare on the other.

In medieval ascetic perfectionism and in Protestant sectarian perfectionism (of the type of Meno Simons, for instance) the effort to achieve a standard of perfect love in individual life was not presented as a political alternative. On the contrary, the political problem and task were specifically disavowed. This perfectionism did not give itself to the illusion that it had discovered a method for eliminating the element of conflict from political strategies. On the contrary, it regarded the mystery of evil as beyond its power of solution. It was content to set up the most perfect and unselfish individual life as a symbol of the Kingdom of God. It knew that this could only be done by disavowing the political task and by freeing the individual of all responsibility for social justice.

It is this kind of pacifism which is not a heresy. It is rather a valuable asset for the Christian faith. It is a reminder to the Christian community that the relative norms of social justice, which justify both coercion and resistance to coercion, are not final norms, and that Christians are in constant peril of forgetting their relative and tentative character and of making them too completely normative.

There is thus a Christian pacifism which is not a heresy. Yet most modern forms of Christian pacifism are heretical. Presumably inspired by the Christian gospel, they have really absorbed the Renaissance faith in the goodness of man, have rejected the Christian doctrine of original sin as an outmoded bit of pessimism, have reinterpreted the Cross so that it is made to stand for the absurd idea that perfect love is guaranteed a simple victory over the world, and have rejected all other profound elements of the Christian gospel as "Pauline" accretions which must be stripped from the "simple gospel of Jesus." This form of pacifism is not only heretical when judged by the standards of the total gospel. It is equally heretical when judged by the facts of human existence. There are no historical realities which remotely conform to it. It is important to recognize this lack of conformity to the facts of experience as a criterion of heresy.

All forms of religious faith are principles of interpretation which we use to organize our experience. Some religions may be adequate principles of interpretation at certain levels of experience, but they break down at deeper levels. No religious faith can maintain itself in defiance of the experience which it supposedly interprets. A religious faith which substitutes faith in man for faith in God cannot finally validate itself in experience. If we believe that the only reason men do not love each other perfectly is because the law of love has not been preached persuasively enough, we believe something to which experience does not conform. If we believe that if Britain had only been fortunate enough to have produced 30 per cent instead of 2 per cent of conscientious objectors to military service, Hitler's heart would have been softened and he would not have dared to attack Poland, we hold a faith which no historic reality justifies.

Such a belief has no more justification in the facts of experience than the communist belief that the sole cause of man's sin is the class organization of society and the corollary faith that a "classless" society will be essentially free of human sinfulness. All of these beliefs are pathetic alternatives to the Christian faith. They all come finally to the same thing. They do not believe that man remains a tragic creature who needs the divine mercy as much at the end as at the beginning of his moral endeavors. They believe rather that there is some fairly easy way out of the human situation of "self-alienation." In this connection it is significant that Christian pacifists, rationalists like Bertrand Russell, and mystics like Aldous Huxley, believe essentially the same thing. The Christians make Christ into the symbol of their faith in man. But their faith is really identical with that of Russell or Huxley.

The common element in these various expressions of faith in man is the belief that man is essentially good at some level of his being. They believe that if you can abstract the rational-universal man from what is finite and contingent in human nature, or if you can only cultivate some mystic-universal element in the deeper levels of man's consciousness, you will be able to eliminate human selfishness and the consequent conflict of life with life. These rational or mystical views of man conform neither to the New Testament's view of human nature nor yet to the complex facts of human experience.

In order to elaborate the thesis more fully, that the refusal of the Christian Church to espouse pacifism is not apostasy and that most modern forms of pacifism are heretical, it is necessary first of all to consider the character of the absolute and unqualified demands which Christ makes and to understand the relation of these demands to the gospel.

II

It is very foolish to deny that the ethic of Jesus is an absolute and uncompromising ethic. It is, in the phrase of Ernst Troeltsch, an ethic of "love universalism and love perfectionism." The injunctions "resist not evil," "love your enemies," "if ye love them that love you what thanks have you?" "be not anxious for your life," and "be ye therefore perfect even as your father in heaven is perfect," are all of one piece, and they are all uncompromising and absolute. Nothing is more futile and pathetic than the effort of some Christian theologians who find it necessary to become involved in the relativities of politics, in resistance to tyranny or in social conflict, to justify themselves by seeking to prove that Christ was also involved in some of these relativities, that he used whips to drive the money-changers out of the Temple, or that he came "not to bring peace but a sword," or that he asked the disciples to sell a cloak and buy a sword. What could be more futile than to build a whole ethical structure upon the exegetical issue whether Jesus accepted the sword with the words: "It is enough," or whether he really meant: "Enough of this"?[1]

1. Luke xxii, 36.

Those of us who regard the ethic of Jesus as finally and ultimately normative, but as not immediately applicable to the task of securing justice in a sinful world, are very foolish if we try to reduce the ethic so that it will cover and justify our prudential and relative standards and strategies. To do this is to reduce the ethic to a new legalism. The significance of the law of love is precisely that it is not just another law, but a law which transcends all law. Every law and every standard which falls short of the law of love embodies contingent factors and makes concessions to the fact that sinful man must achieve tentative harmonies of life with life which are less than the best. It is dangerous and confusing to give these tentative and relative standards final and absolute religious sanction.

Curiously enough the pacifists are just as guilty as their less absolutist brethren of diluting the ethic of Jesus for the purpose of justifying their position. They are forced to recognize that an ethic of pure non-resistance can have no immediate relevance to any political situation; for in every political situation it is necessary to achieve justice by resisting pride and power. They therefore declare that the ethic of Jesus is not an ethic of non-resistance, but one of non-violent resistance; that it allows one to resist evil provided the resistance does not involve the destruction of life or property.

There is not the slightest support in Scripture for this doctrine of non-violence. Nothing could be plainer than that the ethic uncompromisingly enjoins non-resistance and not non-violent resistance. Furthermore, it is obvious that the distinction between violent and non-violent resistance is not an absolute distinction. If it is made absolute, we arrive at the morally absurd position of giving moral preference to the non-violent power which Doctor Goebbels wields over the type of power wielded by a general. This absurdity is really derived from the modern (and yet probably very ancient and very Platonic) heresy of regarding the "physical" as evil and the "spiritual" as good. The *reductio ad absurdum* of this position is achieved in a book which has become something of a textbook for modern pacifists, Richard Gregg's *The Power of Non-Violence.* In this book non-violent resistance is commended as the best method of defeating your foe, particularly as the best method of breaking his morale. It is suggested that Christ ended his life on the Cross because he had not completely mastered the technique of non-violence, and must for this reason be regarded as a guide who is inferior to Gandhi, but whose significance lies in initiating a movement which culminates in Gandhi.

One may well concede that a wise and decent statesmanship will seek not only to avoid conflict, but to avoid violence in conflict. Parliamentary political controversy is one method of sublimating political struggles in such a way as to avoid violent collisions of interest. But this pragmatic distinction has nothing to do with the more basic distinction between the ethic of the "Kingdom of God," in which no concession is made to human sin, and all relative political strategies which, assuming human sinfulness, seek to secure the highest measure of peace and justice among selfish and sinful men.

III

If pacifists were less anxious to dilute the ethic of Christ to make it conform to their particular type of non-violent politics, and if they were less obsessed with the obvious contradiction between the ethic of Christ and the fact of war, they might have noticed that the injunction "resist not evil" is only part and parcel of a total ethic which we violate not only in war-time, but every day of our life, and that overt conflict is but a final and vivid revelation of the character of human existence. This total ethic can be summarized most succinctly in the two injunctions "Be not anxious for your life" and "love thy neighbor as thyself."

In the first of these, attention is called to the fact that the root and source of all undue self-assertion lies in the anxiety which all men have in regard to their existence: The ideal possibility is that perfect trust in God's providence ("for your heavenly father knoweth what things ye have need of") and perfect unconcern for the physical life ("fear not them which are able to kill the body") would create a state of serenity in which one life would not seek to take advantage of another life. But the fact is that anxiety is an inevitable concomitant of human freedom, and is the root of the inevitable sin which expresses itself in every human activity and creativity. Not even the most idealistic preacher who admonishes his congregation to obey the law of Christ is free of the sin which arises from anxiety. He may or may not be anxious for his job, but he is certainly anxious about his prestige. Perhaps he is anxious for his reputation as a righteous man. He may be tempted to preach a perfect ethic the more vehemently in order to hide an unconscious apprehension of the fact that his own life does not conform to it. There is no life which does not violate the injunction "Be not anxious." That is the tragedy of human sin. It is the tragedy of man who is dependent upon God, but seeks to make himself independent and self-sufficing.

In the same way there is no life which is not involved in a violation of the injunction, "Thou shalt love thy neighbor as thyself." No one is so blind as the idealist who tells us that war would be unnecessary "if only" nations obeyed the law of Christ, but who remains unconscious of the fact that even the most saintly life is involved in some measure of contradiction to this law. Have we not all known loving fathers and mothers who, despite a very genuine love for their children, had to be resisted if justice and freedom were to be gained for the children? Do we not know that the sinful will-to-power may be compounded with the most ideal motives and may use the latter as its instruments and vehicles? The collective life of man undoubtedly stands on a lower moral plane than the life of individuals; yet nothing revealed in the life of races and nations is un-known in individual life. The sins of pride and of lust for power and the consequent tyranny and injustice are all present, at least in an inchoate form, in individual life. Even as I write my little five-year-old boy comes to me with the tale of an attack made upon him by his year-old sister. This tale is concocted to escape paternal judgment for being too rough in play-ing with his sister. One is reminded of Germany's claim that Poland was the aggressor and the similar Russian charge against Finland.

The pacifists do not know human nature well enough to be concerned about the contradictions between the law of love and the sin of man, until sin has conceived and brought forth death. They do not see that sin intro-duces an element of conflict into the world and that even the most loving relations are not free of it. They are, consequently, unable to appreciate the complexity of the problem of justice. They merely assert that if only men loved one another, all the complex, and sometimes horrible, realities of the political order could be dispensed with. They do not see that their "if" begs the most basic problem of human history. It is because men are sinners that justice can be achieved only by a certain degree of coercion on the one hand, and by resistance to coercion and tyranny on the other hand. The political life of man must constantly steer between the Scylla of anarchy and the Charybdis of tyranny.

Human egotism makes large-scale co-operation upon a purely volun-tary basis impossible. Governments must coerce. Yet there is an element of evil in this coercion. It is always in danger of serving the purposes of the coercing power rather than the general weal. We cannot fully trust the motives of any ruling class or power. That is why it is important to maintain democratic checks upon the centers of power. It may also be necessary to resist a ruling class, nation or race, if it violates the standards of relative justice which have been set up for it. Such resistance means war. It need not mean overt conflict or violence. But if those who resist tyranny publish their scruples against violence too publicly the tyrannical power need only threaten the use of violence against non-violent pressure to persuade the resisters to quiescence. (The relation of pacifism to the abortive effort to apply non-violent sanctions against Italy in the Ethio-pian dispute is instructive at this point.)

The refusal to recognize that sin introduces an element of conflict into the world invariably means that a morally perverse preference is given to tyranny over anarchy (war). If we are told that tyranny would destroy itself, if only we would not challenge it, the obvious answer is that tyr-anny continues to grow if it is not resisted. If it is to be resisted, the risk of overt conflict must be taken. The thesis that German tyranny must not be challenged by other nations because Germany will throw off this yoke in due time, merely means that an unjustified moral preference is given to civil war over international war, for internal resistance runs the risk of conflict as much as external resistance. Furthermore, no consideration is given to the fact that a tyrannical State may grow too powerful to be successfully resisted by purely internal pressure, and that the injustices which it does to other than its own nationals may rightfully lay the problem of the tyranny upon other nations.

It is not unfair to assert that most pacifists who seek to present their religious absolutism as a political alternative to the claims and counter-claims, the pressures and counter-pressures of the political order, invariably betray themselves into this preference for tyranny. Tyranny is not war. It is peace, but it is a peace which has nothing to do with the peace of the Kingdom of God. It is a peace which results from one will establishing a complete dominion over other wills and reducing them to acquiescence.

One of the most terrible consequences of a confused religious absolutism is that it is forced to condone such tyranny as that of Germany in the nations which it has conquered and now cruelly oppresses. It usually does this by insisting that the tyranny is no worse than that which is practised in the so-called democratic nations. Whatever may be the moral ambiguities of the so-called democratic nations, and however serious may be their failure to conform perfectly to their democratic ideals, it is sheer moral perversity to equate the inconsistencies of a democratic civilization with the brutalities which modern tyrannical States practise. If we cannot make a distinction here, there are no historical distinctions which have any value. All the distinctions upon which the fate of civilization has turned in the history of mankind have been just such relative distinctions.

One is persuaded to thank God in such times as these that the common people maintain a degree of "common sense," that they preserve an uncorrupted ability to react against injustice and the cruelty of racial bigotry. This ability has been lost among some Christian idealists who preach the law of love but forget that they, as well as all other men, are involved in the violation of that law; and who must (in order to obscure this glaring defect in their theory) eliminate all relative distinctions in history and praise the peace of tyranny as if it were nearer to the peace of the Kingdom of God than war. The overt conflicts of human history are periods of judgment when what has been hidden becomes revealed. It is the business of Christian prophecy to anticipate these judgments to some degree at least, to call attention to the fact that when men say "peace and quiet" "destruction will come upon them unaware," and reveal to what degree this overt destruction is a vivid portrayal of the constant factor of sin in human life. A theology which fails to come to grips with this tragic factor of sin is heretical, both from the standpoint of the gospel and in terms of its blindness to obvious facts of human experience in every realm and on every level of moral goodness.

IV

The gospel is something more than the law of love. The gospel deals with the fact that men violate the law of love. The gospel presents Christ as the pledge and revelation of God's mercy which finds man in his rebellion and overcomes his sin.

The question is whether the grace of Christ is primarily a power of righteousness which so heals the sinful heart that henceforth it is able to fulfil the law of love; or whether it is primarily the assurance of divine mercy for a persistent sinfulness which man never overcomes completely. When St. Paul declared: "I am crucified with Christ; nevertheless I live, yet it is no more I that live but Christ that dwelleth in me," did he mean that the new life in Christ was not his own by reason of the fact that grace, rather than his own power, enabled him to live on the new level of righteousness? Or did he mean that the new life was his only in intention and by reason of God's willingness to accept intention for achievement? Was the emphasis upon sanctification or justification?

This is the issue upon which the Protestant Reformation separated itself from classical Catholicism, believing that Thomistic interpretations of grace lent themselves to new forms of self-righteousness in place of the Judaistic-legalistic self-righteousness which St. Paul condemned. If one studies the whole thought of St. Paul, one is almost forced to the conclusion that he was not himself quite certain whether the peace which he had found in Christ was a moral peace, the peace of having become what man truly is; or whether it was primarily a religious peace, the peace of being "completely known and all forgiven," of being accepted by God despite the continued sinfulness of the heart. Perhaps St. Paul could not be quite sure about where the emphasis was to be placed, for the simple reason that no one can be quite certain about the character of this ultimate peace. There must be, and there is, moral content in it, a fact which Reformation theology tends to deny and which Catholic and sectarian theology emphasizes. But there is never such perfect moral content in it that any man could find perfect peace through his moral achievements, not even the achievements which he attributes to grace rather than the power of his own will. This is the truth which the Reformation and which modern Protestant Christianity has almost completely forgotten.

We are, therefore, living in a state of sorry moral and religious confusion. In the very moment of world history in which every contemporary historical event justifies the Reformation emphasis upon the persistence of sin on every level of moral achievement, we not only identify Protestant faith with a moralistic sentimentality which neglects and obscures truths in the Christian gospel (which it was the mission of the Reformation to rescue from obscurity), but we even neglect those reservations and qualifications upon the theory of sanctification upon which classical Catholicism wisely insisted.

We have, in other words, reinterpreted the Christian gospel in terms of the Renaissance faith in man. Modern pacifism is merely a final fruit of this Renaissance spirit, which has pervaded the whole of modern Protestantism. We have interpreted world history as a gradual ascent to the Kingdom of God which waits for final triumph only upon the willingness of Christians to "take Christ seriously." There is nothing in Christ's own teachings, except dubious interpretations of the parable of the leaven and the mustard seed, to justify this interpretation of world history. In the whole of the New Testament, Gospels and Epistles alike, there is only one interpretation of world history. That pictures history as moving toward a climax in which both Christ and anti-Christ are revealed.

The New Testament does not, in other words, envisage a simple triumph of good over evil in history. It sees human history involved in the contradictions of sin to the end. That is why it sees no simple resolution of the problem of history. It believes that the Kingdom of God will finally resolve the contradictions of history; but for it the Kingdom of God is no simple historical possibility. The grace of God for man and the Kingdom of God for history are both divine realities and not human possibilities.

The Christian faith believes that the Atonement reveals God's mercy as an ultimate resource by which God alone overcomes the judgment which sin deserves. If this final truth of the Christian religion has no meaning to modern men, including modern Christians, that is because even the tragic character of contemporary history has not yet persuaded them to take the fact of human sinfulness seriously.

V

The contradiction between the law of love and the sinfulness of man raises not only the ultimate religious problem how men are to have peace if they do not overcome the contradiction, and how history will culminate if the contradiction remains on every level of historic achievement; it also raises the immediate problem how men are to achieve a tolerable harmony of life with life, if human pride and selfishness prevent the realization of the law of love.

The pacifists are quite right in one emphasis. They are right in asserting that love is really the law of life. It is not some ultimate possibility which has nothing to do with human history. The freedom of man, his transcendence over the limitations of nature and over all historic and traditional social situations, makes any form of human community which falls short of the law of love less than the best. Only by a voluntary giving of life to life and a free interpenetration of personalities could man do justice both to the freedom of other personalities and the necessity of community between personalities. The law of love therefore remains a principle of criticism over all forms of community in which elements of coercion and conflict destroy the highest type of fellowship.

To look at human communities from the perspective of the Kingdom of God is to know that there is a sinful element in all the expedients which the political order uses to establish justice. That is why even the seemingly most stable justice degenerates periodically into either tyranny or anarchy. But it must also be recognized that it is not possible to eliminate the sinful element in the political expedients. They are, in the words of St. Augustine, both the consequence of, and the remedy for, sin. If they are the remedy for sin, the ideal of love is not merely a principle of indiscriminate criticism upon all approximations of justice. It is also a principle of discriminate criticism between forms of justice.

As a principle of indiscriminate criticism upon all forms of justice, the law of love reminds us that the injustice and tyranny against which we contend in the foe is partially the consequence of our own injustice, that the pathology of modern Germans is partially a consequence of the vindictiveness of the peace of Versailles, and that the ambition of a tyrannical imperialism is different only in degree and not in kind from the imperial impulse which characterizes all of human life.

The Christian faith ought to persuade us that political controversies are always conflicts between sinners and not between righteous men and sinners. It ought to mitigate the self-righteousness which is an inevitable concomitant of all human conflict. The spirit of contrition is an important ingredient in the sense of justice. If it is powerful enough it may be able to restrain the impulse of vengeance sufficiently to allow a decent justice to emerge. This is an important issue facing Europe in anticipation of the conclusion of the present war. It cannot be denied that the Christian conscience failed terribly in restraining vengeance after the last war. It is also quite obvious that the natural inclination to self-righteousness was the primary force of this vengeance (expressed particularly in the war guilt clause of the peace treaty). The pacifists draw the conclusion from the fact that justice is never free from vindictiveness, that we ought not for this reason ever to contend against a foe. This argument leaves out of account that capitulation to the foe might well subject us to a worse vindictiveness. It is as foolish to imagine that the foe is free of the sin which we deplore in ourselves as it is to regard ourselves as free of the sin which we deplore in the foe.

The fact that our own sin is always partly the cause of the sins against which we must contend is regarded by simple moral purists as proof that we have no right to contend against the foe. They regard the injunction "Let him who is without sin cast the first stone" as a simple alternative to the schemes of justice which society has devised and whereby it prevents the worst forms of anti-social conduct. This injunction of Christ ought to remind *every* judge and every juridical tribunal that the crime of the criminal is partly the consequence of the sins of society: But if pacifists are to be consistent they ought to advocate the abolition of the whole judicial process in society. It is perfectly true that national societies have more impartial instruments of justice than international society possesses to date. Nevertheless, no impartial court is as impartial as it pretends to be, and there is no judicial process which is completely free of vindictiveness. Yet we cannot dispense with it; and we will have to continue to put criminals into jail. There is a point where the final cause of the criminal's anti-social conduct becomes a fairly irrelevant issue in comparison with the task of preventing his conduct from injuring innocent fellows.

The ultimate principles of the Kingdom of God are never irrelevant to any problem of justice, and they hover over every social situation as an ideal possibility; but that does not mean that they can be made into simple alternatives for the present schemes of relative justice. The thesis that the so-called democratic nations have no right to resist overt forms of tyranny, because their own history betrays imperialistic motives, would have meaning only if it were possible to achieve a perfect form of justice in any nation and to free national life completely of the imperialistic motive. This is impossible; for imperialism is the collective expression of the sinful will-to-power which characterizes all human existence. The pacifist argument on this issue betrays how completely pacifism gives itself to illusions about the stuff with which it is dealing in human nature. These illusions deserve particular censure, because no one who knows his own heart very well ought to be given to such illusions.

The recognition of the law of love as an indiscriminate principle of criticism over all attempts at social and international justice is actually a resource of justice, for it prevents the pride, self-righteousness and vindictiveness of men from corrupting their efforts at justice. But it must be recognized that love is also a principle of discriminate criticism between various forms of community and various attempts at justice. The closest approximation to a love in which life supports life in voluntary community is a justice in which life is prevented from destroying life and the interests of the one are guarded against unjust claims by the other. Such justice is achieved when impartial tribunals of society prevent men "from being judges in their own cases," in the words of John Locke. But the tribunals of justice merely codify certain equilibria of power. Justice is basically dependent upon a balance of power. Whenever an individual or a group or a nation possesses undue power, and whenever this power is not checked by the possibility of criticizing and resisting it, it grows inordinate. The equilibrium of power upon which every structure of justice rests would degenerate into anarchy but for the organizing center which controls it. One reason why the balances of power, which prevent injustice in international relations, periodically degenerate into overt anarchy is because no way has yet been found to establish an adequate organizing center, a stable international judicatory, for this balance of power.

A balance of power is something different from, and inferior to, the harmony of love. It is a basic condition of justice, given the sinfulness of man. Such a balance of power does not exclude love. In fact, without love the frictions and tensions of a balance of power would become intolerable. But without the balance of power even the most loving relations may degenerate into unjust relations, and love may become the screen which hides the injustice. Family relations are instructive at this point. Women did not gain justice from men, despite the intimacy of family relations, until they secured sufficient economic power to challenge male autocracy. There are Christian "idealists" today who speak sentimentally of love as the only way to justice, whose family life might benefit from a more delicate "balance of power."

Naturally the tensions of such a balance may become overt; and overt tensions may degenerate into conflict. The center of power, which has the function of preventing this anarchy of conflict, may also degenerate into tyranny. There is no perfectly adequate method of preventing either anarchy or tyranny. But obviously the justice established in the so-called democratic nations represents a high degree of achievement; and the achievement becomes the more impressive when it is compared with the tyranny into which alternative forms of society have fallen. The obvious evils of tyranny, however, will not inevitably persuade the victims of economic anarchy in democratic society to eschew tyranny. When men suffer from anarchy they may foolishly regard the evils of tyranny as the lesser evils. Yet the evils of tyranny in fascist and communist nations are so patent, that we may dare to hope that what is still left of democratic civilizations will not lightly sacrifice the virtues of democracy for the sake of escaping its defects.

We have a very vivid and conclusive evidence about the probable consequences of a tyrannical unification of Europe. The nature of the German rule in the conquered nations of Europe gives us the evidence. There are too many contingent factors in various national and international schemes of justice to justify any unqualified endorsement of even the most democratic structure of justice as "Christian." Yet it must be obvious that any social structure in which power has been made responsible, and in which anarchy has been overcome by methods of mutual accommodation, is preferable to either anarchy or tyranny. If it is not possible to express a moral preference for the justice achieved in democratic societies, in comparison with tyrannical societies, no historical preference has any meaning. This kind of justice approximates the harmony of love more than either anarchy or tyranny.

If we do not make discriminate judgments between social systems we weaken the resolution to defend and extend civilization. Pacifism either tempts us to make no judgments at all, or to give an undue preference to tyranny in comparison with the momentary anarchy which is necessary to overcome tyranny. It must be admitted that the anarchy of war which results from resistance to tyranny is not always creative; that, at given periods of history, civilization may lack the resource to fashion a new and higher form of unity out of momentary anarchy. The defeat of

Germany and the frustration of the Nazi effort to unify Europe in tyrannical terms is a negative task. It does not guarantee the emergence of a new Europe with a higher level of international cohesion and new organs of international justice. But it is a negative task which cannot be avoided. All schemes for avoiding this negative task rest upon illusions about human nature. Specifically, these illusions express themselves in the failure to understand the stubbornness and persistence of the tyrannical will, once it is fully conceived. It would not require great argumentative skill to prove that Nazi tyranny never could have reached such proportions as to be able to place the whole of Europe under its ban, if sentimental illusions about the character of the evil which Europe was facing had not been combined with less noble motives for tolerating Nazi aggression.

A simple Christian moralism is senseless and confusing. It is senseless when, as in the World War, it seeks uncritically to identify the cause of Christ with the cause of democracy without a religious reservation. It is just as senseless when it seeks to purge itself of this error by an uncritical refusal to make any distinctions between relative values in history. The fact is that we might as well dispense with the Christian faith entirely if it is our conviction that we can act in history only if we are guiltless. This means that we must either prove our guiltlessness in order to be able to act; or refuse to act because we cannot achieve guiltlessness. Self-righteousness or inaction are the alternatives of secular moralism. If they are also the only alternatives of Christian moralism, one rightly suspects that Christian faith has become diluted with secular perspectives.

In its profoundest insights the Christian faith sees the whole of human history as involved in guilt, and finds no release from guilt except in the grace of God. The Christian is freed by that grace to act in history; to give his devotion to the highest values he knows; to defend those citadels of civilization of which necessity and historic destiny have made him the defender; and he is persuaded by that grace to remember the ambiguity of even his best actions. If the providence of God does not enter the affairs of men to bring good out of evil, the evil in our good may easily destroy our most ambitious efforts and frustrate our highest hopes.

VI

Despite our conviction that most modern pacifism is too filled with secular and moralistic illusions to be of the highest value to the Christian community, we may be grateful for the fact that the Christian Church has learned, since the last war, to protect its pacifists and to appreciate their testimony. Even when this testimony is marred by self-righteousness, because it does not proceed from a sufficiently profound understanding of the tragedy of human history, it has its value.

It is a terrible thing to take human life. The conflict between man and man and nation and nation is tragic. If there are men who declare that, no matter what the consequences, they cannot bring themselves to participate in this slaughter, the Church ought to be able to say to the general community: We quite understand this scruple and we respect it. It proceeds from the conviction that the true end of man is brotherhood, and that love is the law of life. We who allow ourselves to become engaged in war need this testimony of the absolutist against us, lest we accept the warfare of the world as normative, lest we become callous to the horror of war, and lest we forget the ambiguity of our own actions and motives and the risk we run of achieving no permanent good from this momentary anarchy in which we are involved.

But we have a right to remind the absolutists that their testimony against us would be more effective if it were not corrupted by self-righteousness and were not accompanied by the implicit or explicit accusation of apostasy. A pacifism which really springs from the Christian faith, without secular accretions and corruptions, could not be as certain as modern pacifism is that it possesses an alternative for the conflicts and tensions from which and through which the world must rescue a precarious justice.

A truly Christian pacifism would set each heart under the judgment of God to such a degree that even the pacifist idealist would know that knowledge of the will of God is no guarantee of his ability or willingness to obey it. The idealist would recognize to what degree he is himself involved in rebellion against God, and would know that this rebellion is too serious to be overcome by just one more sermon on love, and one more challenge to man to obey the law of Christ.

Source

Reinhold Niebuhr, "Why the Christian Church Is Not Pacifist," in *Christianity and Power Politics* (1940; New York: Charles Scribner's Sons, 1952), 1–32. Reprinted with the permission of the Estate of Reinhold Niebuhr.

Further Reading

Fox, Richard Wightman. *Reinhold Niebuhr: A Biography.* New York: Harper and Row, 1985.

Gilkey, Langdon. *On Niebuhr: A Theological Study.* Chicago: University of Chicago Press, 2001.

Hollinger, David A. *After Cloven Tongues of Fire: Protestant Liberalism in Modern American History.* Princeton: Princeton University Press, 2013.

Sittser, Gerald Lawson. *A Cautious Patriotism: The American Churches and the Second World War.* Chapel Hill: University of North Carolina Press, 1997.

DOROTHY DAY,
"WARS ARE CAUSED BY MAN'S LOSS
OF HIS FAITH IN MAN" (1940)

Like Reinhold Niebuhr, Dorothy Day (1897–1980) was deeply shaped by the economic and political upheavals of the 1930s and

1940s. Early in her career, she worked as a journalist in New York City, participating in the radical political and cultural experiments centered in Greenwich Village. Then, in 1926, the year her daughter Tamar was born, Day began a spiritual transformation that culminated in her joining the Catholic Church, to the astonishment of her radical friends.

Day and the French mystic Peter Maurin began the Catholic Worker Movement in 1933. Sometimes described as an experiment in Christian anarchism, this venture combined Day's talent for journalism, her left-wing politics, and her newfound faith commitment. The Catholic Worker's most visible attributes were its eponymous newspaper and its Houses of Hospitality, decentralized sites of communal living and poverty relief established around the country during the Depression decade.

The confident tone of this 1940 selection from Day's newspaper belies the rift that the Second World War would create within the movement. Although Catholic Workers had preached peace since their earliest days, they were deeply divided after Pearl Harbor. Day exercised considerable authority over the group, despite its anarchist ethos, and she insisted that the Catholic Worker Movement maintain its pacifism. In response, many Houses of Hospitality closed down as nonpacifist members dropped out.

The Catholic Worker recovered after the war to form a vanguard of antinuclear protest and opposition to the Vietnam War, inspiring such figures as the radical priests Daniel and Philip Berrigan. In the 1960s, the "personalist" theology of Day and Maurin appealed as well to many non-Catholic members of the New Left and the counterculture who sought alternatives to the bureaucratic soullessness of big business and big government. Recently, Dorothy Day has been claimed by libertarians on the right, socialists on the left, and many others in between. She is also being considered for canonization as a Catholic saint.

Dorothy Day, "Wars Are Caused by Man's Loss of His Faith in Man"

NON-VIOLENT RESISTANCE IS PATH TO PEACE

They are fighting for freedom in England, they say, but men have already lost their freedom.

We must prepare to fight for freedom here in America, they say, but we have lost our freedom here. People have come to accept the idea that we are a nation of industrial slaves, creatures of the State which doles out relief and jobs, and which is now going to seize the young and the strong for defense.

We have lost our democracy because we have lost our faith in men,— we no longer look upon them as creatures of body and soul, temples of the Holy Ghost, made to the image and likeness of God. If we have no faith in their spiritual capacities, we make no call on their spiritual resources.

The leaders of thought have failed the people because they have lost touch with the common man. They have lived in ivory towers; they have made themselves gross and comfortable. They have sacrificed their integrity for a mess of pottage. They have trusted to mass movements and mass responses, and have not appealed to personalist response. They have trusted to words, ideas,—they have not gone to the worker as Pope Pius XI appealed; they have not led by example. Or in those cases where they *have* gone to the workers they have been discouraged at finding the same vices and greed and dishonesty among the poor, and, looking for quick results, have become discouraged and aloof.

And war has come upon the world, and they have turned everywhere to the use of force, compulsion, denying freedom.

THESE THINGS WE ARE TO DO

But all times are troublous times, as one Saint has said. So what then are we to do in the midst of this disorder?

First to remember, the first duty of man, to know God, to love Him, to serve Him in our neighbor. To see all men as our brothers, to see Christ in all men, in our enemy and in our friend. If we do not see them so, we can not love them. We must overcome any sense of futility or hopelessness, for that is the beginning of despair. "Hope is the most sinned against of all virtues."

If we love our fellows, we have faith in them. But the loss of faith in men is epitomized now by the war spirit throughout the world, the belief that only force can overcome force. That only by war can we retain freedom and escape from the slavery of the totalitarian States. That men are not strong enough spiritually to use good means, so they are compelled to use evil means.

"Blackfriars" in its leading editorial this month states: "Whether man likes it or not, his nature is such that he cannot but possess freedom of will. Even the totalitarian powers cannot crush this. Even though they impose the strongest pressure to compel their subjects to act in a certain way, the will can always refuse its assent to the Government's decree. If assent is refused, of course the subject must be prepared to face the penalty, and, as this is usually of the gravest kind, there are very few who are prepared to exercise their will in a manner contrary to the command of the State."

LIFE CAN FLOWER BEHIND BARS

This seems to me to indicate plainly the loss of faith in man. Dostoievsky has said in several of his books (and Father Pierre Charles has quoted it in "Prayers for Our Times") that it is possible for a man to lead a perfect life even in jail.

There is a book about the last war which tells of a Belgian in a concentration camp who retains his integrity, who is not debased, who leads a life of high virtue, all during the war. Then he is released, to a land filled with war profiteers. Even the humblest of villagers has been contaminated by dishonesty and vice, the fruits of war. *They have fared worse outside of jail than he has within.* Pius XII has written, "There is nothing to be gained by war, everything to be lost."

We live with the poor, the destitute. Every day, here, 1,200 men and women come to our doors for food. In all our Houses there are probably 15,000 coming to us daily. We bear, all of us, the ugliness, the filth, the humiliations, of poverty. To leave out of account for a moment our good friends who give us too much credit, we wish to call attention only to our opponents, those within our households, as well as without, who heap scorn and bitterness upon us, when we are not able to take care of all their needs, those goods to which they feel themselves entitled; who accuse us of mishandling funds, who speak of us as hypocrites, vainglorious, liars and deceivers.

IF WE DWELT ON THIS PICTURE

We see the worst of the poor, as we see the worst of the rich. We see idleness in a generation which has been brought up in idleness. We see drunkenness and vice in their worst forms. If we dwelt on this dark picture we should lose hope; we would dream of an authoritarian State to bring man out of this Egypt in which he has dwelt so long.

But we cannot lose hope, just as we cannot lose faith in the teaching and examples of Jesus Christ. We know that men are but dust, but we know too that they are little less than the angels. We know them to be capable of high heroism, of sacrifice, of endurance. They respond to this call in wartime. But the call is never made to them to oppose violence *with non-resistance,* a strengthening of the will, an increase in love and faith.

We make this call, and we feel we have a right to make this call by the very circumstances of our lives. We know the sufferings which people are already able to endure; we know their capacity for suffering as the comfortable, those in high places, can never know it. We know it in the response which The Catholic Worker has met with throughout the land. We know it in the response of those very poor upon our breadlines who are helping us in carrying on the work all over the country.

THE OPPRESSOR SHALL FAIL

ιo respond in this way is to do away with war. A people thus trained to recognition of spiritual values will overcome the oppressor, the conquered will overcome the conquerors.

A faith which will be crushed by war, will be built up by such a peace. There is no dishonor in such a peace. Men will lay down their lives for their friends, and in losing their lives they will save them.

Source

Dorothy Day, "Wars Are Caused by Man's Loss of His Faith in Man," *Catholic Worker*, September 1940, 1–2.

The Catholic Worker Movement website: http://www.catholicworker.org/dorothy day/articles/366.html

Further Reading

Fisher, James Terence. *The Catholic Counterculture in America, 1933–1962.* Chapel Hill: University of North Carolina Press, 1989.

McKanan, Dan. *Prophetic Encounters: Religion and the American Radical Tradition.* Boston: Beacon, 2011.

Piehl, Mel. *Breaking Bread: The Catholic Worker and the Origin of Catholic Radicalism in America.* Philadelphia: Temple University Press, 1982.

JEHOVAH'S WITNESS FLAG SALUTE CASES: *GOBITIS* (1940) AND *BARNETTE* (1943)

The pair of Supreme Court cases excerpted here show how a religious group on the margins of American society could raise central questions about the limits of toleration. Jehovah's Witnesses, heirs of the Adventist tradition that began with the nineteenth-century prophet William Miller, emphasize the imminent Second Coming of Christ and carefully study biblical texts for clues about the "last days." Beginning in the late nineteenth century with the name "Bible Students," American Witnesses numbered about 40,000 on the eve of World War II.

Jehovah's Witnesses resemble other evangelicals in many ways. However, in midcentury America, a few highly visible differences provoked hostility. Witnesses practice especially active forms of proselytizing, which used to include pointed denunciations of other Christian traditions. The organization is strongly hierarchical, and critics compared the group's powerful president Joseph Rutherford to a dictator. Most importantly, Jehovah's Witnesses choose to not participate in rituals expressing loyalty to the nation, for they view human government as sinful and nationalism as nothing less than idolatry. The Nazis sent large numbers of German Witnesses to concentration camps because they would not recognize Hitler's regime.

In the United States, Jehovah's Witnesses Lillian Gobitas, age twelve, and Billy Gobitas, age ten, were expelled from their Pennsylvania school in 1935 for declining to salute the flag and recite the Pledge of Allegiance (oddly, the court decision has their name misspelled). Backed by the American Civil Liberties Union, the Gobitas family took their case to the Supreme Court, but the court upheld the school district's policy. The ruling, along with the Witnesses' opposition to the Second World War, brought violent persecution upon them. The war years saw hundreds of physical attacks on Witnesses, who were deemed by many of their fellow citizens to be as anti-American as the Nazis themselves.

In this climate of repression, the Supreme Court undertook an unusual reversal. Three years after *Minersville School District v. Gobitis*, the justices decided the very similar *West Virginia State Board of Education v. Barnette* case in favor of the defendants' right to forgo the flag salute. Given the significance of these cases and others involving the Witnesses, most notably *Cantwell v. Connecticut* and *Chaplinsky v. New Hampshire*, the group ended up providing a profound test of wartime American democracy. Indeed, it is no exaggeration to say that the Jehovah's Witness cases inaugurated a transformative expansion of First Amendment rights, not only for religions but for a wide range of minority groups.

Minersville School District v. Gobitis

MR. JUSTICE FRANKFURTER delivered the opinion of the Court.

A grave responsibility confronts this Court whenever in course of litigation it must reconcile the conflicting claims of liberty and authority. But when the liberty invoked is liberty of conscience, and the authority is authority to safeguard the nation's fellowship; judicial conscience is put to its severest test. Of such a nature is the present controversy.

Lillian Gobitis, aged twelve, and her brother William, aged ten, were expelled from the public schools of Minersville, Pennsylvania, for refusing to salute the national flag as part of a daily school exercise. The local Board of Education required both teachers and pupils to participate in this ceremony. The ceremony is a familiar one. The right hand is placed on the breast and the following pledge recited in unison: "I pledge allegiance to my flag, and to the Republic for which it stands; one nation indivisible, with liberty and justice for all." While the words are spoken, teachers and pupils extend their right hands in salute to the flag. The Gobitis family are affiliated with "Jehovah's Witnesses," for whom the Bible as the Word of God is the supreme authority. The children had been brought up conscientiously to believe that such a gesture of respect for the flag was forbidden by command of Scripture.

The Gobitis children were of an age for which Pennsylvania makes school attendance compulsory. Thus they were denied a free education, and their parents had to put them into private schools. To be relieved of the financial burden thereby entailed, their father, on behalf of the children and in his own behalf, brought this suit. He sought to enjoin the authorities from continuing to exact participation in the flag-salute ceremony as a condition of his children's attendance at the Minersville school.

[...]

We must decide whether the requirement of participation in such a ceremony, exacted from a child who refuses upon sincere religious grounds, infringes without due process of law the liberty guaranteed by the Fourteenth Amendment.

Centuries of strife over the erection of particular dogmas as exclusive or all-comprehending faiths led to the inclusion of a guarantee for religious freedom in the Bill of Rights. The First Amendment, and the Fourteenth through its absorption of the First, sought to guard against repetition of those bitter religious struggles by prohibiting the establishment of a state religion and by securing to every sect the free exercise of its faith. So pervasive is the acceptance of this precious right that its scope is brought into question, as here, only when the conscience of individuals collides with the felt necessities of society.

Certainly the affirmative pursuit of one's convictions about the ultimate mystery of the universe and man's relation to it is placed beyond the reach of law. Government may not interfere with organized or individual expression of belief or disbelief. Propagation of belief—or even of disbelief—in the supernatural is protected, whether in church or chapel, mosque or synagogue, tabernacle or meeting-house. Likewise the Constitution assures generous immunity to the individual from imposition of penalties for offending, in the course of his own religious activities, the religious views of others, be they a minority or those who are dominant in government.

But the manifold character of man's relations may bring his conception of religious duty into conflict with the secular interests of his fellowmen. When does the constitutional guarantee compel exemption from doing what society thinks necessary for the promotion of some great common end, or from a penalty for conduct which appears dangerous to the general good? To state the problem is to recall the truth that no single principle can answer all of life's complexities. The right to freedom of religious belief, however dissident and however obnoxious to the cherished beliefs of others—even of a majority—is itself the denial of an absolute. But to affirm that the freedom to follow conscience has itself no limits in the life of a society would deny that very plurality of principles which, as a matter of history, underlies protection of religious toleration. Our present task, then, as so often the case with courts, is to reconcile two rights in order to prevent either from destroying the other. But, because in safeguarding conscience we are dealing with interests so subtle and so dear, every possible leeway should be given to the claims of religious faith.

In the judicial enforcement of religious freedom we are concerned with a historic concept. The religious liberty which the Constitution protects has never excluded legislation of general scope not directed against doctrinal loyalties of particular sects. Judicial nullification of legislation cannot be justified by attributing to the framers of the Bill of Rights views for which there is no historic warrant. Conscientious scruples have not, in the course of the long struggle for religious toleration, relieved the individual from obedience to a general law not aimed at the promotion or restriction of religious beliefs. The mere possession of religious convictions which contradict the relevant concerns of a political society does not relieve the citizen from the discharge of political responsibilities. The necessity for this adjustment has again and again been recognized. In a number of situations the exertion of political authority has been sustained, while basic considerations of religious freedom have been left inviolate. In all these cases the general laws in question, upheld in their application to those who refused obedience from religious conviction, were manifestations of specific powers of government deemed by the legislature essential to secure and maintain that orderly, tranquil, and free society without which religious toleration itself is unattainable. Nor does the freedom of speech assured by Due Process move in a more absolute circle of immunity than that enjoyed by religious freedom. Even if it were assumed that freedom of speech goes beyond the historic concept of full opportunity to utter and to disseminate views, however heretical or offensive to dominant opinion, and includes freedom from conveying what may be deemed an implied but rejected affirmation, the question remains whether school children, like the Gobitis children, must be excused from conduct required of all the other children in the promotion of national cohesion. We are dealing with an interest inferior to none in the hierarchy of legal values. National unity is the basis of national security. To deny the legislature the right to select appropriate means for its attainment presents a totally different order of problem from that of the propriety of subordinating the possible ugliness of littered streets to the free expression of opinion through distribution of handbills.

Situations like the present are phases of the profoundest problem confronting a democracy—the problem which Lincoln cast in memorable dilemma: "Must a government of necessity be too *strong* for the liberties of its people, or too *weak* to maintain its own existence?" No mere textual reading or logical talisman can solve the dilemma. And when the issue demands judicial determination, it is not the personal notion of judges of what wise adjustment requires which must prevail.

Unlike the instances we have cited, the case before us is not concerned with an exertion of legislative power for the promotion of some specific need or interest of secular society—the protection of the family, the promotion of health, the common defense, the raising of public revenues to defray the cost of government. But all these specific activities of government presuppose the existence of an organized political society. The ultimate foundation of a free society is the binding tie of cohesive sentiment. Such a sentiment is fostered by all those agencies of the mind and spirit which may serve to gather up the traditions of a people, transmit them from generation to generation, and thereby create that continuity of a treasured common life which constitutes a civilization. "We live by symbols." The flag is the symbol of our national unity, transcending all internal differences, however large, within the framework of the Constitution. This Court has had occasion to say that ". . . the flag is the symbol of the Nation's power, the emblem of freedom in its truest, best sense. . . . it signifies government resting on the consent of the governed; liberty regulated by law; the protection of the weak against the strong; security against the exercise of arbitrary power; and absolute safety for free institutions against foreign aggression."

The case before us must be viewed as though the legislature of Pennsylvania had itself formally directed the flag-salute for the children of Minersville; had made no exemption for children whose parents were possessed of conscientious scruples like those of the Gobitis family; and had indicated its belief in the desirable ends to be secured by having its public school children share a common experience at those periods of development when their minds are supposedly receptive to its assimilation, by an exercise appropriate in time and place and setting, and one designed to evoke in them appreciation of the nation's hopes and dreams, its sufferings and sacrifices. The precise issue, then, for us to decide is whether the legislatures of the various states and the authorities in a thousand counties and school districts of this country are barred from determining the appropriateness of various means to evoke that unifying sentiment without which there can ultimately be no liberties, civil or religious. To stigmatize legislative judgment in providing for this universal gesture of respect for the symbol of our national life in the setting of the common school as a lawless inroad on that freedom of conscience which the Constitution protects, would amount to no less than the pronouncement of pedagogical and psychological dogma in a field where courts possess no marked and certainly no controlling competence. The influences which help toward a common feeling for the common country are manifold. Some may seem harsh and others no doubt are foolish. Surely, however, the end is legitimate. And the effective means for its attainment are still so uncertain and so unauthenticated by science as to preclude us from putting the widely prevalent belief in flag-saluting beyond the pale of legislative power. It mocks reason and denies our whole history to find in the allowance of a requirement to salute our flag on fitting occasions the seeds of sanction for obeisance to a leader.

The wisdom of training children in patriotic impulses by those compulsions which necessarily pervade so much of the educational process is not for our independent judgment. Even were we convinced of the folly of such a measure, such belief would be no proof of its unconstitutionality. For ourselves, we might be tempted to say that the deepest patriotism is best engendered by giving unfettered scope to the most crochety beliefs. Perhaps it is best, even from the standpoint of those interests which ordinances like the one under review seek to promote, to give to the least popular sect leave from conformities like those here in issue. But the courtroom is not the arena for debating issues of educational policy. It is not our province to choose among competing considerations in the subtle process of securing effective loyalty to the traditional ideals of democracy, while respecting at the same time individual idiosyncracies among a people so diversified in racial origins and religious allegiances. So to hold would in effect make us the school board for the country. That authority has not been given to this Court, nor should we assume it.

We are dealing here with the formative period in the development of citizenship. Great diversity of psychological and ethical opinion exists among us concerning the best way to train children for their place in society. Because of these differences and because of reluctance to permit a single, iron-cast system of education to be imposed upon a nation compounded of so many strains, we have held that, even though public education is one of our most cherished democratic institutions, the Bill of Rights bars a state from compelling all children to attend the public schools. But it is a very different thing for this Court to exercise censorship over the conviction of legislatures that a particular program or exercise will best promote in the minds of children who attend the common schools an attachment to the institutions of their country.

What the school authorities are really asserting is the right to awaken in the child's mind considerations as to the significance of the flag contrary to those implanted by the parent. In such an attempt the state is normally at a disadvantage in competing with the parent's authority, so long—and this is the vital aspect of religious toleration—as parents are unmolested in their right to counteract by their own persuasiveness the wisdom and rightness of those loyalties which the state's educational system is seeking to promote. Except where the transgression of constitutional liberty is too plain for argument, personal freedom is best maintained—so long as the remedial channels of the democratic process remain open and unobstructed—when it is ingrained in a people's habits and not enforced against popular policy by the coercion of adjudicated law. That the flag-salute is an allowable portion of a school program for those who do not invoke conscientious scruples is surely not debatable. But for us to insist that, though the ceremony may be required, exceptional immunity must be given to dissidents, is to maintain that there is no basis for a legislative judgment that such an exemption might introduce elements of difficulty into the school discipline, might cast doubts in the minds of the other children which would themselves weaken the effect of the exercise.

The preciousness of the family relation, the authority and independence which give dignity to parenthood, indeed the enjoyment of all freedom, presuppose the kind of ordered society which is summarized by our flag. A society which is dedicated to the preservation of these ultimate values of civilization may in self-protection utilize the educational process for inculcating those almost unconscious feelings which bind men together in a comprehending loyalty, whatever may be their lesser differences and difficulties. That is to say, the process may be utilized so long as men's right to believe as they please, to win others to their way of belief, and their right to assemble in their chosen places of worship for the devotional ceremonies of their faith, are all fully respected.

Judicial review, itself a limitation on popular government, is a fundamental part of our constitutional scheme. But to the legislature no less than to courts is committed the guardianship of deeply-cherished liberties. Where all the effective means of inducing political changes are left free from interference, education in the abandonment of foolish legislation is itself a training in liberty. To fight out the wise use of legislative authority in the forum of public opinion and before legislative assemblies rather than to transfer such a contest to the judicial arena, serves to vindicate the self-confidence of a free people.

Reversed.

West Virginia State Board of Education v. Barnette

Mr. Justice Jackson delivered the opinion of the Court.

Following the decision by this Court on June 3, 1940, in *Minersville School District* v. *Gobitis,* 310 U. S. 586, the West Virginia legislature amended its statutes to require all schools therein to conduct courses of instruction in history, civics, and in the Constitutions of the United States and of the State "for the purpose of teaching, fostering and perpetuating the ideals, principles and spirit of Americanism, and increasing the knowledge of the organization and machinery of the government." Appellant Board of Education was directed, with advice of the State Superintendent of Schools, to "prescribe the courses of study covering these subjects" for public schools. The Act made it the duty of private, parochial and denominational schools to prescribe courses of study "similar to those required for the public schools."

The Board of Education on January 9, 1942, adopted a resolution containing recitals taken largely from the Court's *Gobitis* opinion and ordering that the salute to the flag become "a regular part of the program of activities in the public schools," that all teachers and pupils "shall be required to participate in the salute honoring the Nation represented by the Flag; provided, however, that refusal to salute the Flag be regarded as an act of insubordination, and shall be dealt with accordingly."

The resolution originally required the "commonly accepted salute to the Flag" which it defined. Objections to the salute as "being too much like Hitler's" were raised by the Parent and Teachers Association, the Boy and Girl Scouts, the Red Cross, and the Federation of Women's Clubs. Some modification appears to have been made in deference to these objections, but no concession was made to Jehovah's Witnesses. What is now required is the "stiff-arm" salute, the saluter to keep the right hand raised with palm turned up while the following is repeated: "I pledge allegiance to the Flag of the United States of America and to the Republic for which it stands; one Nation, indivisible, with liberty and justice for all."

Failure to conform is "insubordination" dealt with by expulsion. Readmission is denied by statute until compliance. Meanwhile the expelled child is "unlawfully absent" and may be proceeded against as a delinquent. His parents or guardians are liable to prosecution, and if convicted are subject to fine not exceeding $50 and jail term not exceeding thirty days.

Appellees, citizens of the United States and of West Virginia, brought suit in the United States District Court for themselves and others similarly situated asking its injunction to restrain enforcement of these laws and regulations against Jehovah's Witnesses. The Witnesses are an unincorporated body teaching that the obligation imposed by law of God is superior to that of laws enacted by temporal government. Their religious beliefs include a literal version of Exodus, Chapter 20, verses 4 and 5, which says: "Thou shalt not make unto thee any graven image, or any likeness of anything that is in heaven above, or that is in the earth beneath, or that is in the water under the earth; thou shalt not bow down thyself to them nor serve them." They consider that the flag is an "image" within this command. For this reason they refuse to salute it.

Children of this faith have been expelled from school and are threatened with exclusion for no other cause. Officials threaten to send them to reformatories maintained for criminally inclined juveniles. Parents of such children have been prosecuted and are threatened with prosecutions for causing delinquency.

[. . .]

This case calls upon us to reconsider a precedent decision, as the Court throughout its history often has been required to do.

[. . .]

The *Gobitis* decision *assumed,* as did the argument in that case and in this, that power exists in the State to impose the flag salute discipline upon school children in general. The Court only examined and rejected a claim based on religious beliefs of immunity from an unquestioned general rule. The question which underlies the flag salute controversy is whether such a ceremony so touching matters of opinion and political attitude may be imposed upon the individual by official authority under powers committed to any political organization under our Constitution. We examine rather than assume existence of this power and, against this broader definition of issues in this case, reëxamine specific grounds assigned for the *Gobitis* decision.

1. It was said that the flag-salute controversy confronted the Court with "the problem which Lincoln cast in memorable dilemma: 'Must a government of necessity be too *strong* for the liberties of its people, or too *weak* to maintain its own existence?'" and that the answer must be in favor of strength.

We think these issues may be examined free of pressure or restraint growing out of such considerations.

It may be doubted whether Mr. Lincoln would have thought that the strength of government to maintain itself would be impressively vindicated by our confirming power of the State to expel a handful of children from school. Such oversimplification, so handy in political debate, often lacks the precision necessary to postulates of judicial reasoning. If validly applied to this problem, the utterance cited would resolve every issue of power in favor of those in authority and would require us to override every liberty thought to weaken or delay execution of their policies.

Government of limited power need not be anemic government. Assurance that rights are secure tends to diminish fear and jealousy of strong government, and by making us feel safe to live under it makes for its better support. Without promise of a limiting Bill of Rights it is doubtful if our Constitution could have mustered enough strength to enable its ratification. To enforce those rights today is not to choose weak government over strong government. It is only to adhere as a means of strength to individual freedom of mind in preference to officially disciplined uniformity for which history indicates a disappointing and disastrous end.

The subject now before us exemplifies this principle. Free public education, if faithful to the ideal of secular instruction and political neutrality, will not be partisan or enemy of any class, creed, party, or faction. If it is to impose any ideological discipline, however, each party or denomination must seek to control, or failing that, to weaken the influence of the educational system. Observance of the limitations of the Constitution will not weaken government in the field appropriate for its exercise.

2. It was also considered in the *Gobitis* case that functions of educational officers in States, counties and school districts were such that to interfere with their authority "would in effect make us the school board for the country."

The Fourteenth Amendment, as now applied to the States, protects the citizen against the State itself and all of its creatures—Boards of Education not excepted. These have, of course, important, delicate, and highly discretionary functions, but none that they may not perform within the limits of the Bill of Rights. That they are educating the young for citizenship is reason for scrupulous protection of Constitutional freedoms of the individual, if we are not to strangle the free mind at its source and teach youth to discount important principles of our government as mere platitudes.

Such Boards are numerous and their territorial jurisdiction often small. But small and local authority may feel less sense of responsibility to the Constitution, and agencies of publicity may be less vigilant in calling it to account. The action of Congress in making flag observance voluntary and respecting the conscience of the objector in a matter so vital as raising the Army contrasts sharply with these local regulations in matters relatively trivial to the welfare of the nation. There are village tyrants as well as village Hampdens, but none who acts under color of law is beyond reach of the Constitution.

3. The *Gobitis* opinion reasoned that this is a field "where courts possess no marked and certainly no controlling competence," that it is committed to the legislatures as well as the courts to guard cherished liberties and that it is constitutionally appropriate to "fight out the wise use of legislative authority in the forum of public opinion and before legislative assemblies rather than to transfer such a contest to the judicial arena," since all the "effective means of inducing political changes are left free."

The very purpose of a Bill of Rights was to withdraw certain subjects from the vicissitudes of political controversy, to place them beyond the reach of majorities and officials and to establish them as legal principles to be applied by the courts. One's right to life, liberty, and property, to free speech, a free press, freedom of worship and assembly, and other fundamental rights may not be submitted to vote; they depend on the outcome of no elections.

In weighing arguments of the parties it is important to distinguish between the due process clause of the Fourteenth Amendment as an instrument for transmitting the principles of the First Amendment and those cases in which it is applied for its own sake. The test of legislation which collides with the Fourteenth Amendment, because it also collides with the principles of the First, is much more definite than the test when only the Fourteenth is involved. Much of the vagueness of the due process clause disappears when the specific prohibitions of the First become its standard. The right of a State to regulate, for example, a public utility may well include, so far as the due process test is concerned, power to impose all of the restrictions which a legislature may have a "rational basis" for adopting. But freedoms of speech and of press, of assembly, and of worship may not be infringed on such slender grounds. They are susceptible of restriction only to prevent grave and immediate danger to interests which the State may lawfully protect. It is important to note that while it is the Fourteenth Amendment which bears directly upon the State it is the more specific limiting principles of the First Amendment that finally govern this case.

Nor does our duty to apply the Bill of Rights to assertions of official authority depend upon our possession of marked competence in the field where the invasion of rights occurs. True, the task of translating the majestic generalities of the Bill of Rights, conceived as part of the pattern of liberal government in the eighteenth century, into concrete restraints on officials dealing with the problems of the twentieth century, is one to disturb self-confidence. These principles grew in soil which also produced a philosophy that the individual was the center of society, that his liberty was attainable through mere absence of governmental restraints, and that government should be entrusted with few controls and only the mildest supervision over men's affairs. We must transplant these rights to a soil in which the *laissez-faire* concept or principle of non-interference has withered at least as to economic affairs, and social advancements are increasingly sought through closer integration of society and through expanded and strengthened governmental controls. These changed conditions often deprive precedents of reliability and cast us more than we would choose upon our own judgment. But we act in these matters not by authority of our competence but by force of our commissions. We cannot, because of modest estimates of our competence in such specialties as public education, withhold the judgment that history authenticates as the function of this Court when liberty is infringed.

4. Lastly, and this is the very heart of the *Gobitis* opinion, it reasons that "National unity is the basis of national security," that the authorities have "the right to select appropriate means for its attainment," and hence reaches the conclusion that such compulsory measures toward "national unity" are constitutional. Upon the verity of this assumption depends our answer in this case.

National unity as an end which officials may foster by persuasion and example is not in question. The problem is whether under our Constitution compulsion as here employed is a permissible means for its achievement.

Struggles to coerce uniformity of sentiment in support of some end thought essential to their time and country have been waged by many good as well as by evil men. Nationalism is a relatively recent phenomenon but at other times and places the ends have been racial or territorial security, support of a dynasty or regime, and particular plans for saving souls. As first and moderate methods to attain unity have failed, those bent on its accomplishment must resort to an ever-increasing severity. As governmental pressure toward unity becomes greater, so strife becomes more bitter as to whose unity it shall be. Probably no deeper division of our people could proceed from any provocation than from finding it necessary to choose what doctrine and whose program public educational officials shall compel youth to unite in embracing. Ultimate futility of such attempts to compel coherence is the lesson of every such effort from the Roman drive to stamp out Christianity as a disturber of its pagan unity, the Inquisition, as a means to religious and dynastic unity, the Siberian exiles as a means to Russian unity, down to the fast failing efforts of our present totalitarian enemies. Those who begin coercive elimination of dissent soon find themselves exterminating dissenters. Compulsory unification of opinion achieves only the unanimity of the graveyard.

It seems trite but necessary to say that the First Amendment to our Constitution was designed to avoid these ends by avoiding these beginnings. There is no mysticism in the American concept of the State or of the nature or origin of its authority. We set up government by consent of the governed, and the Bill of Rights denies those in power any legal opportunity to coerce that consent. Authority here is to be controlled by public opinion, not public opinion by authority.

The case is made difficult not because the principles of its decision are obscure but because the flag involved is our own. Nevertheless, we apply the limitations of the Constitution with no fear that freedom to be intellectually and spiritually diverse or even contrary will disintegrate the social organization. To believe that patriotism will not flourish if patriotic ceremonies are voluntary and spontaneous instead of a compulsory routine is to make an unflattering estimate of the appeal of our institutions to free minds. We can have intellectual individualism and the rich cultural diversities that we owe to exceptional minds only at the price of occasional eccentricity and abnormal attitudes. When they are so harmless to others or to the State as those we deal with here, the price is not too great. But freedom to differ is not limited to things that do not matter much. That would be a mere shadow of freedom. The test of its substance is the right to differ as to things that touch the heart of the existing order.

If there is any fixed star in our constitutional constellation, it is that no official, high or petty, can prescribe what shall be orthodox in politics, nationalism, religion, or other matters of opinion or force citizens to confess by word or act their faith therein. If there are any circumstances which permit an exception, they do not now occur to us.

We think the action of the local authorities in compelling the flag salute and pledge transcends constitutional limitations on their power and invades the sphere of intellect and spirit which it is the purpose of the First Amendment to our Constitution to reserve from all official control.

The decision of this Court in *Minersville School District v. Gobitis* and the holdings of those few *per curiam* decisions which preceded and foreshadowed it are overruled, and the judgment enjoining enforcement of the West Virginia Regulation is

Affirmed.

Sources

Minersville School District v. Gobitis, 310 U.S. 586 (1940).
West Virginia State Board of Education v. Barnette, 319 U.S. 624 (1943).

Further Reading

Gordon, Sarah Barringer. *The Spirit of the Law: Religious Voices and the Constitution in Modern America.* Cambridge, MA: Harvard University Press, 2010.
Peters, Shawn Francis. *Judging Jehovah's Witnesses: Religious Persecution and the Dawn of the Rights Revolution.* Lawrence: University Press of Kansas, 2000.

GEORGE DOCHERTY,
"A NEW BIRTH OF FREEDOM" (1954)

The end of the Second World War was a triumph for the United States, but the good feeling was short-lived. In the years immediately following the war the Soviet Union expanded its influence across Eastern Europe; the United States tried to stop that expansion. These events produced a new "Cold War" between the two wartime allies, a lengthy struggle that would last until the breakup of the Soviet Union in 1991. Although the contest was "cold" in the sense that the principals never engaged in direct military confrontation, "hot" wars in Korea, Vietnam, and elsewhere served as deadly proxies for the fight between the superpowers. At the same time, the threat of global devastation by nuclear weapons added an undercurrent of fear to everyday life.

The early Cold War coincided with an American religious revival, and many citizens came to see the conflict in spiritual terms. In this view, a more fundamental difference lay beneath disagreements about capitalist and Communist economics: the difference between faith and atheism. During the 1950s religious themes became increasingly visible in American conceptions of politics. Political theorists claimed to discover that democracy itself had religious roots. The extraordinarily popular evangelistic campaigns of Billy Graham mixed the Christian gospel and anticommunism, while unbelievers were viewed with suspicion or simply rendered invisible in the nation's public life.

This 1954 sermon by the Presbyterian minister George M. Docherty (1911–2008) exemplifies the tenor of Cold War religious politics. Docherty was the pastor at New York Avenue Presbyterian Church, a prominent place of worship located just a few blocks from the White House. Indeed, President Dwight Eisenhower was in attendance when Docherty gave this call to recognize the godly foundations of American freedom. The preacher proposed adding the words "under God" to the Pledge of Allegiance, which did not originally contain them. Docherty's suggestion proved wildly popular and was soon signed by Eisenhower into law. In 1956, the government would establish "In God We Trust" as the national motto, providing another potent symbol of the nation's spiritual opposition to Communism.

George Docherty, "A New Birth of Freedom"

The famous city of Sparta was once visited by an ambassador from another kingdom. He expected to find this great city surrounded by thick protecting walls; he was surprised when he saw no battlements at all.

"Where are the walls to defend the city?" he asked of the King of Sparta.

"Here are the walls of Sparta," replied the king, showing him his army of first line crack troops.

Had this ambassador visited our United States today, he would also be surprised to find no wall around our cities. (I should think, as a matter of fact, it would be extremely difficult even for American know-how to build a wall around Los Angeles.) And if our visitor were to ask the question, "Where is the defense of the Nation?", he could be shown something of the awesome power of the mighty American Army, Navy, and Air Force; not to mention the enormous economic potential of the country. But the true strength of the United States of America lies deeper, as it lay in Sparta. It is the spirit of both military and people—a flaming devotion to the cause of freedom within these borders.

At this season of anniversary of the birth of Abraham Lincoln, it will not be inappropriate to speak about this freedom, and what is called the American way of life.

Freedom is a subject everyone seems to be talking about without seemingly stopping to ask the rather basic question, "What do we mean by freedom?" In this matter, apparently, we all are experts.

The world of Mr. Lincoln's day is unbelievably different from this modern age. Yet there is a sense in which history is always repeating itself. The issues we face today are precisely the issues he spent his life seeking to resolve. In his day, the issue was sparked by Negro slavery; today, it is sparked by a militantly atheistic communism that has already enslaved 800 million of the peoples of the earth, and now menaces the rest of the free world.

Lincoln, in his day, saw this country as a nation that "was conceived in liberty and dedicated to the proposition that all men are created equal." And the question he asks is the timeless, and timely, one—"whether that Nation, or any nation so conceived and so dedicated, can long endure."

I recall once discussing the "American way of life" with a newspaper editor. He had been using the phrase rather freely. When asked to define the phrase "the American way of life," he became very wordy and verbose. "It is live and let live; it is freedom to act," and other such platitudes.

Let me tell what "the American way of life" is. It is going to the ball game and eating popcorn, and drinking Coca Cola, and rooting for the Senators. It is shopping in Sears, Roebuck. It is losing heart and hat on a roller coaster. It is driving on the right side of the road and putting up at motels on a long journey. It is being bored with television commercials. It is setting off firecrackers with your children on the Fourth of July. It is sitting for 7 hours to see the pageantry of the presidential inauguration.

But, it is deeper than that.

It is gardens with no fences to bar you from the neighborliness of your neighbor. It is the perfume of honeysuckle, and the sound of katydids in the warm night air of summer, when you go out into the garden, the children long ago asleep, and you feel the pulse and throb of nature around you. It is Negro spirituals and colonial architecture. It is Thanksgiving turkey and pumpkin pie. It is the sweep of broad rivers and the sea of wheat and grass. It is a view from the air of the conflux of muddy rivers and neat little excavations and columns of smoke that is the mighty Pittsburgh. It is canyons of skyscrapers in New York, and the sweep of Lakeshore Drive that is Chicago. It is the lonely, proud status of Lee on Gettysburg field. It is schoolgirls wearing jeans and schoolboys riding enormous push bikes. It is color comics. It is the Sunday New York Times. It is sitting on the porch of a Sunday afternoon, after morning church, rocking in a creeking wicker chair. It is a lad and a lass looking at you intently in the marriage service. It is sickness and a home empty, quieted, and stilled by grief. It is the sound of the bell at the railroad crossing, and children's laughter. It is a solitary bugler playing taps, clear and long-noted, at Arlington.

And where did all this come from?

It has been with us so long, we have to recall it was brought here by people who laid stress on fundamentals. They called themselves Puritans because they wished to live the pure and noble life purged of all idolatry and enslavement of the mind, even by the church. They did not realize that in fleeing from tyranny and setting up a new life in a new world they were to be the fathers of a mighty nation.

These fundamental concepts of life had been given to the world from Sinai, where the moral law was graven upon tablets of stone, symbolizing the universal application to all men; and they came from the New Testament, where they heard in the words of Jesus of Nazareth the living word of God for the world.

This is the American way of life. Lincoln saw this clearly. History for him was the Divine Comedy, though he would not use that phrase. The providence of God was being fulfilled.

Wherefore, he claims that it is under God that this Nation shall know a new birth of freedom. And by implication, it is under God that "government of the people, by the people, and for the people, shall not perish from the earth." For Lincoln, since God was in His Heaven, all must ultimately be right for his country.

Now, all this may seem obvious, until one sits down and takes these implications of freedom really seriously. For me, it came in a flash one day sometime ago when our children came home from school. Almost casually, I asked what happened at school when they arrived there in the morning. They described to me, in great detail and with strange solemnity, the ritual of the salute to the flag. The children turn to the flag, and with their hand across their heart, they repeat the words:

"I pledge allegiance to the flag of the United States and the Republic for which it stands; one nation, indivisible, with liberty and justice for all."

They were very proud of the pledge; and rightly so.

I don't suppose you fathers would have paid much attention to that as I did. I had the advantage over you. I could listen to those noble words as if for the first time. You have learned them so long ago, like the arithmetic table or the shorter catechism, something you can repeat without realizing what it all really means. But I could sit down and brood upon it, going over each word slowly in my mind.

And I came to a strange conclusion. There was something missing in this pledge, and that which was missing was the characteristic and definitive factor in the American way of life. Indeed, apart from the mention of the phrase, the United States of America, this could be a pledge of any republic. In fact, I could hear little Muscovites repeat a similar pledge to their hammer-and-sickle flag in Moscow with equal solemnity, for Russia is also a republic that claims to have overthrown the tyranny of kingship.

Russia also claims to be indivisible. Mr. Stalin admitted to Sir Winston Churchill that the uniting of the peasants was the most difficult of all tasks. (He did not mention the massacre of the 3 million Kulak farmers in this blood-and-iron unification.)

Russia claims to have liberty. You will never understand the Communist mind until you realize this aberration of their judgment. Marx, in his dialectic, makes it clear that the Communist state is only an imperfect stage toward world socialism. When that day comes the state will wither away and true socialism will reign forever. Utopia will have dawned. Until that day there must be personal limitations. As the capitalist state limits freedom in the day of war, so must the workers of the world accept this form of restricted freedom. Besides, claims Marx, trouble arises when you give men their unrestricted freedom. Human freedom always degenerates into license and gives rise to greed and war. They might claim that their "servitude is perfect freedom."

Again the Communists claim there is justice in Russia. They have their law courts. They have their elections with universal suffrage. When pressed to the point, they will admit there is really only one candidate because the people are so unanimous about that way of life.

They call their way of life "democratic." One of the problems statesmen find in dealing with Russia is one of semantics, of definition. Russia says she is democratic and we are Fascist; we claim to be democratic and call Russia Communists.

What, therefore, is missing in the pledge of allegiance that Americans have been saying on and off since 1892, and officially since 1942? The one fundamental concept that completely and ultimately separates Communist Russia from the democratic institutions of this country. This was seen clearly by Lincoln. Under God this people shall know a new birth of freedom, and "under God" are the definitive words.

Now, Lincoln was not being original in that phrase. He was simply reminding the people of the basis upon which the Nation won its freedom in its Declaration of Independence. He went back to Jefferson as he did in so much of his thinking. Indeed, he acknowledges his debt to Jefferson in a famous speech delivered at Independence Hall in Philadelphia on February 22, 1861, 2 years before the Gettysburg Address. "All the political sentiments I entertain have been drawn from the sentiments which originated and were given to the world from this hall. I have never had a feeling politically that did not spring from sentiments embodied in the Declaration of Independence."

Listen again to the fundamentals of this Declaration:

"We hold these truths to be self-evident, that all men are created equal; that they are endowed by their Creator with certain unalienable rights; that among these are life, liberty, and the pursuit of happiness."

At Gettysburg Lincoln poses the question: "Now we are engaged in a great civil war, testing whether that nation, or any nation so conceived and so dedicated, can long endure."

That is the text of our day and generation also.

The tragedy of the 19th century democratic liberalism, when nation after nation set up parliamentary forms of government, was that two world convulsions shattered the illusion that you can build a nation on human ideas without a fundamental belief in God's providence. Crowns in Europe toppled, not because of autocracy but because the peoples had lost the vision of God.

We face, today, a theological war. It is not basically a conflict between two political philosophies—Thomas Jefferson's political democracy over against Lenin's communistic state.

Nor is it a conflict fundamentally between two economic systems between, shall we say, Adam Smith's Wealth of Nations and Karl Marx's Das Capital.

It is a fight for the freedom of the human personality. It is not simply man's inhumanity to man. It is Armageddon, a battle of the gods. It is the view of man as it comes down to us from Judaio-Christian civilization in mortal combat against modern, secularized, godless humanity.

The pledge of allegiance seems to me to omit this theological implication that is fundamental to the American way of life. It should be "One nation, indivisible, under God." Once "under God," then we can define what we mean by "liberty and justice for all." To omit the words "under God" in the pledge of allegiance is to omit the definitive character of the American way of life.

Some might assert this to be a violation of the first amendment to the Constitution. It is quite the opposite. The first amendment states concerning the question of religion: "Congress shall make no law respecting the establishment of religion."

Now, "establishment of religion" is a technical term. It means Congress will permit no state church in this land such as exists in England. In England the bishops are appointed by Her Majesty. The church, by law, is supported by teinds or rent. The church, therefore, can call upon the support of the law of the land to carry out its own ecclesiastical laws. What the declaration says, in effect, is that no state church shall exist in this land. This is separation of church and state; it is not, and never was meant to be, a separation of religion and life. Such objection is a confusion of the first amendment with the First Commandment.

If we were to add the phrase "under the church" that would be different. In fact, it would be dangerous. The question arises, which church? Now, I could give good Methodists an excellent dissertation upon the virtues of the Presbyterian Church, and show how much superior John Knox was to John Wesley. But the whole sad story of church history shows how, of all tyrants, often the church could be the worst for the best of reasons. The Jewish Church persecuted unto death the Christian Church in the first decade of Christianity; and for 1,200 years the Christian Church persecuted the Jewish Church. The Roman Church persecuted the Protestants; and the Protestants, in turn, persecuted the Roman Church; the Presbyterians and the Episcopalians brought low the very name of Christian charity, both in Scotland and America. It is not for nothing that

Thomas Jefferson, on his tombstone at Monticello, claimed that one of the three achievements of his life was his fight for religious freedom in Virginia—that even above the exalted office as President of these United States. No church is infallible; and no churchman is infallible.

Of course, as Christians, we might include the words "under Jesus Christ" or "under the King of Kings." But one of the glories of this land is that it has opened its gates to all men of every religious faith.

The word of welcome to these shores is epitomized on the Statue of Liberty:

> "Give me your tired, your poor,
> Your huddled masses yearning to breathe free,
> The wretched refuse of your teeming shore,
> Send these, the homeless, tempest tossed to me:
> I lift my lamp beside the golden door."

There is no religious examination on entering the United States of America—no persecution because a man's faith differs even from the Christian religion. So, it must be "under God" to include the great Jewish community, and the people of the Moslem faith, and the myriad of denominations of Christians in the land.

What then of the honest atheist?

Philosophically speaking, an atheistic American is a contradiction in terms. Now don't misunderstand me. This age has thrown up a new type of man—we call him a secular; he does not believe in God; not because he is a wicked man, but because he is dialectically honest, and would rather walk with the unbelievers than sit hypocritically with people of the faith. These men, and many have I known, are fine in character; and in their obligations as citizens and good neighbors, quite excellent.

But they really are spiritual parasites. And I mean no term of abuse in this. I'm simply classifying them. A parasite is an organism that lives upon the life force of another organism without contributing to the life of the other. These excellent ethical seculars are living upon the accumulated spiritual capital of Judaio-Christian civilization, and at the same time, deny the God who revealed the divine principles upon which the ethics of this country grow. The dilemma of the secular is quite simple.

He cannot deny the Christian revelation and logically live by the Christian ethic.

And if he denies the Christian ethic, he falls short of the American ideal of life.

In Jefferson's phrase, if we deny the existence of the God who gave us life. How can we live by the liberty He gave us at the same time? This is a God-fearing nation. On our coins, bearing the imprint of Lincoln and Jefferson, are the words "In God we trust." Congress is opened with prayer.

It is upon the Holy Bible the President takes his oath of office. Naturalized citizens, when they take their oath of allegiance, conclude, solemnly, with the words "so help me God."

This is the issue we face today: A freedom that respects the rights of the minorities, but is defined by a fundamental belief in God. A way of life that sees man, not as the ultimate outcome of a mysterious concatenation of evolutionary process, but a sentient being created by God and seeking to know His will, and "Whose soul is restless till he rest in God."

In this land, there is neither Jew nor Greek, neither bond nor free, neither male nor female, for we are one nation indivisible under God, and humbly as God has given us the light we seek liberty and justice for all. This quest is not only within these United States, but to the four corners of the globe wherever man will lift up his head toward the vision of his true and divine manhood.

Source

[George Docherty, "A New Birth of Freedom."] 100 Cong. Rec. A1794–95 (1954).

Further Reading

Inboden, William. *Religion and American Foreign Policy, 1945–1960: The Soul of Containment.* New York: Cambridge University Press, 2008.

Kruse, Kevin M. *One Nation Under God: How Corporate America Invented Christian America.* New York: Basic, 2015.

Stevens, Jason W. *God-Fearing and Free: A Spiritual History of America's Cold War.* Cambridge, MA: Harvard University Press, 2010.

5

Social Movements and Spiritual Diversity

The 1960s and 1970s were decades of great upheaval in American life. The civil rights movement, along with the repeal of immigration restrictions, overthrew white supremacy as the nation's reigning racial ideology and helped bring about a new age of multiculturalism. The politics of gender, sexuality, and family also changed, transformed by new reproductive technologies (most notably the birth control pill) and a resurgent feminist movement. Meanwhile, the Vietnam War and the Watergate scandal eroded Americans' confidence in political institutions.

New religious configurations supplanted old systems of authority. Even though the nation had always been religiously diverse, Protestants had played a dominant role in public life for much of American history, leading some scholars to posit the existence of an unofficial "Protestant Establishment." This regime began to change significantly in the mid twentieth century, as the vision took hold of a "tri-faith America" that included Catholics and Jews alongside Protestants. In the 1960s and 1970s, the diversification of religious life intensified with the growth of Hinduism and Buddhism, the revitalization of Native American traditions, the emergence of feminist spiritualities, and the reshaping of Protestant, Catholic, and Jewish faiths by new waves of immigrants.

This period saw a remarkable intellectual ferment of American religious liberalism, which assumed that religion had to adapt to a changing culture and that social and political reform were necessary imperatives for committed people of faith. Much of the liberals' thinking would be strongly opposed by the religious right, represented here in an early sermon by Jerry Falwell and more extensively in the next section.

JOHN F. KENNEDY, "ADDRESS TO THE GREATER HOUSTON MINISTERIAL ASSOCIATION" (1960)

The 1960 election of John F. Kennedy (1917–1963), the nation's first Catholic president, marked a shift in the American religious landscape. In the preceding decades, Catholics and Protestants had begun to overcome their historic hostility. Restrictions on immigration imposed in the 1920s meant that, over time, fewer U.S. Catholics were foreign-born, so the accusation that Catholicism was un-American grew less convincing. Meanwhile, the Second World War and the early Cold War gave strength to the idea of an inclusive "Judeo-Christian tradition" as the basis of American democracy, a heritage that encompassed Protestants, Catholics, and Jews. Given these gains, Richard Nixon, Kennedy's Republican opponent, was reluctant to raise the issue of religion during the campaign for fear of alienating Catholic voters.

Many Americans did, however, oppose Kennedy because of his faith. Powerful Protestant ministers such as Billy Graham and Norman Vincent Peale feared having a Catholic in the White House and worked quietly to build support for Nixon. Kennedy's detractors suggested that a Catholic president would be more loyal to the pope than to the American people. This unease grew so widespread that Kennedy felt the need to clarify publicly his views on religion, which he attempted to do in this speech to an assembly of Protestant ministers in Houston.

The 1960 election was one of the closest in American history. No one can know exactly what pushed Kennedy over the top, but many historians feel that his deft handling of the religion question helped his campaign. For the new president's coreligionists, the victory provided special cause for celebration. When, in 1962, Pope John XXIII convened the Second Vatican Council to reform church traditions, many American Catholics envisioned "the two Johns" bringing their faith fully into the modern world. Perhaps the greatest sign of Kennedy's success is that he is seldom remembered today as a Catholic president, but simply as a beloved and tragic leader of Cold War America.

John F. Kennedy, "Address to the Greater Houston Ministerial Association"

Reverend Meza, Reverend Reck, I'm grateful for your generous invitation to speak my views.

While the so-called religious issue is necessarily and properly the chief topic here tonight, I want to emphasize from the outset that we have far more critical issues to face in the 1960 election; the spread of Communist influence, until it now festers 90 miles off the coast of Florida—the humiliating treatment of our President and Vice President by those who no longer respect our power—the hungry children I saw in West Virginia, the old people who cannot pay their doctor bills, the families forced to give up their farms—an America with too many slums, with too few schools, and too late to the moon and outer space.

These are the real issues which should decide this campaign. And they are not religious issues—for war and hunger and ignorance and despair know no religious barriers.

But because I am a Catholic, and no Catholic has ever been elected President, the real issues in this campaign have been obscured—perhaps deliberately, in some quarters less responsible than this. So it is apparently necessary for me to state once again—not what kind of church I believe in, for that should be important only to me—but what kind of America I believe in.

I believe in an America where the separation of church and state is absolute—where no Catholic prelate would tell the President (should he be Catholic) how to act, and no Protestant minister would tell his parishioners for whom to vote—where no church or church school is granted any public funds or political preference—and where no man is denied public office merely because his religion differs from the President who might appoint him or the people who might elect him.

I believe in an America that is officially neither Catholic, Protestant nor Jewish—where no public official either requests or accepts instructions on public policy from the Pope, the National Council of Churches or any other ecclesiastical source—where no religious body seeks to impose its will directly or indirectly upon the general populace or the public acts of its officials—and where religious liberty is so indivisible that an act against one church is treated as an act against all.

For while this year it may be a Catholic against whom the finger of suspicion is pointed, in other years it has been, and may someday be again, a Jew—or a Quaker—or a Unitarian—or a Baptist. It was Virginia's harassment of Baptist preachers, for example, that helped lead to Jefferson's statute of religious freedom. Today I may be the victim—but tomorrow it may be you—until the whole fabric of our harmonious society is ripped at a time of great national peril.

Finally, I believe in an America where religious intolerance will some-day end—where all men and all churches are treated as equal—where every man has the same right to attend or not attend the church of his choice—where there is no Catholic vote, no anti-Catholic vote, no bloc voting of any kind—and where Catholics, Protestants and Jews, at both the lay and pastoral level, will refrain from those attitudes of disdain and division which have so often marred their works in the past, and promote instead the American ideal of brotherhood.

That is the kind of America in which I believe. And it represents the kind of Presidency in which I believe—a great office that must neither be humbled by making it the instrument of any one religious group nor tarnished by arbitrarily withholding its occupancy from the members of any one religious group. I believe in a President whose religious views are his own private affair, neither imposed by him upon the nation or imposed by the nation upon him as a condition to holding that office.

I would not look with favor upon a President working to subvert the first amendment's guarantees of religious liberty. Nor would our system of checks and balances permit him to do so—and neither do I look with favor upon those who would work to subvert Article VI of the Constitution by requiring a religious test—even by indirection—for it. If they disagree with that safeguard they should be out openly working to repeal it.

I want a Chief Executive whose public acts are responsible to all groups and obligated to none—who can attend any ceremony, service or dinner his office may appropriately require of him—and whose fulfillment of his Presidential oath is not limited or conditioned by any religious oath, ritual or obligation.

This is the kind of America I believe in—and this is the kind I fought for in the South Pacific, and the kind my brother died for in Europe. No one suggested then that we may have a "divided loyalty," that we did "not believe in liberty," or that we belonged to a disloyal group that threatened the "freedoms for which our forefathers died."

And in fact this is the kind of America for which our forefathers died—when they fled here to escape religious test oaths that denied office to members of less favored churches—when they fought for the Constitution, the Bill of Rights, and the Virginia Statute of Religious Freedom—and when they fought at the shrine I visited today, the Alamo. For side by side with Bowie and Crockett died McCafferty and Bailey and Carey—but no one knows whether they were Catholic or not. For there was no religious test at the Alamo.

I ask you tonight to follow in that tradition—to judge me on the basis of my record of fourteen years in Congress—on my declared stands against an Ambassador to the Vatican, against unconstitutional aid to parochial schools, and against any boycott of the public schools (which I have attended myself)—instead of judging me on the basis of these pamphlets and publications we all have seen that carefully select quotations out of context from the statements of Catholic church leaders, usually in other countries, frequently in other centuries, and always omitting, of course, the statement of the American Bishops in 1948 which strongly endorsed church-state separation, and which more nearly reflects the views of almost every American Catholic.

I do not consider these other quotations binding upon my public acts— why should you? But let me say, with respect to other countries, that I am wholly opposed to the state being used by any religious group, Catholic or Protestant, to compel, prohibit, or persecute the free exercise of any other religion. And I hope that you and I condemn with equal fervor those nations which deny their Presidency to Protestants and those which deny it to Catholics. And rather than cite the misdeeds of those who differ, I would cite the record of the Catholic Church in such nations as Ireland and France—and the independence of such statesmen as Adenauer and De Gaulle.

But let me stress again that these are my views—for contrary to common newspaper usage, I am not the Catholic candidate for President. I am the Democratic Party's candidate for President who happens also to be a Catholic. I do not speak for my church on public matters—and the church does not speak for me.

Whatever issue may come before me as President—on birth control, divorce, censorship, gambling or any other subject—I will make my decision in accordance with these views, in accordance with what my conscience tells me to be the national interest, and without regard to outside religious pressures or dictates. And no power or threat of punishment could cause me to decide otherwise.

But if the time should ever come—and I do not concede any conflict to be even remotely possible—when my office would require me to either violate my conscience or violate the national interest, then I would resign the office; and I hope any conscientious public servant would do the same.

But I do not intend to apologize for these views to my critics of either Catholic or Protestant faith—nor do I intend to disavow either my views or my church in order to win this election.

If I should lose on the real issues, I shall return to my seat in the Senate, satisfied that I had tried my best and was fairly judged. But if this election is decided on the basis that 40 million Americans lost their chance of being President on the day they were baptized, then it is the whole nation that will be the loser, in the eyes of Catholics and non-Catholics around the world, in the eyes of history, and in the eyes of our own people.

But if, on the other hand, I should win the election, then I shall devote every effort of mind and spirit to fulfilling the oath of the Presidency— practically identical, I might add, to the oath I have taken for fourteen years in the Congress. For without reservation, I can "solemnly swear that I will faithfully execute the office of President of the United States, and will to the best of my ability preserve, protect, and defend the Constitution . . . so help me God."

Source

John F. Kennedy, "Address to the Greater Houston Ministerial Association," September 12, 1960.

John F. Kennedy Presidential Library and Museum. http://www.jfklibrary.org/Asset-Viewer/ALL6YEBJMEKYGMCntnSCvg.aspx

Further Reading

Carty, Thomas J. *A Catholic in the White House? Religion, Politics, and John F. Kennedy's Presidential Campaign.* New York: Palgrave Macmillan, 2004.

Casey, Shaun. *The Making of a Catholic President: Kennedy vs. Nixon 1960.* New York: Oxford University Press, 2009.

McGreevy, John T. *Catholicism and American Freedom: A History.* New York: Norton, 2003.

MARTIN LUTHER KING, JR., "LETTER FROM BIRMINGHAM JAIL" (1963)

Despite the brevity of his life, Martin Luther King, Jr. (1929–1968), became the most prominent figure in twentieth-century American religious politics. He was unexpectedly catapulted to national prominence during the Montgomery bus boycott of 1955–56, then reigned as the leader of the civil rights movement until his assassination in 1968. His use of Christian nonviolence overthrew legal segregation (though other forms of racial division persisted) and made antiracism a religious imperative.

King's larger-than-life persona often obscures the specific faith traditions that shaped him. At one level, his outlook was rooted in the African American Baptist church. His father, Martin Luther King, Sr., was a prominent Atlanta minister and an official in the National Association for the Advancement of Colored People (NAACP). The younger King drew his speaking style and his commitment to black freedom from that heritage. Yet King also imbibed the theological tenets of midcentury liberal Protestantism at Boston University, where he received his doctoral degree. Indeed, King's theology was in many ways a continuation of the Social Gospel, and he cited Walter Rauschenbusch as one of his most vital influences. Much of King's success sprang from his ability to work on different spiritual registers, appealing at once to ordinary African American Southerners and to white Northern intellectuals.

The "Letter from Birmingham Jail," excerpted here, is considered a classic of American literature and political philosophy, yet it too sprang from a religious context. King wrote in response to a public statement by white Southern ministers criticizing his use of civil disobedience (which had landed him behind bars) as "unwise and untimely." Although many of his arguments have contributed to general theories of dissent, he focuses much of the essay on the specific failure of white Southern churches to support civil rights. Indeed, one of King's great accomplishments was to convince his fellow Americans that the teachings of Christianity demanded racial equality, a contention that his Southern religious opponents were ultimately unable to refute.

Martin Luther King, Jr., "Letter from Birmingham Jail"

We have waited for more than 340 years for our constitutional and God-given rights. The nations of Asia and Africa are moving with jet-like speed toward gaining political independence, but we still creep at horse-and-buggy pace toward gaining a cup of coffee at a lunch counter. Perhaps it is easy for those who have never felt the stinging darts of segregation to say "Wait." But when you have seen vicious mobs lynch your mothers and fathers at will and drown your sisters and brothers at whim; when you have seen hate-filled policemen curse, kick and even kill your black brothers and sisters with impunity; when you see the vast majority of your 20 million Negro brothers smothering in an air-tight cage of poverty in the midst of an affluent society; when you suddenly find your tongue twisted as you seek to explain to your six-year-old daughter why she can't go to the public amusement park that has just been advertised on television, and see tears welling up when she is told that Funtown is closed to colored children, and see ominous clouds of inferiority beginning to form in her little mental sky, and see her beginning to distort her personality by unconsciously developing a bitterness toward white people; when you have to concoct an answer for a five-year-old son asking, "Daddy, why do white people treat colored people so mean?"; when you take a cross-country drive and find it necessary to sleep night after night in the uncomfortable corners of your automobile because no motel will accept you; when you are humiliated day in and day out by nagging signs reading "white" and "colored"; when your first name becomes "nigger," your middle name becomes "boy" (however old you are) and your last name becomes "John," and your wife and mother are never given the respected title "Mrs."; when you are harried by day and haunted by night by the fact that you are a Negro, never quite knowing what to expect next, and are plagued with inner fears and outer resentments; when you are forever fighting a degenerating sense of "nobodiness"—then you will understand why we find it difficult to wait. There comes a time when the cup of endurance runs over, and men are no longer willing to be plunged into an abyss of injustice where they experience the bleakness of corroding despair. I hope, sirs, you can understand our legitimate and unavoidable impatience.

You express a great deal of anxiety over our willingness to break laws. This is certainly a legitimate concern. Since we so diligently urge people to obey the Supreme Court's decision of 1954 outlawing segregation in the public schools, at first glance it may seem rather paradoxical for us consciously to break laws. One may well ask, "How can you advocate breaking some laws and obeying others?" The answer lies in the fact that there are two types of laws: just and unjust. I agree with St. Augustine that "an unjust law is no law at all."

Now what is the difference between the two? How does one determine whether a law is just or unjust? A just law is a man-made code that squares with the moral law or the law of God. An unjust law is a code that is out of harmony with the moral law. To put it in the terms of St. Thomas Aquinas, an unjust law is a human law that is not rooted in eternal law and natural law. Any law that uplifts human personality is just. Any law that degrades human personality is unjust. All segregation statutes are unjust because segregation distorts the soul and damages the personality. It gives the segregator a false sense of superiority and the segregated a false sense of inferiority. Segregation, to use the terminology of the Jewish philosopher Martin Buber, substitutes an "I-it" relationship for an "I-thou" relationship and ends up relegating persons to the status of things. Hence segregation is not only politically, economically and sociologically unsound, it is sinful. Paul Tillich has said that sin is separation. Is not segregation an existential expression of man's tragic separation, his awful estrangement, his terrible sinfulness? Thus it is that I can urge men to disobey segregation ordinances, for such ordinances are morally wrong.

Let us consider some of the ways in which a law can be unjust. A law is unjust, for example, if the majority group compels a minority group to obey the statute but does not make it binding on itself. By the same token a law in all probability is just if the majority is itself willing to obey it. Also, a law is unjust if it is inflicted on a minority that, as a result of being denied the right to vote, had no part in enacting or devising the law. Who can say that the legislature of Alabama which set up that state's segregation laws was democratically elected? Throughout Alabama all sorts of devious methods are used to prevent Negroes from becoming registered voters, and there are some counties in which, even though Negroes constitute a majority of the population, not a single Negro is registered. Can any law enacted under such circumstances be considered democratically structured?

Sometimes a law is just on its face and unjust in its application. For instance, I have been arrested on a charge of parading without a permit. Now there is nothing wrong in having an ordinance which requires a permit for a parade. But such an ordinance becomes unjust when it is used to maintain segregation and to deny citizens the First-amendment privilege of peaceful assembly and protest.

I hope you are able to see the distinction I am trying to point out. In no sense do I advocate evading the law, as would the rabid segregationist. That would lead to anarchy. One who breaks an unjust law must do so *openly, lovingly,* and with a willingness to accept the penalty. I submit that an individual who breaks a law that conscience tells him is unjust and who willingly accepts the penalty of imprisonment in order to arouse the conscience of the community over its injustice is in reality expressing the highest respect for law.

Of course, there is nothing new about this kind of civil disobedience. It was evidenced sublimely in the refusal of Shadrach, Meshach and Abednego to obey the laws of Nebuchadnezzar, on the ground that a higher moral law was at stake. It was practiced superbly by the early Christians who were willing to face hungry lions rather than submit to certain unjust laws of the Roman empire. To a degree, academic freedom is a reality today because Socrates practiced civil disobedience. We should never forget that everything Adolf Hitler did in Germany was "legal" and everything the Hungarian freedom fighters did in Hungary was "illegal." It was "illegal" to aid and comfort a Jew in Hitler's Germany. Even so, I am sure that had I lived in Germany at the time I would have aided and comforted my Jewish brothers. If today I lived in a communist country where certain principles dear to the Christian faith are suppressed, I would openly advocate disobeying that country's antireligious laws.

I must make two honest confessions to you, my Christian and Jewish brothers. First, I must confess that over the past few years I have been gravely disappointed with the white moderate. I have almost reached the regrettable conclusion that the Negro's great stumbling block in his stride toward freedom is not the White Citizen's Counciler or the Ku Klux Klanner but the white moderate who is more devoted to "order" than to justice; who prefers a negative peace which is the absence of tension to a positive peace which is the presence of justice; who constantly says "I agree with you in the goal you seek, but I cannot agree with your methods"; who paternalistically believes he can set the timetable for another man's freedom; who lives by a mythical concept of time and who constantly advises the Negro to wait for a "more convenient season." Shallow understanding from people of good will is more frustrating than absolute misunderstanding from people of ill will. Lukewarm acceptance is much more bewildering than outright rejection.

I had hoped that the white moderate would understand that law and order exist for the purpose of establishing justice and that when they fail in this purpose they block social progress. I had hoped that the white moderate would understand that the present tension in the south is a necessary phase of the transition from an obnoxious negative peace, in which the Negro passively accepted his unjust plight, to a substantive and positive peace, in which all men will respect the dignity and worth of human personality. Actually, we who engage in nonviolent direct action are not the creators of tension. We merely bring to the surface the hidden tension that is already alive. We bring it out in the open where it can be seen and dealt with. Like a boil that can never be cured so long as it is covered up but must be opened with all its pus-flowing ugliness to the natural medicines of air and light, injustice must be exposed, with all the tension its exposure creates, to the light of human conscience and the air of national opinion before it can be cured.

In your statement you assert that our actions, even though peaceful, must be condemned because they precipitate violence. But is this a logical assertion? Isn't this like condemning a robbed man because his possession of money precipitated an act of robbery? Isn't this like condemning Socrates because his unswerving commitment to truth and his philosophical inquiries precipitated the act by the misguided populace in which they made him drink hemlock? Isn't this like condemning Jesus because his unique God-consciousness and never-ceasing devotion to God's will precipitated the evil act of crucifixion? We must come to see that, as the federal courts have consistently affirmed, it is wrong to urge an individual to cease his efforts to gain his basic constitutional rights because the quest may precipitate violence. Society must protect the robbed and punish the robber.

I had also hoped that the white moderate would reject the myth concerning time in relation to the struggle for freedom. I have just received a letter from a white brother in Texas. He writes: "All Christians know that the colored people will receive equal rights eventually, but it is possible that you are in too great a religious hurry. It has taken Christianity almost 2,000 years to accomplish what it has. The teachings of Christ take time to come to earth." Such an attitude stems from a tragic misconception of time, from the strangely irrational notion that there is something in the very flow of time that will inevitably cure all ills. Actually, time itself is neutral; it can be used either destructively or constructively. More and more I feel that the people of ill will have used time much more effectively than have the people of good will. We will have to repent in this generation not merely for the hateful words and actions of the bad people but for the appalling silence of the good people. Human progress never rolls in on wheels of inevitability; it comes through the tireless efforts of men willing to be coworkers with God, and without this hard work time itself becomes an ally of the forces of social stagnation. We must use time creatively, in the knowledge that the time is always ripe to do right. Now is the time to make real the promise of democracy and transform our pending national elegy into a creative psalm of brotherhood. Now is the time to lift our national policy from the quicksand of racial injustice to the solid rock of human dignity.

You speak of our activity in Birmingham as extreme. At first I was rather disappointed that fellow clergymen would see my nonviolent efforts as those of an extremist. I began thinking about the fact that I stand in the middle of two opposing forces in the Negro community. One is a force of complacency made up of Negroes who, as a result of long years of oppression, are so completely drained of self-respect and a sense of "somebodiness" that they have adjusted to segregation, and of a few middle class Negroes who, because of a degree of academic and economic security and because in some ways they profit by segregation, have unconsciously become insensitive to the problems of the masses. The other force is one of bitterness and hatred, and it comes perilously close to advocating violence. It is expressed in the various black nationalist groups that are springing up across the nation, the largest and best-known being Elijah Muhammad's Muslim movement. Nourished by the Negro's frustration over the continued existence of racial discrimination, this movement is made up of people who have lost faith in America, who have absolutely repudiated Christianity, and who have concluded that the white man is an incorrigible "devil."

I have tried to stand between these two forces, saying that we need emulate neither the "do-nothingism" of the complacent nor the hatred of the black nationalist. For there is the more excellent way of love and nonviolent protest. I am grateful to God that, through the influence of the Negro church, the way of nonviolence became an integral part of our struggle.

If this philosophy had not emerged, by now many streets of the south would, I am convinced, be flowing with blood. And I am further convinced that if our white brothers dismiss as "rabble-rousers" and "outside agitators" those of us who employ nonviolent direct action and if they refuse to support our nonviolent efforts, millions of Negroes will, out of frustration and despair, seek solace and security in black nationalist ideologies—a development that would inevitably lead to a frightening racial nightmare.

Oppressed people cannot remain oppressed forever. The yearning for freedom eventually manifests itself, and that is what has happened to the

American Negro. Something within has reminded him of his birthright of freedom, and something without has reminded him that it can be gained. Consciously or unconsciously, he has been caught up by the *Zeitgeist,* and with his black brothers of Africa and his brown and yellow brothers of Asia, South America and the Caribbean, the U.S. Negro is moving with a sense of great urgency toward the promised land of racial justice. If one recognizes this vital urge that has engulfed the Negro community, he should readily understand why public demonstrations are taking place. The Negro has many pent-up resentments and latent frustrations, and he must release them. So let him march; let him make prayer pilgrimages to the city hall; let him go on freedom rides—and try to understand why he must do so. If his repressed emotions are not released in nonviolent ways, they will seek expression through violence; this is not a threat but a fact of history. I have not said to my people, "Get rid of your discontent." Rather, I have tried to say that this normal and healthy discontent can be channeled into the creative outlet of nonviolent direct action. And now this approach is being termed extremist.

But though I was initially disappointed at being categorized as an extremist, as I continued to think about the matter I gradually gained a measure of satisfaction from the label. Was not Jesus an extremist for love: "Love your enemies, bless them that curse you, do good to them that hate you, and pray for them which despitefully use you, and persecute you." Was not Amos an extremist for justice: "Let justice roll down like waters and righteousness like an everflowing stream." Was not Paul an extremist for the Christian gospel: "I bear in my body the marks of the Lord Jesus." Was not Martin Luther an extremist: "Here I stand; I can do no other so help me God." And John Bunyan: "I will stay in jail to the end of my days before I make a butchery of my conscience." And Abraham Lincoln: "This nation cannot survive half slave and half free." And Thomas Jefferson: "We hold these truths to be self-evident, that all men are created equal . . ." So the question is not whether we will be extremists but what kind of extremists we will be. Will we be extremists for hate or for love? Will we be extremists for the preservation of injustice or for the extension of justice? Perhaps the south, the nation and the world are in dire need of creative extremists.

I had hoped that the white moderate would see this need. Perhaps I was too optimistic; perhaps I expected too much. I suppose I should have realized that few members of the oppressor race can understand the deep groans and passionate yearnings of the oppressed race, and still fewer have the vision to see that injustice must be rooted out by strong, persistent and determined action. I am thankful, however, that some of our white brothers have grasped the meaning of this social revolution and committed themselves to it. They are still all too few in quantity, but they are big in quality. Some—such as Ralph McGill, Lillian Smith, Harry

Golden and James McBride Dabbs—have written about our struggle in eloquent and prophetic terms. Others have marched with us down nameless streets of the south. They have languished in filthy, roach-infested jails, suffering the abuse and brutality of policemen who view them as "dirty nigger lovers." Unlike so many of their moderate brothers and sisters, they have recognized the urgency of the moment and sensed the need for powerful "action" antidotes to combat the disease of segregation.

Let me take note of my other major disappointment. Though there are some notable exceptions, I have also been disappointed with the white church and its leadership. I do not say this as one of those negative critics who can always find something wrong with the church. I say this as a minister of the gospel, who loves the church; who was nurtured in its bosom; who has been sustained by its spiritual blessings and who will remain true to it as long as the cord of life shall lengthen.

When I was suddenly catapulted into the leadership of the bus protest in Montgomery, Alabama, a few years ago I felt we would be supported by the white church. I felt that the white ministers, priests and rabbis of the south would be among our strongest allies. Instead, some have been outright opponents, refusing to understand the freedom movement and misrepresenting its leaders; all too many others have been more cautious than courageous and have remained silent and secure behind stained-glass windows.

In spite of my shattered dreams I came to Birmingham with the hope that the white religious leadership of this community would see the justice of our cause and with deep moral concern would serve as the channel through which our just grievances could reach the power structure. But again I have been disappointed.

I have heard numerous southern religious leaders admonish their worshipers to comply with a desegregation decision because it is the *law*, but I have longed to hear white ministers declare, "Follow this decree because integration is morally *right* and because the Negro is your brother." In the midst of blatant injustices inflicted upon the Negro I have watched white churchmen stand on the sideline and mouth pious irrelevancies and sanctimonious trivialities. In the midst of a mighty struggle to rid our nation of racial and economic injustice I have heard many ministers say, "Those are social issues with which the gospel has no real concern," and I have watched many churches commit themselves to a completely otherworldly religion which makes a strange, unbiblical distinction between body and soul, between the sacred and the secular.

We are moving toward the close of the 20th century with a religious community largely adjusted to the status quo—a taillight behind other community agencies rather than a headlight leading men to higher levels of justice.

I have traveled the length and breadth of Alabama, Mississippi and all the other southern states. On sweltering summer days and crisp autumn mornings I have looked at the south's beautiful churches with their lofty spires pointing heavenward, and at her impressive religious education buildings. Over and over I have found myself asking: "What kind of people worship here? Who is their God? Where were their voices when the lips of Governor Barnett dripped with words of interposition and nullification? Where were they when Governor Wallace gave a clarion call for defiance and hatred? Where were their voices of support when bruised and weary Negro men and women decided to rise from the dark dungeons of complacency to the bright hills of creative protest?"

Yes, these questions are still in my mind. In deep disappointment I have wept over the laxity of the church. But be assured that my tears have been tears of love. There can be no deep disappointment where there is not deep love. Yes, I love the church. How could I do otherwise? I am in the rather unique position of being the son, the grandson and the great-grandson of preachers. Yes, I see the church as the body of Christ. But, oh! How we have blemished and scarred that body through social neglect and through fear of being nonconformists.

There was a time when the church was very powerful—in the time when the early Christians rejoiced at being deemed worthy to suffer for what they believed. In those days the church was not merely a thermometer that recorded the ideas and principles of popular opinion; it was a thermostat that transformed the mores of society. Whenever the early Christians entered a town the power structure immediately sought to convict them for being "disturbers of the peace" and "outside agitators." But the Christians pressed on, in the conviction that they were "a colony of heaven," called to obey God rather than man. Small in number, they were big in commitment. By their effort and example they brought an end to such ancient evils as infanticide and gladiatorial contest.

Things are different now. So often the contemporary church is a weak, ineffectual voice with an uncertain sound. So often it is an archdefender of the status quo. Far from being disturbed by the presence of the church, the power structure of the average community is consoled by the church's silent—and often even vocal—sanction of things as they are.

But the judgment of God is upon the church as never before. If today's church does not recapture the sacrificial spirit of the early church, it will lose its authenticity, forfeit the loyalty of millions, and be dismissed as an irrelevant social club with no meaning for the 20th century. Every day I meet young people whose disappointment with the church has turned into outright disgust.

Perhaps I have once again been too optimistic. Is organized religion too inextricably bound to the status quo to save our nation and the world?

Perhaps I must turn my faith to the inner spiritual church, the church within the church, as the true *ecclesia* and the hope of the world. But again I am thankful to God that some noble souls from the ranks of organized religion have broken loose from the paralyzing chains of conformity and joined us as active partners in the struggle for freedom. They have left their secure congregations and walked the streets of Albany, Georgia, with us. They have gone down the highways of the south on torturous rides for freedom. Yes, they have gone to jail with us. Some have been kicked out of their churches, have lost the support of their bishops and fellow ministers. But they have acted in the faith that right defeated is stronger than evil triumphant. Their witness has been the spiritual salt that has preserved the true meaning of the gospel in these troubled times. They have carved a tunnel of hope through the dark mountain of disappointment.

I hope the church as a whole will meet the challenge of this decisive hour. But even if the church does not come to the aid of justice, I have no despair about the future. I have no fear about the outcome of our struggle in Birmingham, even if our motives are at present misunderstood. We will reach the goal of freedom in Birmingham and all over the nation, because the goal of America is freedom. Abused and scorned though we may be, our destiny is tied up with America's destiny. Before the pilgrims landed at Plymouth we were here. Before the pen of Jefferson etched across the pages of history the mighty words of the Declaration of Independence, we were here. For more than two centuries our forebears labored in this country without wages; they made cotton king; they built the homes of their masters while suffering gross injustice and shameful humiliation— and yet out of a bottomless vitality they continued to thrive and develop. If the inexpressible cruelties of slavery could not stop us, the opposition we now face will surely fail. We will win our freedom because the sacred heritage of our nation and the eternal will of God are embodied in our echoing demands.

Before closing I feel impelled to mention one other point in your statement that has troubled me profoundly. You warmly commended the Birmingham police force for keeping "order" and "preventing violence." I doubt that you would have so warmly commended the police force if you had seen its angry dogs sinking their teeth into six unarmed, nonviolent Negroes. I doubt that you would so quickly commend the policemen if you were to observe their ugly and inhuman treatment of Negroes here in the city jail; if you were to watch them push and curse old Negro women and young Negro girls; if you were to see them slap and kick old Negro men and young boys; if you were to observe them, as they did on two occasions, refuse to give us food because we wanted to sing our grace together. I cannot join you in your praise of the Birmingham police department.

It is true that the police have exercised discipline in handling the demonstrators. In this sense they have conducted themselves rather "nonviolently" in public. But for what purpose? To preserve the evil system of segregation. Over the past few years I have consistently preached that nonviolence demands that the means we use must be as pure as the ends we seek. I have tried to make clear that it is wrong to use immoral means to attain moral ends. But now I must affirm that it is just as wrong, or perhaps even more so, to use moral means to preserve immoral ends. Perhaps Mr. Connor and his policemen have been rather nonviolent in public, as was Chief Pritchett in Albany, Georgia, but they have used the moral means of nonviolence to maintain the immoral end of racial injustice. As T. S. Eliot has said, there is no greater treason than to do the right deed for the wrong reason.

I wish you had commended the Negro sit-inners and demonstrators of Birmingham for their sublime courage, their willingness to suffer and their amazing discipline in the midst of great provocation. One day the south will recognize its real heroes. They will be the James Merediths, with a noble sense of purpose facing jeering and hostile mobs and the agonizing loneliness that characterizes the life of the pioneer. They will be old, oppressed, battered Negro women, symbolized in a 72-year-old woman in Montgomery, Alabama, who rose up with a sense of dignity and with her people decided not to ride segregated buses, and who responded with ungrammatical profundity to one who inquired about her: "My feet is tired, but my soul is rested." They will be the young high school and college students, the young ministers of the gospel and a host of their elders courageously and nonviolently sitting in at lunch counters and willingly going to jail for conscience' sake. One day the south will know that when these disinherited children of God sat down at lunch counters they were in reality standing up for what is best in the American dream and for the most sacred values in our Judeo-Christian heritage, thereby bringing our nation back to those great wells of democracy which were dug deep by the founding fathers in their formulation of the Constitution and the Declaration of Independence.

Never before have I written so long a letter. I can assure you that it would have been much shorter if I had been writing from a comfortable desk, but what else can one do when he is alone for days in a narrow jail cell, other than write long letters, think long thoughts and pray long prayers?

If I have said anything in this letter that overstates the truth and indicates an unreasonable impatience, I beg you to forgive me. If I have said anything that *under*states the truth and indicates my having a patience that allows me to settle for anything less than brotherhood, I beg God to forgive me.

I hope this letter finds you strong in the faith. I also hope that circumstances will soon make it possible for me to meet each of you, not as an integrationist or a civil rights leader but as a fellow clergyman and a Christian brother. Let us all hope that the dark clouds of racial prejudice will soon pass away and the deep fog of misunderstanding will be lifted from our fear-drenched communities and in some not too distant tomorrow the radiant stars of love and brotherhood will shine over our great nation with all their scintillating beauty.

Source

Martin Luther King, Jr., "Letter from Birmingham Jail." *Christian Century*, June 12, 1963, 768–73. Reprinted by arrangement with The Heirs to the Estate of Martin Luther King Jr., c/o Writers House as agent for the proprietor, New York, NY. Copyright © 1963 Dr. Martin Luther King Jr. © renewed 1991 Coretta Scott King.

Further Reading

Branch, Taylor. *Parting the Waters: America in the King Years, 1954–1963*. New York: Simon and Schuster, 1988.

Chappell, David. *A Stone of Hope: Prophetic Religion and the Death of Jim Crow*. Chapel Hill: University of North Carolina Press, 2004.

Miller, Keith D. *Voice of Deliverance: The Language of Martin Luther King, Jr., and Its Sources*. Athens, GA: University of Georgia Press, 1998.

Rieder, Jonathan. *Gospel of Freedom: Martin Luther King, Jr.'s Letter from Birmingham Jail and the Struggle That Changed a Nation*. New York: Bloomsbury, 2013.

JERRY FALWELL, "MINISTERS AND MARCHES" (1965)

The civil rights movement generated enormous opposition among the South's white Christians, who, given the high rates of religious participation in the region, frequently represented the leadership of white Southern culture as a whole. The movement's foes continued to defend racial segregation, which in religious terms meant that most white churches barred African Americans from membership, whether through official rules or informal agreement. The anti-integration forces also objected to the mixing of religion and politics by Martin Luther King, Jr. and other black leaders, especially when those leaders undertook civil disobedience in the name of a higher spiritual law. That objection forms the basis of Jerry Falwell's 1965 sermon "Ministers and Marches."

Falwell (1933–2007) was a captivating Southern preacher only a few years younger than King. He founded Thomas Road Baptist Church in Lynchburg, Virginia, in 1956, the year that King led the famous bus boycott in Montgomery, Alabama. "Ministers and Marches" was preached near the high point of the civil rights movement's legislative success, just after the Civil Rights Act and shortly before the Voting Rights Act. Falwell speaks out of a fundamentalist Baptist theology that sought to maintain the purity of religion against the corruption of politics.

Eventually, Falwell changed his mind in two ways. First, he repudiated his defense of racial segregation. Second, he asserted by the 1970s that Christians should in fact enter the political arena. In his 1980 book *Listen, America!* he called for like-minded religious conservatives to defend the traditional family and the nation against the forces of liberalism, Communism, and feminism. The previous year, Falwell helped start the Moral Majority, an activist group promoting conservative causes and voter registration that led to the minister's alliance with Ronald Reagan. Americans of the 1960s would have most likely associated religious politics with progressive causes such as civil rights, but Falwell and his allies ensured that the most visible forms of religious politics in the 1980s and 1990s were conservative, a far cry from the separatism advocated in "Ministers and Marches."

Jerry Falwell, "Ministers and Marches"

Under the Constitution of the United States, every American has the right to "peacefully" petition the government for a redress of grievances. This simply means that, in the present racial crises, all Americans, white, negro, or otherwise, have the legal right to "peacefully" demonstrate in order to obtain voting rights in Alabama—or elsewhere—if these rights are not allowed to the citizens. The purpose of this message is not to question such constitutional rights. Neither is it the intention of this message to discuss the subject of integration or segregation. It is my desire, in this sermon, to open the Bible and, from God's Word, answer the question—*"Does the 'CHURCH' have any command from God to involve itself in marches, demonstrations, or any other actions, such as many ministers and church leaders are so doing today in the name of civil rights reforms?"*

At the outset of this message, I do wish to speak frankly about one particular matter. There are, no doubt, many very sincere Christians who have felt a compulsion to join in civil rights efforts across the nation. At the same time, I must personally say that I do question the sincerity and non-violent intentions of some civil rights leaders such as Dr. Martin Luther King Jr., Mr. James Farmer, and others, who are known to have left-wing associations. It is very obvious that the Communists, as they do in all parts of the world, are taking advantage of a tense situation in our land, and are exploiting every incident to bring about violence and bloodshed. But I must repeat that I do believe many sincere persons are participating. I must also say that I believe these demonstrations and marches have done more to damage race relations and to gender hate than to help!

CHURCH RESPONSIBILITY

Since all orthodox Christians accept the Bible to be the verbally inspired Word of God, let us look into this Bible and see what the commands to the church are. In the first book of the New Testament, Matthew 28:18–20, Jesus commissioned the church to: "Go ye therefore and teach all nations, baptizing them in the name of the Father and of the Son and of the Holy Ghost: teaching them to observe all things whatsoever I have commanded you." You will notice here three specific commands: (1) Make disciples, or as we sometimes say, win souls; (2) baptize these new converts in the name of the Trinity; (3) teach them the Christ-life. In Mark 16, you will find the same command in slightly different words. In Luke 24 and in John 20, the same commands are given. As we move to the Book of the Acts of the Apostles, we find in the 1st chapter and the 8th verse the very same command. As we search through the letters of Paul, and all the other New Testament letters, we see that the church is given no command other than this Great Commission to take the message of Christ to a dying world. As far as the relationship of the church to the world, it can be expressed as simply as the three words which Paul gave to Timothy—"preach the Word." We have a message of redeeming grace through a crucified and risen Lord. This message is designed to go right to the heart of man and there meet his deep spiritual need. Nowhere are we commissioned to reform the externals. We are not told to wage wars against bootleggers, liquor stores, gamblers, murderers, prostitutes, racketeers, prejudiced persons or institutions, or any other existing evil as such. Our ministry is not reformation but transformation. The gospel does not clean up the outside but rather regenerates the inside. I have had no greater joy as a minister of the gospel than to witness the marvelous changes wrought in the lives of many people to whom I have preached the gospel. Right here in the Thomas Road Baptist Church, I look into the faces of many people each Sunday who once were involved in the worst kinds of sin. Today they are God-fearing servants of Christ Jesus. What changed them? Did we lead a march down to their bootlegging joint and demand that they stop selling liquor? Did we go to Richmond and try to get laws passed which would send these persons to jail? No! In Christian love, we went to them prayerfully with the message of a crucified Christ. They received this Christ as their own personal Lord and Saviour. When

Christ came in, sin went out. They no longer live their former lives. Not because we demanded they stop these things, but because now, they no longer want to do these things. As Paul says it in II Cor. 5:17: "Therefore if any man be in Christ, he is a new creature: old things are passed away; behold, all things are become new."

You may search the Bible and yet find no other command than the one mentioned above. Some, who are not acquainted with the Bible, will lift out such instances as Moses and his leading of the Jews out of Egyptian bondage, and thereby try to prove that Christians today are supposed to lead people out of bondage in situations where they are being discriminated against. Any Bible student would know first of all that the Jews spent 400 years in Egypt because of their own rebellion and because of a spiritual lesson which God was pointing out to all generations to come. Any Bible scholar would also know that the Jews were and are God's chosen people. His dealings with the Jews are very unique indeed. Likewise, the lessons of the Old Testament are related to the Law, while the New Testament lessons are all related to Grace. If we are going to lift out of the Old Testament things that are convenient for proving our contentions, we are also forced to accept other things. For instance, we would be forced to stone to death everybody who does any work on the Sabbath, or who commits adultery, or who fails to tithe. You can see how absurd such applications are under the Grace of God. The 400 years of Egyptian bondage is a type of the sinner's experience before he is converted. We all live in bondage to sin until we know the truth of the new birth. When the Jews came out of Egypt, they immediately came into 40 years of wilderness wandering. This is a parallel to our infant and carnal Christian life as we struggle before learning the lessons of faith and rest in God. If church leaders are going to use Moses and the Jews in Egypt as a justification for what they are doing today with the negro in the South, they should also go on and tell the Jews that they are going to lead them into 40 years of wandering in which everyone of them except two will die. That is exactly what happened to all the Jews. Only Caleb and Joshua lived through that experience. Then, a new generation went into the Promised Land. The Promised Land is a parallel to the victorious Christian life on the earthly level, and our eventual Heaven on the eternal plain. To try to force any other meaning than this is simply making the Bible say what you want it to say. One atheist said that he could prove anything by the Bible. This is true, if you are not fair to the full and complete revelation.

THE CHRISTIAN'S CITIZENSHIP

Philippians 3:20 is a key verse in getting to the heart of this matter. Paul said "For our citizenship is in Heaven." The King James version uses the word "conversation" in verse 20, but a study of the Greek reveals that the word should be "citizenship." The Christian has his citizenship in the Royal Nation in Heaven. While we are told to "render unto Caesar, the things that are Caesar's," in the true interpretation, we have very few ties on this earth. We pay our taxes, cast our votes as a responsibility of citizenship, obey the laws of the land, and other things demanded of us by the society in which we live. But, at the same time, we are cognizant that our only purpose on this earth is to know Christ and to make Him known. Believing the Bible as I do, I would find it impossible to stop preaching the pure saving gospel of Jesus Christ, and begin doing anything else—including fighting communism, or participating in civil rights reforms. As a God-called preacher, I find that there is no time left after I give the proper time and attention to winning people to Christ. Preachers are not called to be politicians but to be soul winners. That is one reason why our church operates the Elim Home for Alcoholics. That is also the reason why we will be taking in 2,000 boys and girls without charge at Treasure Island this year. That is another reason why we support missionaries all over the world who are preaching the gospel of Christ. That is why we conduct daily radio and television programs. That is why we print tens of thousands of books and booklets with the Christian message in them. That is why we have established chapels and missions in needy areas in and around our city. When the 2,000 members of Thomas Road Baptist Church attend our services, they do not hear sermons on communism, civil rights, or any other subject except the gospel of Christ. If the many thousands of churches and pastors of America would suddenly begin preaching the old fashioned gospel of Jesus Christ and the power that is in His atoning blood, a revival would grip our land such as we have never known before. If as much effort could be put into winning people to Jesus Christ across the land as is being exerted in the present civil rights movement, America would be turned upside down for God. Hate and prejudice would certainly be in a great measure overcome. Churches would be filled with sincere souls seeking God. Good relations between the races would soon be evidenced. God is Love, and when He is put first in the individual life and in the church, God's people become messengers of love. May we pray toward this goal.

JESUS CHRIST AND POLITICS

In Matthew 22:15–22, we have the story of the Pharisees coming to Jesus for the purpose of entangling Him in His words. They asked Him "Is it lawful to give tribute unto Caesar, or not?" There never was a more discriminatory and cruel government as that of the Roman Empire. Christians were slaughtered. Non-Romans were considered to be nothing. The tax system was most dishonest and unfair. The Pharisees assumed that Jesus would lash out at the Roman government. Surely He would take some political stand here. But He did not. He asked for a penny and, upon receiving the penny, asked whose image was on that penny. They answered by saying "Caesar's." He then said "Render therefore unto Caesar the things which are Caesar's: and unto God the things that are God's." In other words, he said: "Pay your taxes, forget politics, and serve Me with all your heart." He very tactfully sidestepped any involvement in a political argument. He was not here to reform the Roman Empire. In Luke 19:10, He said: "For the Son of man is come to seek and to save that which was lost."

On another occasion, John 4:6–13 gives the story of Jesus and His meeting with the immoral woman at Jacob's well. Jesus was tired after his long journey into Samaria. A woman of Samaria came to draw water and Jesus asked her for a drink. She replied: "How is it that thou, being a Jew, askest drink of me, which am a woman of Samaria? for the Jews have no dealings with the Samarians." This woman was saying to Jesus that the Jews were segregated from the Samaritans. They discriminated against the Samaritans. It was much like many of the situations existing today in America and in other countries between different nations and races. But as we read the rest of the account, we see that Jesus totally ignored her attempt to involve Him in a discussion about segregation. He immediately began to tell her that her need was spiritual water. He told her all about her sinful life and her great need of salvation. She was converted and then, through her testimony, her home town turned to God. Jesus could have spent the rest of the day telling her how terrible it was for her to be a segregationist. He did not. He told her that her need was in the heart. She was a prejudiced person because she was a sinner in need of a Saviour. He did not work from the outside in, but rather from the inside out. When she became a Christian, she forgot all about any racial differences. She immediately became a soul winner herself. She even brought other Samaritans to this formerly despised Jew. What a wonderful lesson for Christians and churches to follow today.

Zacchaeus was a dishonest tax collector. When Jesus came to his town, he was very desirous to see Him. Being a very short man in stature, it was necessary for him to climb a tree in order to see over the heads of the throng who gathered around the Lord Jesus. If Jesus had been like some ministers and church leaders today, He would have led a demonstration against Zacchaeus and demanded that he give back all the money which he had wrongfully taken from the poor people. Instead, He looked up lovingly into the tree where Zacchaeus was. He asked Zacchaeus to come down, for He desired to go to his house and sup with him. This display of love won Zacchaeus to Christ. After his conversion, he offered to give back fourfold everything he had taken unfairly. This is another example of working from the inside out. Jesus was constantly found eating with publicans and sinners. The Pharisees, the church leaders of that day, criticised Him for such identification with sinners. He never attacked sinful people—but rather displayed love toward them. The only thing Jesus ever demonstrated against was the desecration of His Temple. When thieves, money changers, and ungodly people invaded the House of God, He quickly cleared them out with a barrel stave. I believe that if we spent enough effort trying to clean up our churches, rather than trying to clean up state and national governments, we would do well. Dances, parties, bingo games, many other forms of gambling, and other disgraceful things are going on right in the churches today. Worse than that, a liberal gospel has come in. The Bible is rejected as being the verbally inspired Word of God. Fundamental Christianity has been junked. And yet, there seems to be very little concern over this spiritual degradation inside our churches today. I'm afraid the church is casting stones while living in a glass house.

THE HYPOCRISY OF THE SOCIAL GOSPEL

One Bible teacher said that we should always require everything we say to travel first through three "gates of gold" before we allow these words to leave our lips. Those three "gates of gold" are: (1) Is it true?; (2) Is it loving?; (3) Is it needful? In relation then to this subject under discussion, I would ask a question: "Does this present civil rights program promote the Love of God?" The leaders are always crying out against prejudice and hate. They are always talking about love. Romans 12:9 says "Let love be without hypocrisy." I am fearful that all of the rioting and demonstrating has produced a great amount of hate as evidenced through the recent murders and other forms of violence. In Romans 13:13 we read: "Let us walk honestly, as in the day; not in rioting." In II Timothy 2:24, Paul says: "And the servant of the Lord must not strive; but be gentle unto all men." The word "strive" could be translated in a modern form as "straining to have one's way." When we as Christians see an existing evil, it is our responsibility to pray. It is also our responsibility to preach the message of a living Christ to those who are in bondage to such sin. But it is never our duty as servants of God to exert physical force or effort which constitutes striving. In II Corinthians 10:3–5, we read: "For though we walk in the flesh, we do not war after the flesh: for the weapons of our warfare are not carnal, but mighty through God to the pulling down of strongholds; casting down imaginations and every high thing that exalteth itself against the knowledge of God, and bringing into captivity every thought to the obedience of Christ." The Bible teaching here is very clear and needs no explanation.

While the church leaders are so obsessed with the alleged discrimination against negroes in the South, very little is said about the same situation in the North. Likewise, very little is said about the very bad conditions under which American Indians live today. This leads one to believe that political expedience is somewhat involved in this so-called freedom movement. Could it possibly be that the American Indians do not present the potential of a strong voting block in the future. One cannot help but wonder. If church leaders feel that the church should take part in social reforms, then I am forced to ask why the church is not concerned about the alcoholism problem in America. There are almost as many alcoholics as there are negroes. Three times as much money is spent annually in America for liquor as for education. More money is spent annually for tobacco than for support of religious institutions. There seems to be a good bit of hypocrisy evident here. Why is the church not concerned about the liberal trend in our theological schools? Why is there not a like display of concern about the lowering of moral standards among our young people today? Many other questions could be put forth. I believe that this suffices to illustrate the point.

THE CHURCH'S LOSS OF DIGNITY

In I Corinthians 14:40 Paul said: "Let all things be done decently and in order." Also in I Thessalonians 5:22, he said: "Abstain from all appearance of evil." The Christian's testimony is the most precious thing he possesses as far as his relationship to others is concerned. If we are going to win people to Christ, they must see us living the same life seven days a week which we preach in the pulpit on Sunday. If the world does not respect us as children of God, then we have no hope of winning them to the Saviour. Many sinners have lost confidence in the church today because of its involvements in many questionable things.

I went to visit a man recently who is a very wicked person. When I began to tell him about the love of God and how that Christ could make him a new person, he quickly gave me a sharp word. He told me that he had been reading the newspapers and seen ministers and their involvements in the riots and mob actions in American streets. He said: "If this is Christianity, I'm glad I'm not a Christian." The world is losing respect for the church because it is lowering its standards. When any part of the church loses its testimony, the whole church suffers. All are judged by what some do. May God help us to run from all appearance of evil. Of course, we all recognize that there is a degree of discrimination in every place and in every land. As Christians, we detest discrimination. But we do need to see that we can never stop it through any other means than that weapon which was given the church 2,000 years ago—the preaching of the gospel of Christ.

CONCLUSION

Love cannot be legislated. Love is found in a Person—His Name is Jesus Christ. The church needs to become dedicated once again to the task of preaching Christ. Education, medicine, social reform, and all the other external ministries cannot meet the needs of the human soul and spirit. If money and education could raise the moral standards of a nation, America would be pure indeed. It cannot be done this way. When the light of the gospel shines into the sinner's heart, his entire life and attitudes are transformed.

I feel that we need to get off the streets and back into the pulpits and into the prayer rooms. I believe we need to take our Bibles and go down into the highways and hedges and bring men to Christ. I believe we need to rededicate ourselves to the great task of turning this world back to God. The preaching of the gospel is the only means by which this can be done.

* * *

PRAYER—O God, grant that this message shall be received in the same spirit in which it is given. May it please Thee to use the humble and simple truths embodied in this sermon to strengthen the hearts of many of Thy children. May Thy church be guided away from all secondary ministries, and into the true commission of preaching the gospel of Christ to every creature. For we pray in Christ's Name, Amen.

Source

Jerry Falwell, "Ministers and Marches," [Lynchburg, VA]: Thomas Road Baptist Church, 1965.

Further Reading

Harding, Susan Friend. *The Book of Jerry Falwell: Fundamentalist Language and Politics.* Princeton: Princeton University Press, 2000.

Sutton, Matthew Avery. *Jerry Falwell and the Rise of the Religious Right: A Brief History with Documents.* Boston: Bedford/St. Martin's, 2013.

Winters, Michael Sean. *God's Right Hand: How Jerry Falwell Made God a Republican and Baptized the American Right.* New York: HarperOne, 2012.

ABRAHAM HESCHEL,
"THE MORAL OUTRAGE OF VIETNAM" (1967)

Abraham Heschel (1907–1972) could hardly have expected to become the most important American Jewish theologian and political activist of his era. Born in Poland, he achieved success at a young age as a rabbi, poet, and scholar, earning his doctorate from the University of Berlin in 1933. Heschel might have had a brilliant career in Europe had his early accomplishments not coincided with the ascendance of Adolf Hitler and the Nazi regime, which sent him on a radically different course. In 1938, along with many other Polish Jews, he was forced out of Germany; he eventually landed in the United States, where he first taught at Hebrew Union College in Cincinnati and then had a long tenure at the Jewish Theological Seminary in New York City.

Man Is Not Alone (1951) and Heschel's other writings made the case for modern religion, a faith that still spoke amid the horrors of total war and genocide. He later became more active in politics, most notably in the civil rights and antiwar movements. The American system of racial discrimination, he argued, was essentially similar to the dehumanization of Jews that resulted in the Nazis' Final Solution.

Heschel's opposition to the Vietnam War moved him to help start an interfaith group eventually known as Clergy and Laity Concerned About Vietnam (CALCAV). CALCAV brought together respected Protestant, Catholic, and Jewish leaders to provide broad spiritual authority for the antiwar position. This excerpt from Heschel's essay "The Moral Outrage of Vietnam" focuses on the responsibility of each individual to speak out against violence and injustice, an imperative no doubt informed by his experience of Nazism.

Abraham Heschel, "The Moral Outrage of Vietnam"

MILITARY VICTORY—A MORAL DEFEAT

It is weird to wake up one morning and find that we have been placed in an insane asylum. It is even more weird to wake up and find that we have been involved in slaughter and destruction without knowing it.

What is being done by our government is done in our name. Our labor, our wealth, our civic power, our tacit consent are invested in the production and use of the napalm, the bombs, and the mines that explode and bring carnage and ruin to Vietnam.

The thought that I live a life of peace and nonviolence turns out to be an illusion. I have been decent in tiny matters on a tiny scale, but have become vicious on a large scale. In my own eyes my existence appears to be upright, but in the eyes of my victims my very being is a nightmare.

A sense of moral integrity, the equation of America with the pursuit of justice and peace, has long been part of our self-understanding. Indeed, for generations the image of America has been associated with the defense of human rights and the hope for world peace. And now history is sneering at us.

A ghastly darkness has set in over our souls. Will there be an end to dismay, an end to agony?

The encounter of man and God is an encounter within the world. We meet within a situation of shared suffering, of shared responsibility.

This is implied in believing in One God in whose eyes there is no dichotomy of here and there, of me and them. They and I are one; here is there, and there is here. What goes on over there happens even here. Oceans divide us, God's presence unites us, and God is present wherever man is afflicted, and all of humanity is embroiled in every agony wherever it may be.

Though not a native of Vietnam, ignorant of its language and traditions, I am involved in the plight of the Vietnamese. To be human means not to be immune to other people's suffering. People in Vietnam, North and South, have suffered, and all of us are hurt.

Unprepared, perplexed, uninformed, ill-advised, our nation finds herself in a spiritual inferno. Where do we stand? Where do we go from here? For a long time we suppressed anxiety, evaded responsibility. Yet the rivers of tears and blood may turn into a flood of guilt, which no excuse will stem.

The blood we shed in Vietnam makes a mockery of all our proclamations, dedications, celebrations. We have been moving from obscurity to confusion, from ignorance to obfuscation. Many are unaware, some acquiesce, most of us detest this unfathomable war, but are unable to envisage a way of getting out of this maze. Millions of Americans who cannot close their minds to the suffering and sorrow are stricken with anguish, and form a large fellowship living in a state of consternation.

We are killing the Vietnamese because we are suspicious of the Chinese. The aim is to kill the elusive Vietcong, yet to come upon one soldier, it is necessary to put an end to a whole village, to the lives of civilians, men, women, and children.

Is it not true that Communists are fellow human beings first, antagonists second? Politically, the concept of the enemy is becoming obsolete; yesterday's enemy is today's ally. The state of cold war between the United States and Soviet Russia has given place to a quest of friendly understanding.

The absurdity of this war is tacitly admitted by almost everyone. Our presence in Vietnam has become a national nightmare, our actions are forced, we dislike what we do; we do what we hate to do. Is this a way to bring democracy to Vietnam: more explosives, more devastation, more human beings crippled, orphaned, killed? Is it not clear that military victory in Vietnam would be a tragic moral defeat? That military triumph would be a human disaster?

The choice is clear. We decide either in favor of further escalation that may lead to a world war or in favor of gradual disengagement followed by negotiation. Refusal to embark upon a course of unlimited massacre will redound only to the honor of America. Did not the retreat of France from Algeria, where her involvement was incomparably more important, add to the glory of France? Did President Kennedy's self-restraint during the ill-planned expedition to the Bay of Pigs tarnish in any way the prestige of America?

Is it not the avowed policy of the United States to insist that there is an alternative to war?

We are fully aware of America's moral commitment to give aid to democratic governments all over the world when they are threatened or attacked by tyrants and dictators. However, we do not fight in Vietnam as allies of a freely elected democratic government but rather as fellow-travelers of anti-Communists, as allies of a despotic military oligarchy. Is it the destiny of our youth to serve as mercenaries in the service of military juntas all over the world?

Our major blunder is the fact that our aid and involvement is a government-to-government operation. Driven by our tendency to suspect social change, by our tendency to measure other peoples' values by our own standards, we have no communication with the people of Vietnam, nor have we sought to relate ourselves to their political understanding. We are in touch with military dictatorship, we ignore the people. We see the power structure, we disregard human beings.

We do not listen to their voice, we are ignorant of their way of thinking, traditions and scale of values. Our failure to convince the Vietnamese that our aim is to save their freedom, to insure their welfare, is not necessarily a sign of their being imbeciles.

Vietnam is a country which has for many decades been the victim of colonial demoralization. Injustice, poverty, exploitation prevail. Revolutionary change is a moral necessity.

Because the government of South Vietnam is corrupt, distrusted by and alienated from the majority of the people, our aid fails to reach the peasants. We are being misguided in maintaining that social revolution can be stopped by military operations. America's identification with Vietnamese juntas not only thwarts any effort to bring aid to the destitute peasants but defames our image in their eyes.

Can an outside power succeed in bringing a recalcitrant heretic community such as the National Liberation Front back to the fold by fire and sword? A major stumbling block to these efforts is our opponents' distrust in our desire for peace. Yet the atmosphere on both sides is infected with suspicion. The Golden Rule seems to be "suspect thy neighbor as thyself."

Indeed, how can there be trust in our desire for peace, if the call for negotiation is consistently followed by further escalation? The groan deepens, the combat burns, the wailing cry does not abate. Every act of escalation has as its effect further aggravation.

For on horror's head horrors accumulate. We are in danger of being swept away—against our will, despite circumspection—by a vehement current and compulsive course which never feels the retiring ebb but keeps on, due to a more violent pace, to an even wider torrent.

War tends to become its own end. Force unleashed moves on its own momentum, breaks all constraint, reaching intensities which man can no longer control. The nation's confidence both in the candor of the

Administration and in the policy which it is pursuing in Vietnam is faltering, while the world's respect for American democracy has been profoundly shaken. America's image is tragically distorted.

For many years the world's eyes were directed to Washington, trusting that the White House, the spirit of America, would secure peace. Should the world's eyes be directed to Moscow, hoping that the Kremlin may use its influence to bring about peace in Vietnam?

What is it that may save us, that may unite men all over the world? The abhorrence of atrocity, the refusal of the conscience to accommodate to the arrogance of military power. Indeed, it is the power of the human conscience which has in the last twenty years inhibited the use of thermonuclear weapons. Yet the power of the conscience is tenuous and exceedingly vulnerable. Its status is undergoing profound upheavals. We are challenged too frequently, too radically to be able to react adequately.

However, the surrender of conscience destroys first the equilibrium of human existence and then existence itself. In the past, war was regarded as an instrument of politics. Today politics is in the process of becoming an instrument of military technology. How long can total war be avoided?

Militarism is whoredom, voluptuous and vicious, first disliked and then relished. To paraphrase the prophet's words "For the spirit of harlotry is within them, and they know not the Lord" (Hosea 5:4): "Samson with his strong body, had a weak head, or he would not have laid it in a harlot's lap."

HAS OUR CONSCIENCE BECOME A FOSSIL?

Has our conscience become a fossil? Is all mercy gone? If mercy, the mother of humanity, is still alive as a demand, how can we say Yes to our bringing agony to the tormented nation of Vietnam?

It is a war we can never win. For, indeed, our superior weapons may well destroy the cities and the hamlets, the fighting forces and the villagers who support them. However, what will our army have left behind? Tombs, tears, havoc, acrimony, and vast incentives to hatred and rage.

The world is not the same since Auschwitz and Hiroshima. The decisions we make, the values we teach must be pondered not only in the halls of learning but also in the presence of inmates in extermination camps, and in the sight of the mushroom of a nuclear explosion.

Those who pray tremble when they realize how staggering are the debts of the religions of the West. We have mortgaged our souls and borrowed so much grace, patience, and forgiveness. We have promised charity, love, guidance, and a way of redemption, and now we are challenged to keep the promise, to honor the pledge. How shall we prevent bankruptcy in the presence of God and man?

We have embarked on this adventure guided by the assumption that those who disagree with us are a threat to us; the assumption that what is good for America is good for Vietnam; that it is better to be dead than red; that communism is the only danger, the only evil which all must fight.

Must we proudly cling to our first mistake? Must Americans and Vietnamese die in order to honor a false decision?

IS WAR AN ANSWER TO HUMAN AGONY?

America has been enticed by her own might. There is nothing so vile as the arrogance of the military mind. Of all the plagues with which the world is cursed, of every ill, militarism is the worst: the assumption that war is an answer to human agony. There are many wild beasts in the human heart, but the beastliest of all is the brutality of arms.

No war remains within its limits; its road is not only downhill but steep. We have sown the wind, and we now reap the whirlwind.

The question addressed to every one of us personally and collectively is this: What shall I do to stop the killing and dying in Vietnam? It is this urgent question that we all have in common at this moment, challenging equally our integrity, our right to invoke the name of Him who is the Father of the Vietnamese as well as of the Americans. The war in Vietnam has plunged every one of us into unknown regions of responsibility. I am personally involved in the torment of the people injured in battle on the front and in the hamlets, in the shipping of explosives, in the triggering of guns. Though deaf to the distant cry of the orphaned and the maimed, I know that my own integrity is being slashed in that slaughter.

There is a deep and awesome power in blood that is spilled, in "the voice of the blood that cries from the earth." The voice of those who die in Vietnam abominates all of us.

The decision to use military force was a failure of statesmanship, a failure of nerve, a moral retreat. To deescalate now, people say, is difficult. What must not be forgotten is that to continue the war will make our situation even more difficult. Remember the price we pay when military pride is hurt. We have gone beyond the policy of brinkmanship. Are we prepared to descend into an abyss? War has ceased to be a human action, carried out with courage and volition. War today is an impersonal, mechanized process. It begins as darkness in the mind and creeps on as a spiritual pestilence, contaminating the power of decision.

There is abundance of weapons and scarcity of compassion. Arms are absolutes, reliable, infallible, while human understanding is relative, vacillating, open to question. So we put our trust in what the arms will do. It is not man any more who ascertains standards, directions. Vast military power tends to cultivate a sense of invincibility and to debilitate the delicate power of political and moral discernment. Decisions are made in terms of monstrosity. Statesmen surrender to the sovereignty of computers. The engine is driving the driver. Frankensteins are here.

Leading American authorities on international law maintain that the unilateral military intervention of the United States in Vietnam violates the charter of the United Nations; that the military presence of the United States in Vietnam violates the Geneva Accords of 1954; that the United States is not committed by the SEATO treaty or otherwise to intervene in Vietnam; that the intensity and destructiveness of United States warfare in Vietnam is contrary to international law; that the United States' actions in Vietnam violate treaties which are part of the supreme law of the land, and hence violate the United States Constitution.

Indeed, this is a war that cannot be waged within the terms of civilized rules of warfare. An advertisement in the *New York Times,* January 15, 1967, sponsored by a group of lawyers, said of the American campaign: "We, unintentionally, are killing and wounding three or four times more people than the Vietcong do. . . . We are not maniacs and monsters; but our planes range the sky all day and all night and our artillery is lavish, and we have much more deadly stuff to kill with. The people are there on the ground, sometimes destroyed by accident, sometimes destroyed because Vietcong are reported to be among them. This is indeed a new kind of war. . . ."

Where are the events leading to? Invasion of North Vietnam? Occupation of Laos and Cambodia? An encounter with the Chinese army?

The State Department and the Pentagon behave as if there were a division of qualities: infallibility of judgment in their possession; ignorance and sentimentality everywhere else.

Those of us who disagree with American policy on Vietnam are told by the State Department that since we do not possess all the facts, we are not competent to evaluate the situation. Yet some of us wonder whether the State Department alone has a monopoly on wisdom and vision. Is it not possible that the minds of those involved in a certain policy become addicted to it, and are hardly capable of undertaking an agonizing reappraisal that may prove how wrong the premises are?

There is a large community of concern for Vietnam which is also a community of concern about the inadequacy of our concern. In Vietnam people die, while we deliver speeches. In Vietnam people bleed, while all we do is send telegrams to Washington. We have succeeded in getting pictures of the moon, but have no picture of the agony of the Vietnamese, no picture of the spiritual agony of millions of Americans who are aghast at what is being done in their names.

THE CRISIS OF RESPONSIBILITY

Responsibility is the essence of being a person, the essence of being human, and many of us are agonized by a grave *crisis of responsibility.* Horrified by the atrocities of this war, we are also dismayed by the ineffectiveness of our protests, by the feebleness of our dissent. Have we done our utmost in expressing our anguish? Does our outcry match the outrage?

This is a unique hour in human history. It is within our might to decide whether this war is a prelude to doom, the beginning of the end, or whether to establish a precedent of solving a most complex crisis by abandoning slogans and clichés.

There is no alternative, we are told. Yet have we really exhausted all possibilities of negotiation? Is the state of humanity so overcome by insanity that all rationality is gone and war left as the only way? Is it really so simple? Are we Americans all innocent, righteous, full of saving grace, while our adversaries are all corrupt, wicked, insensitive to human rights?

Collision between states is not always due to a conflict of vital interests. It is often due to the tendency toward self-enhancement inherent in the monstrosity of power.

Worse than war is the belief in the inevitability of war. There is no such thing as inevitable war. And certainly the war in Vietnam was not inevitable. It came about as a failure of vision, as a result of political clichés, of thinking by analogies, of false comparisons, of blindness to the uniqueness of an extraordinary constellation. This war will not end by dropping bigger and better bombs, by an increase in ferocity, and by the merciless use of force. Vietnam is primarily a human problem, a human emergency, human anguish. There are no military solutions to human problems; violence and bloodshed are no answer to human anguish.

We feel alarmed by a policy that continues to be dogmatic, devoid of elasticity. The root of the tragedy is in the combination of global power and parochial philosophy, of most efficient weapons and pedestrian ideas. New thinking is called for; new contacts must be made. Leaders not directly involved in present operations must be consulted.

Let the American presence in Vietnam be a presence of understanding and compassion. America's war potential is great, but America's peace potential is even greater. Let there be an effort for friendship for Vietnam. Modern war is a mechanical operation. But peace is a personal effort, requiring deep commitment, hard, honest vision, wisdom and patience, facing one another as human beings, elasticity rather than dogmatism.

Would not sending a Peace Corps prove more helpful than sending more armed divisions?

We have entered an age in which military victories are tragic defeats, in which even small wars are exercises in immense disaster.

The public enemy number one is the nuclear bomb, the population explosion, starvation, and disease. It is the fear of nuclear war that unites men all over the world, East and West, North and South. It is fear that unites us today. Let us hope that the conquest of fear and the elimination of misery will unite us tomorrow.

This war, I am afraid, will not leave the nation where it found it. Its conclusion may be the beginning of a grave alienation. The speed and the spirit in which this war will end will fashion our own lives in the years that lie ahead.

On January 22, 1917, President Woodrow Wilson in his address to the Senate uttered a point of view which we pray President Lyndon Johnson would adopt as his own: "It must be a peace without victory." Let our goal be compromise, not victory.

In the name of our kinship of being human, the American people meet the Vietnamese face to face. Only few men are marble-hearted. And even marble can be pierced with patience and compassion. Let us create a climate of reconciliation. Reducing violence and tension, acts of goodwill are necessary prerequisites for negotiations. We must seek neither victory nor defeat. Our aim is to enable the South Vietnamese to find themselves as free and independent people.

The initiative for peace must come from the strong, out of a position of strength.

We will all have to strain our energies, crack our sinews, tax and exert our brains, cultivate understanding, open our hearts, and meet with all Vietnamese, North as well as South.

This is the demand of the hour: not to rest until—by excluding fallacies, stereotypes, prejudices, exaggerations which perpetual contention and the consequent hostilities breed—we succeed in reaching the people of Vietnam as brothers.

There is still time to unlearn old follies, there is still time to seek honest reconciliation. A few months from now it may be too late; a few months from now our folly may be beyond repair, sin beyond repentance.

It is not for man to decide who shall live and who shall die, who shall kill and who shall sigh. May no one win this war; may all sides win the right to live in peace.

Source

Abraham J. Heschel, "The Moral Outrage of Vietnam," in Robert McAfee Brown, Abraham J. Heschel, and Michael Novak, *Vietnam: Crisis of Conscience* (New York: Association Press, 1967), 48–61.

Further Reading

Hall, Mitchell K. *Because of Their Faith: CALCAV and Religious Opposition to the Vietnam War.* New York: Columbia University Press, 1990.

Kaplan, Edward K. *Spiritual Radical: Abraham Joshua Heschel in America, 1940–1972.* New Haven: Yale University Press, 2007.

Staub, Michael E. *Torn at the Roots: The Crisis of Jewish Liberalism in Postwar America.* New York: Columbia University Press, 2002.

MARY DALY, *BEYOND GOD THE FATHER* (1973)

During the late 1960s and 1970s, the women's liberation movement transformed the politics of gender. Now more commonly known as the women's movement or second-wave feminism, "women's lib" took shape amid growing female participation in the workforce, widespread availability of birth control, and demands for justice raised by the civil rights movement and the New Left. Although this reform effort did not eliminate sexism or economic discrimination, it did eventually establish gender equality as the reigning ideology of American public life.

Feminists were often hostile to organized religion. Unlike the civil rights and the antiwar movements, where clergy played central roles, the women's movement featured mostly secular leadership. Indeed, the gender hierarchies that defined American religion seemed to offer little to women seeking power and influence. Yet those hierarchies did not remain unchanged by the churning of this period. Fulfilling Frances Willard's demand from decades earlier, increasing numbers of religious organizations started ordaining women. Liberal Protestants and Jews in particular began to accept women as clergy and experimented with gender-neutral language for God; these soon became divisive issues, as conservatives maintained the desirability of male spiritual leadership.

The radical feminist Mary Daly (1928–2010) tried to reimagine Christianity in the light of women's liberation. Trained as a Catholic theologian, Daly had a stormy career at Boston College, where she incited controversy by banning men from some of her classes. In this excerpt from the first chapter of *Beyond God the Father,* she draws on and criticizes concepts from the liberal theologian Paul Tillich to argue for a more authentic faith free of the distortions of patriarchal social relations. Daly would eventually move outside of Christianity to develop an unorthodox woman-centered spirituality. She remains relevant in an age when politics is dominated by questions of gender and sexuality, from abortion to same-sex marriage.

Mary Daly, *Beyond God the Father*

> The first step in the elevation of women under all systems of religion is to convince them that the great Spirit of the Universe is in no way responsible for any of these absurdities.
> —Elizabeth Cady Stanton

The biblical and popular image of God as a great patriarch in heaven, rewarding and punishing according to his mysterious and seemingly arbitrary will, has dominated the imagination of millions over thousands of years. The symbol of the Father God, spawned in the human imagination and sustained as plausible by patriarchy, has in turn rendered service to this type of society by making its mechanisms for the oppression of women appear right and fitting. If God in "his" heaven is a father ruling "his" people, then it is in the "nature" of things and according to divine plan and the order of the universe that society be male-dominated.

Within this context a mystification of roles takes place: the husband dominating his wife represents God "himself." The images and values of a given society have been projected into the realm of dogmas and "Articles of Faith," and these in turn justify the social structures which have given rise to them and which sustain their plausibility. The belief system becomes hardened and objectified, seeming to have an unchangeable independent existence and validity of its own. It resists social change that would rob it of its plausibility. Despite the vicious circle, however, change can occur in society, and ideologies can die, though they die hard.

As the women's movement begins to have its effect upon the fabric of society, transforming it from patriarchy into something that never existed before—into a diarchal situation that is radically new—it can become the greatest single challenge to the major religions of the world, Western and Eastern. Beliefs and values that have held sway for thousands of years will be questioned as never before. This revolution may well be also the greatest single hope for survival of spiritual consciousness on this planet.

THE CHALLENGE: EMERGENCE OF WHOLE HUMAN BEINGS

There are some who persist in claiming that the liberation of women will only mean that new characters will assume the same old roles, and that nothing will change essentially in structures, ideologies, and values. This supposition is often based on the observation that the very few women in "masculine" occupations often behave much as men do. This kind of reasoning is not at all to the point, for it fails to take into account the fact that tokenism does not change stereotypes or social systems but works to preserve them, since it dulls the revolutionary impulse. The minute proportion of women in the United States who occupy such roles (such as senators, judges, business executives, doctors, etc.) have been trained by men in institutions defined and designed by men, and they have been pressured subtly to operate according to male rules. There are no alternate models. As sociologist Alice Rossi has suggested, this is not what the women's movement in its most revolutionary potential is all about.[1]

What *is* to the point is an emergence of woman-consciousness such as has never before taken place. It is unimaginative and out of touch with what is happening in the women's movement to assume that the becoming of women will simply mean uncritical acceptance of structures,

---

1. Alice Rossi, "Sex Equality: The Beginning of Ideology," *Masculine/Feminine,* edited by Betty Roszak and Theodore Roszak (New York: Harper and Row, 1969), pp. 173–86. Rossi points out some inadequacies of assimilation into male models.

beliefs, symbols, norms, and patterns of behavior that have been given priority by society under male domination. Rather, this becoming will act as catalyst for radical change in our culture. It has been argued cogently by Piaget that structure is maintained by an interplay of transformation laws that never yield results beyond the system and never tend to employ elements external to the system.[2] This is indicative of what *can* effect basic alteration in the system, that is, a potent influence *from without*. Women who reject patriarchy have this power and indeed *are* this power of transformation that is ultimately threatening to things as they are.

The roles and structures of patriarchy have been developed and sustained in accordance with an artificial polarization of human qualities into the traditional sexual stereotypes. The image of the person in authority and the accepted understanding of "his" role has corresponded to the eternal masculine stereotype, which implies hyper-rationality (in reality, frequently reducible to pseudo-rationality), "objectivity," aggressivity, the possession of dominating and manipulative attitudes toward persons and the environment, and the tendency to construct boundaries between the self (and those identified with the self) and "the Other." The caricature of human being which is represented by this stereotype depends for its existence upon the opposite caricature—the eternal feminine. This implies hyper-emotionalism, passivity, self-abnegation, etc. By becoming whole persons women can generate a counterforce to the stereotype of the leader, challenging the artificial polarization of human characteristics into sex-role identification. There is no reason to assume that women who have the support of each other to criticize not only the feminine stereotype but the masculine stereotype as well will simply adopt the latter as a model for ourselves. On the contrary, what is happening is that women are developing a wider range of qualities and skills. This is beginning to encourage and in fact demand a comparably liberating process in men—a phenomenon which has begun in men's liberation groups and which is taking place every day within the context of personal relationships. The becoming of androgynous human persons implies a radical change in the fabric of human consciousness and in styles of human behavior.

This change is already threatening the credibility of the religious symbols of our culture. Since many of these have been used to justify oppression, such a challenge should be seen as redemptive. Religious symbols fade and die when the cultural situation that gave rise to them and supported them ceases to give them plausibility. Such an event generates anxiety, but it is part of the risk involved in a faith which accepts the relativity of all symbols and recognizes that clinging to these as fixed and ultimate is self-destructive and idolatrous.

2. See Jean Piaget, *Structuralism* (New York: Basic Books, Inc., 1970).

The becoming of new symbols is not a matter that can be decided arbitrarily around a conference table. Rather, symbols grow out of a changing communal situation and experience. This does not mean that we are confined to the role of passive spectators. The experience of the becoming of women cannot be understood merely conceptually and abstractly but through active participation in the overcoming of servitude. Both activism and creative thought flow from and feed into the evolving woman-consciousness. The cumulative effect is a surge of awareness beyond the symbols and doctrines of patriarchal religion.

THE INADEQUATE GOD OF POPULAR PREACHING

The image of the divine Father in heaven has not always been conducive to humane behavior, as any perceptive reader of history knows. The often cruel behavior of Christians toward unbelievers and toward dissenters among themselves suggests a great deal not only about the values of the society dominated by that image, but also about how that image itself functions in relation to behavior. There has been a basic ambivalence in the image of the heavenly patriarch—a split between the God of love and the jealous God who represents the collective power of "his" chosen people. As historian Arnold Toynbee has indicated, this has reflected and perpetuated a double standard of behavior.[3] Without debating the details of his historical analysis, the insight is available on an experiential level. The character of Vito Corleone in *The Godfather* is a vivid illustration of the marriage of tenderness and violence so intricately blended in the patriarchal ideal. The worshippers of the loving Father may in a sense love their neighbors, but in fact the term applies only to those within a restricted and unstable circumference, and these worshippers can "justifiably" be intolerant and fanatic persecutors of those outside the sacred circle.

How this God operates is illustrated in contemporary American civil religion.[4] In one of the White House sermons given during the first term of Richard Nixon, Rabbi Louis Finkelstein expressed the hope that a future historian may say "that in the period of great trials and great tribulations, the finger of God pointed to Richard Milhous Nixon, giving the vision and the wisdom to save the world and civilization; and also to open the way for our country to realize the good that the twentieth century offers mankind."[5] Within this context, as Charles Henderson has shown, God

---

3. Arnold Toynbee, *Christianity among the Religions of the World* (New York: Charles Scribner's Sons, 1957), p. 19.
4. See Robert N. Bellah, "Civil Religion in America," *Daedalus,* XCVI (Winter 1967), pp. 1–21. Bellah points out that the inauguration of a president is an important ceremonial event in American civil religion. It involves religious legitimation of the highest political authority. At Nixon's inauguration in 1973, Cardinal Cooke of New York was reported to have used the expression "heavenly Father" approximately seven times (conversation with Janice Raymond, who counted, January 20, 1973).
5. Rabbi Louis Finkelstein, in *White House Sermons,* edited by Ben Hibbs (New York: Harper and Row, 1972), p. 68. This sermon was delivered June 29, 1969. Similar sentiments have been expressed

is an American and Nixon is "his" anointed one.[6] The preachers carefully selected for the White House sermons stress that this nation is "under God." The logical conclusion is that its policies are right. Under God, the President becomes a Christ figure. In 1969, the day the astronauts would set foot on the moon, and when the President was preparing to cross the Pacific "in search of peace," one of these preachers proclaimed:

And my hope for mankind is strengthened in the knowledge that our intrepid President himself will soon go into orbit, reaching boldly for the moon of peace. God grant that he, too, may return in glory and that countless millions of prayers that follow him shall not have been in vain.[7]

A fundamental dynamic of this "theology" was suggested by one of Nixon's speech writers, Ray Price, who wrote:

Selection of a President has to be an act of faith. . . . This faith isn't achieved by reason: it's achieved by charisma, by a *feeling* of trust. . . .[8]

Price also argued that the campaign would be effective only "if we can get people to make the *emotional* leap, or what theologians call 'leap of faith.'"[9] This is, of course, precisely the inauthentic leap that Camus labeled as philosophical suicide. It is the suicide demanded by a civil religion in which "God," the Savior-President, and "our nation" more or less merge. When the "leap" is made, it is possible simply not to see what the great God-Father and his anointed one are actually doing. Among the chosen ones are scientists and professors who design perverse methods of torture and death such as flechette pellets that shred the internal organs of "the enemy" and other comparable inhumane "anti-personnel" weapons. Also among the elect are politicians and priests who justify and bestow their blessing upon the system that perpetrates such atrocities. "Under God" are included the powerful industrialists who are making the planet uninhabitable.

Sophisticated thinkers, of course, have never intellectually identified God with a Superfather in heaven. Nevertheless it is important to recognize that even when very abstract conceptualizations of God are

by the Rev. John McLaughlin, S.J., "the Catholic Billy Graham." See *National Catholic Reporter,* October 6, 1972, p. 9.

6. Charles Henderson, *The Nixon Theology* (New York: Harper and Row, 1972). See also Henderson's article "The [Social] Gospel according to 1) Richard Nixon 2) George McGovern," *Commonweal,* XCVI (September 29, 1972), pp. 518–25.

7. Dr. Paul S. Smith, in *White House Sermons,* pp. 82–83.

8. Cited in Henderson, *The Nixon Theology,* p. 175.

9. *Ibid.,* p. 176.

formulated in the mind, images survive in the imagination in such a way that a person can function on two different and even apparently contradictory levels at the same time. Thus one can speak of God as spirit and at the same time imagine "him" as belonging to the male sex.[10] Such primitive images can profoundly affect conceptualizations which appear to be very refined and abstract. So too the Yahweh of the future, so cherished by the theology of hope, comes through on an imaginative level as exclusively a He-God, and it is consistent with this that theologians of hope have attempted to develop a political theology which takes no explicit cognizance of the devastation wrought by sexual politics.

The widespread conception of the "Supreme Being" as an entity distinct from this world but controlling it according to plan and keeping human beings in a state of infantile subjection has been a not too subtle mask of the divine patriarch. The Supreme Being's plausibility and that of the static worldview which accompanies this projection has of course declined, at least among the more sophisticated, as Nietzsche prophesied. This was a projection grounded in specifically patriarchal societal structures and sustained as subjectively real by the usual processes of producing plausibility such as preaching, religious indoctrination, and cult. The sustaining power of the social structure has been eroded by a number of developments in recent history, including the general trend toward democratization of society and the emergence of technology. However, it is the women's movement which appears destined to play the key role in the overthrow of such oppressive elements in traditional theism, precisely because it strikes at the source of the societal dualism that is reflected in traditional beliefs. It presents a growing threat to the plausibility of the inadequate popular "God" not so much by attacking "him" as by leaving "him" behind. Few major feminists display great interest in institutional religion. Yet this disinterest can hardly be equated with lack of spiritual consciousness. Rather, in our present experience the woman-consciousness is being wrenched free to find its own religious expression.

It can legitimately be pointed out that the Judeo-Christian tradition is not entirely bereft of elements that can foster intimations of transcendence. Yet the liberating potential of these elements is choked off in the surrounding atmosphere of the images, ideas, values, and structures of patriarchy. The social change coming from radical feminism has the potential to bring about a more acute and widespread perception of qualitative differences between the conceptualizations of "God" and of the human relationship to God which have been oppressive in their connotations, and the kind of language that is spoken from and to the rising woman-consciousness.

---

10. This is exemplified in a statement of John L. McKenzie, S.J., in *The Two Edged Sword* (New York: Bruce, 1956), pp. 93–94: "God is of course masculine, but not in the sense of sexual distinction. . . ."

CASTRATING "GOD"

I have already suggested that if God is male, then the male is God. The divine patriarch castrates women as long as he is allowed to live on in the human imagination. The process of cutting away the Supreme Phallus can hardly be a merely "rational" affair. The problem is one of transforming the collective imagination so that this distortion of the human aspiration to transcendence loses its credibility.

Some religious leaders, notably Mary Baker Eddy and Ann Lee, showed insight into the problem to some extent and tried to stress the "maternal" aspect of what they called "God."[11] A number of feminists have referred to "God" as "she." While all of this has a point, the analysis has to reach a deeper level. The most basic change has to take place in women—in our being and self-image. Otherwise there is danger of settling for mere reform, reflected in the phenomenon of "crossing," that is, of attempting to use the oppressor's weapons against him. Black theology's image of the Black God illustrates this. It can legitimately be argued that a transsexual operation upon "God," changing "him" to "her," would be a far more profound alteration than a mere pigmentation change. However, to stop at this level of discourse would be a trivialization of the deep problem of human becoming in women.

BEYOND THE INADEQUATE GOD

The various theologies that hypostatize transcendence, that is, those which in one way or another objectify "God" as a *being,* thereby attempt in a self-contradictory way to envisage transcendent reality as finite. "God" then functions to legitimate the existing social, economic, and political status quo, in which women and other victimized groups are subordinate.

"God" can be used oppressively against women in a number of ways. First, it occurs in an overt manner when theologians proclaim women's subordination to be God's will. This of course has been done throughout the centuries, and residues remain in varying degrees of subtlety and explicitness in the writings of twentieth century thinkers such as Barth, Bonhoeffer, Reinhold Niebuhr, and Teilhard de Chardin.[12]

---

11. See Mary Baker Eddy, *Science and Health* (Boston: Published by the Trustees under the Will of Mary Baker G. Eddy, 1934). Eddy wrote what she believed to be the "spiritual sense" of "The Lord's Prayer." It begins: "Our Father-Mother God, all-harmonious . . ." (p. 16). In the same work she uses the image of God's motherhood a number of times. Ann Lee's ideas have been studied by sociologist Henri Desroches. See, for example, *The American Shakers: From Neo-Christianity to Presocialism,* translated and edited by John K. Savocool (Amherst: University of Massachusetts Press, 1971).
12. See Karl Barth, *Church Dogmatics,* edited by G. W. Bromiley and T. F. Torrance (Edinburgh: T. & T. Clark, 1956–1962), III/4, pp. 116–240. Barth goes on and on about woman's subordination to man, ordained by God. Although he goes through a quasi-infinite number of qualifications, using such jargon as "mutual subordination," he warns that we must not overlook the "concrete subordination of woman to man" (p. 175). He writes: "Properly speaking, the business of woman, her task and function, is to actualize the fellowship in which man can only precede her, stimulating, leading, and inspiring. . . . To wish to replace him in this, or to do it with him, would be to wish not to be a woman." In case the

Second, even in the absence of such explicitly oppressive justification, the phenomenon is present when one-sex symbolism for God and for the human relationship to God is used. The following passage illustrates the point:

> To believe that God is Father is to become aware of oneself not as a stranger, not as an outsider or an alienated person, but as a son who belongs or a person appointed to a marvelous destiny, which he shares with the whole community. To believe that God is Father means to be able to say "we" in regard to all men.[13]

A woman whose consciousness has been aroused can say that such language makes her aware of herself as a stranger, as an outsider, as an alienated person, not as a daughter who belongs or who is appointed to a marvelous destiny. She cannot belong to *this* without assenting to her own lobotomy.

Third, even when the basic assumptions of God-language appear to be nonsexist, and when language is somewhat purified of fixation upon maleness, it is damaging and implicitly compatible with sexism if it encourages detachment from the reality of the human struggle against oppression in its concrete manifestations. That is, the lack of explicit relevance of intellection to the fact of oppression in its precise forms, such as sexual hierarchy, is itself oppressive. This is the case when theologians write long treatises on creative hope, political theology, or revolution without any specific acknowledgment of or application to the problem of sexism or other specific forms of injustice. Such irrelevance is conspicuous in the major works of "theologians of hope" such as Moltmann, Pannenberg, and Metz. This is not to say that the vision of creative eschatology is completely irrelevant, but that it lacks specific grounding in the concrete experiences of the oppressed. The theorizing then has a quality of unreal-

---

point is not clear, he adds the rhetorical question: "What other choice has she [than to be second] seeing she can be nothing at all apart from this sequence and her place within it?" (p. 171). This is justified as being the divine order, according to Barth. See also Dietrich Bonhoeffer, *Letters and Papers from Prison,* edited by Eberhard Bethge, translated by Reginald H. Fuller (New York: Macmillan Paperback, 1966), p. 47: "You may order your home as you like, save in one particular: the woman must be subject to her husband, and the husband must love his wife." See also Reinhold Niebuhr, *The Nature and Destiny of Man: A Christian Interpretation,* Vol. 1 (New York: Charles Scribner's Sons, 1941), p. 282. Niebuhr writes: "A rationalistic feminism is undoubtedly inclined to transgress inexorable bounds set by nature. On the other hand, any premature fixation of certain historical standards in regard to the family will inevitably tend to reinforce male arrogance and to retard *justified efforts* [italics mine] on the part of the female to achieve such freedom as is not incompatible with the *primary function of motherhood* [italics mine]." As for Teilhard de Chardin, his writings are replete with spiritualized androcentrism. For examples, see Henri de Lubac, S.J., *The Eternal Feminine: A Study on the Text of Teilhard de Chardin,* translated by René Hague (New York: Harper and Row, 1971). The sexism is of course unrecognized by de Lubac. See also André A. Devaux, *Teilhard et la vocation de la femme* (Paris: Editions universitaires, 1963).

13. Gregory Baum, *Man Becoming* (New York: Herder and Herder, 1970), p. 195.

ity. Perhaps an obvious reason for this is that the theologians themselves have not shared in the experience of oppression and therefore write from the privileged distance of those who have at best a "knowledge about" the subject.

Tillich's ontological theology, too, even though it is potentially liberating in a very radical sense, fails to be adequate in this regard. It is true that Tillich *tries* to avoid hypostatization of "God" (though the effort is not completely successful) and that his manner of speaking about the ground and power of being would be difficult to use for the legitimation of any sort of oppression.[14] However, the specific relevance of "power of being" to the fact of sexual oppression is not indicated. Moreover, just as his discussion of God is "detached," so is the rest of his theology—a point that I will pursue later on. This detachment from the problem of relevance of God-language to the struggle against demonic power structures characterizes not only Tillich but also other male theoreticians who have developed a relatively nonsexist language for transcendence. Thinkers such as Whitehead, James, and Jaspers employ God-language that soars beyond sexual hierarchy as a specific problem to be confronted in the process of human becoming.

The new insight of women is bringing us to a point beyond such direct and indirect theological oppressiveness that traditionally has centered around discussions of "God." It is becoming clear that if God-language is even implicitly compatible with oppressiveness, failing to make clear the relation between intellection and liberation, then it will either have to be developed in such a way that it becomes explicitly relevant to the problem of sexism or else dismissed. In asserting this I am employing a pragmatic yardstick or verification process to God-language in a manner not totally dissimilar to that of William James. In my thinking, the specific criterion which implies a mandate to reject certain forms of God-talk is expressed in the question: Does this language hinder human becoming by reinforcing sex-role socialization? Expressed positively—a point to be developed later on—the question is: Does it *encourage* human becoming toward psychological and social fulfillment, toward an androgynous mode of living, toward transcendence?

It is probable that the movement will eventually generate a new language of transcendence. There is no reason to assume that the term "God" will always be necessary, as if the three-letter word, materially speaking, could capture and encapsulate transcendent being. At this point in history, however, it is probable that the new God-word's essential newness will be conveyed more genuinely by its being placed in a different

14. I would agree with Gordon Kaufman that Tillich himself does not completely escape hypostatization in his God language. The "Unconditioned" and the "Ground" are almost reified. See Gordon D. Kaufman, "On the Meaning of 'God,'" in *Transcendence,* edited by Herbert W. Richardson and Donald R. Cutler (Boston: Beacon Press, 1969), pp. 114–42.

semantic field than by a mere material alteration in sound or appearance of the word. Since the women's revolution implies the liberation of all human beings, it is impossible to believe that during the course of its realization the religious imagination and intelligence will simply lie dormant. Part of the challenge is to recognize the poverty of all words and symbols and the fact of our past idolatry regarding them, and then to turn to our own resources for bringing about the radically new in our own lives.

Source

Mary Daly, *Beyond God the Father: Toward a Philosophy of Women's Liberation* (1973; Boston: Beacon, 1985), 13–22. Copyright © 1973, 1985 by Mary Daly. Reprinted by permission of Beacon Press, Boston.

Further Reading

Chaves, Mark. *Ordaining Women: Culture and Conflict in Religious Organizations.* Cambridge, MA: Harvard University Press, 1997.

Oppenheimer, Mark. *Knocking on Heaven's Door: American Religion in the Age of Counterculture.* New Haven: Yale University Press, 2003.

6

The Religious Right and Its Critics

The conservative ascendancy of the 1970s and 1980s marked a substantial reversal of American political power. In the mid twentieth century, liberals had consistently gained the upper hand in American government. For instance, excepting an interlude for the moderate Republican Dwight Eisenhower, New Deal Democrats and their heirs held the presidency from the election of Franklin Roosevelt in 1932 until Richard Nixon's triumph in 1968. Nixon's victory, and Ronald Reagan's election in 1980, were the most dramatic evidence of the demise of the Roosevelt legacy.

Those Republican presidents did not elevate conservatism single-handedly; they came to power on the strength of broader trends. The change from an industrial to a postindustrial economy decimated organized labor, a crucial element in the New Deal coalition, and shifted power from the Rust Belt of the Northeast and Midwest to the more conservative Sun Belt of the South and West. Meanwhile, the successes of the social movements of the 1960s, most notably civil rights, feminism, and gay liberation, produced strong reactions by defenders of racial and gender hierarchy.

Conservative people of faith had been active in politics ever since the modern framework of left and right coalesced in the New Deal years. However, in the 1970s and 1980s, the religious right mobilized as never before. In particular, groups that had once looked with suspicion at the corruptions and compromises inherent in politics now decided to join the fray.

The religious right was never unified, but most of its participants agreed on a few central issues. They were strong anticommunists and supported a powerful military to counteract the influence of the Soviet

Union. Armaments excepted, they fought against the expansion of the federal government, often viewing it as a major threat to spiritual life. One of the prime targets of this ideology was *Roe v. Wade*, the 1973 Supreme Court decision that legalized abortion. Initial reactions by religious people were mixed, but opposition to the decision soon became a unifying cause for many Catholics and evangelical Protestants, who accused the American government of sanctioning a mass murder of unborn babies (*Roe*'s supporters countered that antiabortion laws themselves represented intolerable government interference with women's rights). The prolife movement epitomized the strident moral rhetoric and suspicion of state power that defined the religious right more generally.

From one perspective, these insurgents had limited success in national politics. Although many restrictions have been placed on abortion, *Roe v. Wade* has not been overturned. On other concerns, such as school prayer or opposition to gay marriage, the religious right has lost support in recent decades. Still, even when their initiatives have failed, the debates that religious conservatives sparked over politics and morality have often set the terms of the nation's public discourse.

ENGEL v. VITALE (1962)

Since the Second World War, the Supreme Court has played a major role in adjudicating questions of religious freedom. In part, this shift reflects the increasingly prominent place of the federal government in American life more generally, and in part it signals, as in the Jehovah's Witness cases earlier in this book, new conflicts generated by the nation's increasing religious diversity. The Constitution produced a religious disestablishment in the new nation, but some scholars have seen another, more thoroughgoing disestablishment happening in the postwar period. The *Engel v. Vitale* ruling against prayer in public schools marked one milestone in this process.

Schools have often been a flashpoint for disputes over religion. The *Engel* case arose in response to an official prayer formulated by the New York State Board of Regents for recitation in public schools, a common practice across the country. The text of the prayer was inclusive, and the state provided exemptions for students who did not wish to recite it. Nonetheless, an alliance of parents, many of them members of non-Christian minority faiths, brought suit against the regents for promoting an unconstitutional establishment of religion. The Supreme Court agreed, ruling 8–1 in favor of the plaintiffs. Along with *McCollum v. Board of Education* (1948), which ended release time from school for religious instruction, and *School District of Abington Township v. Schempp* (1963), which struck down Bible reading in schools, *Engel v. Vitale* inaugurated the climate of religious neutrality that most public school students today take for granted. Conservative evangelicals were not uniformly opposed to the decision at first, but "prayer in school" eventually became a rallying cry for some segments of the religious right. Despite the persistence of unofficial prayers at graduations and football games, however, conservatives have had little success bringing overt religious practice back into public education.

Hugo Black's decision and Potter Stewart's lone dissent are both remarkable for their uses of history to justify their positions. For Black, school prayer goes against the Founders' intentions in the First Amendment, while Stewart finds such prayer consistent with long traditions of officially sanctioned religious ritual. The two sides illustrate that history writing is not simply a record of things that happened but a site of competing interpretations shaped by the imperatives of the present.

Engel v. Vitale

Mr. Justice Black delivered the opinion of the Court.

The respondent Board of Education of Union Free School District No. 9, New Hyde Park, New York, acting in its official capacity under state law, directed the School District's principal to cause the following prayer to be said aloud by each class in the presence of a teacher at the beginning of each school day:

> "Almighty God, we acknowledge our dependence upon Thee, and we beg Thy blessings upon us, our parents, our teachers and our Country."

This daily procedure was adopted on the recommendation of the State Board of Regents, a governmental agency created by the State Constitution to which the New York Legislature has granted broad supervisory, executive, and legislative powers over the State's public school system. These state officials composed the prayer which they recommended and published as a part of their "Statement on Moral and Spiritual Training in the Schools," saying: "We believe that this Statement will be subscribed to by all men and women of good will, and we call upon all of them to aid in giving life to our program."

Shortly after the practice of reciting the Regents' prayer was adopted by the School District, the parents of ten pupils brought this action in a New York State Court insisting that use of this official prayer in the public schools was contrary to the beliefs, religions, or religious practices of both themselves and their children. Among other things, these parents challenged the constitutionality of both the state law authorizing the School District to direct the use of prayer in public schools and the School District's regulation ordering the recitation of this particular prayer on the ground that these actions of official governmental agencies violate that part of the First Amendment of the Federal Constitution which commands that "Congress shall make no law respecting an establishment of religion"—a command which was "made applicable to the State of New York by the Fourteenth Amendment of the said Constitution."

[. . .]

We think that by using its public school system to encourage recitation of the Regents' prayer, the State of New York has adopted a practice wholly inconsistent with the Establishment Clause. There can, of course, be no doubt that New York's program of daily classroom invocation of God's blessings as prescribed in the Regents' prayer is a religious activity. It is a solemn avowal of divine faith and supplication for the blessings of the Almighty. The nature of such a prayer has always been religious, none of the respondents has denied this and the trial court expressly so found:

> "The religious nature of prayer was recognized by Jefferson and has been concurred in by theological writers, the United States Supreme Court and State courts and administrative officials, including New York's Commissioner of Education. A committee of the New York Legislature has agreed.
>
> "The Board of Regents as *amicus curiae,* the respondents and intervenors all concede the religious nature of prayer, but seek to distinguish this prayer because it is based on our spiritual heritage. . . ."

The petitioners contend among other things that the state laws requiring or permitting use of the Regents' prayer must be struck down as a violation of the Establishment Clause because that prayer was composed by governmental officials as a part of a governmental program to further religious beliefs. For this reason, petitioners argue, the State's use of the Regents' prayer in its public school system breaches the constitutional wall of separation between Church and State. We agree with that contention since we think that the constitutional prohibition against laws respecting an establishment of religion must at least mean that in this country it is no part of the business of government to compose official prayers for any group of the American people to recite as a part of a religious program carried on by government.

It is a matter of history that this very practice of establishing governmentally composed prayers for religious services was one of the reasons which caused many of our early colonists to leave England and seek religious freedom in America. The Book of Common Prayer, which was created under governmental direction and which was approved by Acts of Parliament in 1548 and 1549, set out in minute detail the accepted form and content of prayer and other religious ceremonies to be used in the established, tax-supported Church of England. The controversies over the Book and what should be its content repeatedly threatened to disrupt the peace of that country as the accepted forms of prayer in the established church changed with the views of the particular ruler that happened to be in control at the time. Powerful groups representing some of the varying religious views of the people struggled among themselves to impress their particular views upon the Government and obtain amendments of the Book more suitable to their respective notions of how religious services should be conducted in order that the official religious establishment would advance their particular religious beliefs. Other groups, lacking the necessary political power to influence the Government on the matter, decided to leave England and its established church and seek freedom in America from England's governmentally ordained and supported religion.

It is an unfortunate fact of history that when some of the very groups which had most strenuously opposed the established Church of England found themselves sufficiently in control of colonial governments in this country to write their own prayers into law, they passed laws making their own religion the official religion of their respective colonies. Indeed, as late as the time of the Revolutionary War, there were established churches in at least eight of the thirteen former colonies and established religions in at least four of the other five. But the successful Revolution against English political domination was shortly followed by intense opposition to the practice of establishing religion by law. This opposition crystallized rapidly into an effective political force in Virginia where the minority religious groups such as Presbyterians, Lutherans, Quakers and Baptists had gained such strength that the adherents to the established Episcopal Church were actually a minority themselves. In 1785–1786, those opposed to the established Church, led by James Madison and Thomas Jefferson, who, though themselves not members of any of these dissenting religious groups, opposed all religious establishments by law on grounds of principle, obtained the enactment of the famous "Virginia Bill for Religious Liberty" by which all religious groups were placed on an equal footing so far as the State was concerned. Similar though less far-reaching legislation was being considered and passed in other States.

By the time of the adoption of the Constitution, our history shows that there was a widespread awareness among many Americans of the dangers of a union of Church and State. These people knew, some of them from bitter personal experience, that one of the greatest dangers to the freedom of the individual to worship in his own way lay in the Government's placing its official stamp of approval upon one particular kind of prayer or one particular form of religious services. They knew the anguish, hardship and bitter strife that could come when zealous religious groups struggled with one another to obtain the Government's stamp of approval from each King, Queen, or Protector that came to temporary power. The Constitution was intended to avert a part of this danger by leaving the government of this country in the hands of the people rather than in the hands of any monarch. But this safeguard was not enough. Our Founders were no more willing to let the content of their prayers and their privilege of praying whenever they pleased be influenced by the ballot box than they were to let these vital matters of personal conscience depend upon the succession of monarchs. The First Amendment was added to the Constitution to stand as a guarantee that neither the power nor the prestige of the Federal Government would be used to control, support or influence the kinds of prayer the American people can say—that the people's religions must not be subjected to the pressures of government for change each time a new political administration is elected to office. Under that Amendment's prohibition against governmental establishment of religion, as reinforced by the provisions of the Fourteenth Amendment, government in this country, be it state or federal, is without power to prescribe by law any particular form of prayer which is to be used as an official prayer in carrying on any program of governmentally sponsored religious activity.

There can be no doubt that New York's state prayer program officially establishes the religious beliefs embodied in the Regents' prayer. The respondents' argument to the contrary, which is largely based upon the contention that the Regents' prayer is "non-denominational" and the fact that the program, as modified and approved by state courts, does not require all pupils to recite the prayer but permits those who wish to do so to remain silent or be excused from the room, ignores the essential nature of the program's constitutional defects. Neither the fact that the prayer may be denominationally neutral nor the fact that its observance on the part of the students is voluntary can serve to free it from the limitations of the Establishment Clause, as it might from the Free Exercise Clause, of the First Amendment, both of which are operative against the States by virtue of the Fourteenth Amendment. Although these two clauses may in certain instances overlap, they forbid two quite different kinds of governmental encroachment upon religious freedom. The Establishment Clause, unlike the Free Exercise Clause, does not depend upon any showing of direct governmental compulsion and is violated by the enactment of laws which establish an official religion whether those laws operate directly to coerce nonobserving individuals or not. This is not to say, of course, that laws officially prescribing a particular form of religious worship do not involve coercion of such individuals. When the power, prestige and financial support of government is placed behind a particular religious belief, the indirect coercive pressure upon religious minorities to conform to the prevailing officially approved religion is plain. But the purposes underlying the Establishment Clause go much further than that. Its first and most immediate purpose rested on the belief that a union of government and religion tends to destroy government and to degrade religion. The history of governmentally established religion, both in England and in this country, showed that whenever government had allied itself with one particular form of religion, the inevitable result had been that it had incurred the hatred, disrespect and even contempt of those who held contrary beliefs. That same history showed that many people had lost their respect for any religion that had relied upon the support of government to spread its faith. The Establishment Clause thus stands as an expression of principle on the part of the Founders of our Constitution that religion is too personal, too sacred, too holy, to permit its "unhallowed perversion" by a civil magistrate. Another purpose of the Establishment Clause rested upon an awareness of the historical fact that governmentally established religions and religious persecutions go hand in hand. The Founders knew that only a few years after the Book of Common Prayer became the only accepted form of religious services in the established Church of England, an Act of Uniformity was passed to compel all Englishmen to attend those services and to make it a criminal offense to conduct or attend religious gatherings of any other kind—a law which was consistently flouted by dissenting religious groups in England and which contributed to widespread persecutions of people like John Bunyan who persisted in holding "unlawful [religious] meetings . . . to the great disturbance and distraction of the good subjects of this kingdom. . . ." And they knew that similar persecutions had received the sanction of law in several of the colonies in this country soon after the establishment of official religions in those colonies. It was in large part to get completely away from this sort of systematic religious persecution that the Founders brought into being our Nation, our Constitution, and our Bill of Rights with its prohibition against any governmental establishment of religion. The New York laws officially prescribing the Regents' prayer are inconsistent both with the purposes of the Establishment Clause and with the Establishment Clause itself.

It has been argued that to apply the Constitution in such a way as to prohibit state laws respecting an establishment of religious services in public schools is to indicate a hostility toward religion or toward prayer. Nothing, of course, could be more wrong. The history of man is inseparable from the history of religion. And perhaps it is not too much to say that since the beginning of that history many people have devoutly believed that "More things are wrought by prayer than this world dreams of." It was doubtless largely due to men who believed this that there grew up a sentiment that caused men to leave the cross-currents of officially established state religions and religious persecution in Europe and come to this country filled with the hope that they could find a place in which they could pray when they pleased to the God of their faith in the language they chose. And there were men of this same faith in the power of prayer who led the fight for adoption of our Constitution and also for our Bill of Rights with the very guarantees of religious freedom that forbid the sort of governmental activity which New York has attempted here. These men knew that the First Amendment, which tried to put an end to governmental control of religion and of prayer, was not written to destroy either. They knew rather that it was written to quiet well-justified fears which nearly all of them felt arising out of an awareness that governments of the past had shackled men's tongues to make them speak only the religious thoughts that government wanted them to speak and to pray only to the God that government wanted them to pray to. It is neither sacrilegious nor antireligious to say that each separate government in this country should stay out of the business of writing or sanctioning official prayers and leave that purely religious function to the people themselves and to those the people choose to look to for religious guidance.

It is true that New York's establishment of its Regents' prayer as an officially approved religious doctrine of that State does not amount to a total establishment of one particular religious sect to the exclusion of all others—that, indeed, the governmental endorsement of that prayer seems relatively insignificant when compared to the governmental encroachments upon religion which were commonplace 200 years ago. To those who may subscribe to the view that because the Regents' official prayer is so brief and general there can be no danger to religious freedom in its governmental establishment, however, it may be appropriate to say in the words of James Madison, the author of the First Amendment:

> "[I]t is proper to take alarm at the first experiment on our liberties. . . . Who does not see that the same authority which can establish Christianity, in exclusion of all other Religions, may establish with the same ease any particular sect of Christians, in exclusion of all other Sects? That the same authority which can force a citizen to contribute three pence only of his property for the support of any one establishment, may force him to conform to any other establishment in all cases whatsoever?"

The judgment of the Court of Appeals of New York is reversed and the cause remanded for further proceedings not inconsistent with this opinion.

Reversed and remanded.

MR. JUSTICE STEWART, dissenting.

A local school board in New York has provided that those pupils who wish to do so may join in a brief prayer at the beginning of each school day, acknowledging their dependence upon God and asking His blessing upon them and upon their parents, their teachers, and their country. The Court today decides that in permitting this brief non-denominational prayer the school board has violated the Constitution of the United States. I think this decision is wrong.

The Court does not hold, nor could it, that New York has interfered with the free exercise of anybody's religion. For the state courts have made clear that those who object to reciting the prayer must be entirely free of any compulsion to do so, including any "embarrassments and pressures." But the Court says that in permitting school children to say this simple prayer, the New York authorities have established "an official religion."

With all respect, I think the Court has misapplied a great constitutional principle. I cannot see how an "official religion" is established by letting those who want to say a prayer say it. On the contrary, I think that to deny the wish of these school children to join in reciting this prayer is to deny them the opportunity of sharing in the spiritual heritage of our Nation.

The Court's historical review of the quarrels over the Book of Common Prayer in England throws no light for me on the issue before us in this case. England had then and has now an established church. Equally unenlightening, I think, is the history of the early establishment and later rejection of an official church in our own States. For we deal here not with the establishment of a state church, which would, of course, be constitutionally impermissible, but with whether school children who want to begin their day by joining in prayer must be prohibited from doing so. Moreover, I think that the Court's task, in this as in all areas of constitutional adjudication, is not responsibly aided by the uncritical invocation of metaphors like the "wall of separation," a phrase nowhere to be found in the Constitution. What is relevant to the issue here is not the history of an established church in sixteenth century England or in eighteenth century America, but the history of the religious traditions of our people, reflected in countless practices of the institutions and officials of our government.

At the opening of each day's Session of this Court we stand, while one of our officials invokes the protection of God. Since the days of John Marshall our Crier has said, "God save the United States and this Honorable Court." Both the Senate and the House of Representatives open their daily Sessions with prayer. Each of our Presidents, from George Washington to John F. Kennedy, has upon assuming his Office asked the protection and help of God.

The Court today says that the state and federal governments are without constitutional power to prescribe any particular form of words to be recited by any group of the American people on any subject touching religion. One of the stanzas of "The Star-Spangled Banner," made our National Anthem by Act of Congress in 1931, contains these verses:

> "Blest with victory and peace, may the heav'n rescued land
>   Praise the Pow'r that hath made and preserved us a nation!
> Then conquer we must, when our cause it is just,
>   And this be our motto 'In God is our Trust.'"

In 1954 Congress added a phrase to the Pledge of Allegiance to the Flag so that it now contains the words "one Nation *under God,* indivisible, with liberty and justice for all." In 1952 Congress enacted legislation calling upon the President each year to proclaim a National Day of Prayer. Since 1865 the words "IN GOD WE TRUST" have been impressed on our coins.

Countless similar examples could be listed, but there is no need to belabor the obvious. It was all summed up by this Court just ten years ago in a single sentence: "We are a religious people whose institutions presuppose a Supreme Being."

I do not believe that this Court, or the Congress, or the President has by the actions and practices I have mentioned established an "official religion" in violation of the Constitution. And I do not believe the State of New York has done so in this case. What each has done has been to recognize and to follow the deeply entrenched and highly cherished spiritual traditions of our Nation—traditions which come down to us from those who almost two hundred years ago avowed their "firm Reliance on the Protection of divine Providence" when they proclaimed the freedom and independence of this brave new world.

I dissent.

Source

Engel v. Vitale, 370 U.S. 421 (1962).

Further Reading

Dierenfield, Bruce. *The Battle over School Prayer: How Engel v. Vitale Changed America.* Lawrence: University Press of Kansas, 2007.

Kruse, Kevin M. *One Nation Under God: How Corporate America Invented Christian America.* New York: Basic, 2015.

PHYLLIS SCHLAFLY,
THE POWER OF THE POSITIVE WOMAN (1977)

Women played key roles in the resurgence of religious conservatism, both in positions of leadership and at the grass roots. This fact vexed

many liberals, who had assumed that the conservatives' endorsement of gender hierarchy and attacks on feminism would alienate female adherents. In fact, many evangelical and Catholic women, among others, identified strongly with conservative cultures that emphasized their importance as wives and mothers. Viewing the women's movement as an assault on the family and a promoter of intrusive state power, activists such as Beverly LaHaye, Marabel Morgan, and Anita Bryant offered bold defenses of heterosexual marriage, motherhood, and domesticity. The religious and political meaning of feminism came to a head in the fight over the Equal Rights Amendment (ERA).

The ERA, which promised to ban gender discrimination, looked certain to become part of the Constitution. It was approved by the House of Representatives in 1971 and by the Senate the next year; at the end of 1973 thirty states had ratified it. Then, seemingly out of nowhere, an energetic anti-ERA campaign reversed the amendment's momentum and eventually defeated it. The most important leader of this surprising opposition movement was a Catholic Republican from Illinois named Phyllis Schlafly (1924–2016).

Schlafly's "STOP ERA" effort worked across religious and secular lines to mobilize the amendment's opponents, bringing many apolitical conservatives into politics for the first time. The ERA, Schlafly warned, would create a genderless society that would ignore God-given sex differences and abolish the special treatment enjoyed by women in many areas of American life, such as exemption from military service (the STOP in STOP ERA was an acronym for "Stop Taking Our Privileges"). After the amendment died, Schlafly continued to champion the prolife movement, anticommunism, and other conservative causes. These excerpts from *The Power of the Positive Woman*, written as the tide was turning against the ERA, are worth comparing with Frances Willard's earlier discussion of gender and religion.

Phyllis Schlafly, *The Power of the Positive Woman*

It is on its women that a civilization depends—on the inspiration they provide, on the moral fabric they weave, on the parameters of behavior they tolerate, and on the new generation that they breathe life into and educate. It is no accident of an artist's fancy that the Statue of Liberty is a woman, that the Scales of Justice are held by a woman, that Winged Victory is a woman. Those three essential bulwarks of civilization are personified in Woman—quite apart from her more widely recognized pictorializations as Beauty and Mother.

The Positive Woman accepts her responsibility to spin the fabric of civilization, to mend its tears, and to reinforce its seams. No matter how wide or how narrow is the scope of her influence, this is her task.

If her influence is limited to her immediate family, she knows that, after all, nothing is more important than building the morals and integrity of the family unit, especially its children, and she addresses herself to that. If circumstance and talent extend the scope of her influence to her club or school or business or community or state or nation, she accepts the responsibility. God has a mission for every Positive Woman. It is up to her to find out what it is and to meet the challenge. Only in so doing can she achieve that inner serenity that brings all-round fulfillment in this uncertain world.

[...]

The energies and dedication of the Positive Woman are needed as never before to fend off the attacks on the moral, the social, and the economic integrity of the family.

Take, for example, the tremendous drive to set up child-care centers—taxpayer-financed, government-managed, "universally" available for "all socioeconomic groups" regardless of means. This adds up to an attempt to make it public policy to remove babies from the family unit and place them in an institutional environment.

Several groups see it as in their self-interest to promote a policy to re-place mother care with government care. The women's liberationists are persistent pushers for this objective, based on their dogma that children are a burden from which women must be liberated.

Certain branches of the teachers' lobby also share this goal because they see it as the solution to the growing problem of empty classrooms and teacher unemployment caused by the severe decline in the American birth rate. Obviously, if our society can be induced to accept and finance the notion that every child should be put in school or a school substitute at age two or three instead of at age five or six, this would eliminate teacher unemployment.

The third force working resourcefully and effectively to move babies out of the home into government kiddy-care centers and mothers out of the home into the job market is the consortium of vested interests that always works toward more government (especially federal) spending and control. It is obvious that the American people are now paying all the taxes they are willing to pay; they vote against higher taxes every chance they get.

Where, then, can the bureaucrats, the planners, the government spend-ers, find new sources of revenue to expand their staffs, increase their budgets, and consolidate their control over our activities? The 40 million homemakers in the United States offer a tempting source of new tax rev-enues. When they stay in their homes, care for their own babies, and cook their own meals, no money changes hands. If these homemakers can be induced to leave their homes and take jobs, thereby having to purchase child care and other domestic services (such as packaged foods), the tax collector gets his share and more and bigger government is required.

Finally, there are the self-appointed planners, convinced that they are better able to mold a child's mind than are his parents and that the earlier they get the child under their supervision, the more thorough the indoctrination can be. The behaviorists and humanists assume that parents are incapable of properly raising their own children and that children's development will be enhanced if they are turned over at an early age to government and welfare workers or to academic and psychological experts.

[. . .]

The Positive Woman starts from the premise—which is self-evident to most people but which can also be scientifically demonstrated—that babies grow and develop better in a family with a mother's loving care than in an institution. The Positive Woman, therefore, will work tirelessly to safeguard the mother-care concept and to defeat government-care proposals.

Based on the dogma that a woman's susceptibility to becoming pregnant is the most oppressive inequality that women suffer, the women's liberation movement is compulsively oriented toward abortion on demand, financed by the government and made socially acceptable any time, any place. For the abortionists, their claimed right to kill an unborn child must take precedence over every other moral, marital, family, social, or legal value.

The Supreme Court abortion decision of January 22, 1973, was just the beginning. Since then, the court has held that a father has no right to protect his unborn child from abortion. Although a young girl cannot get her ears pierced or go on a school field trip to the zoo without parental permission, she can have an abortion without parental knowledge or consent. Many kinds of state laws designed to put reasonable limits on the abortion business have been invalidated by the courts. The Department of Health, Education and Welfare has been spending large federal sums to finance abortions.

Until January 22, 1973, the worst decision of the United States Supreme Court was that in the Dred Scott case, which legalized slavery. But the Supreme Court decisions that legalized abortion are even worse. The United States Supreme Court in effect espoused the view that human life does not begin until live birth. No medical evidence whatsoever was presented in the Supreme Court cases to support this most unscientific conclusion. None of the Supreme Court justices is a doctor of medicine.

Every advance in medical knowledge and science proves further that the unborn infant is a separate human life, with separate unique fingerprints, a separate heart that starts beating at twenty-four days, and separate brainwaves that can be detected at forty-three days. No one could look at a photograph of any of the 4 million babies who have been aborted in the United States and conclude it was anything other than human.

The abortionists argue that a woman has a right to do what she wants with her own body. All medical textbooks and professors of embryology and obstetrics are witnesses to the fact that an unborn infant is not a mere extension of the mother's body, like an appendix or tonsils. Abortion involves the destruction of somebody else's body—which is living within the life-support system of the mother, as the astronauts lived within their life-support systems on the moon.

The abortionists argue that unwanted babies should be eliminated. There are no unwanted babies in the United States. The demand for babies far exceeds the supply. Couples are now paying up to $24,000 for a baby they can adopt.

A few decades ago, the famous physician, Sir William Osler, said that most people over sixty are unproductive and should be chloroformed. After he reached sixty, he changed his views, but his antilife suggestion has lingered on. In recent years, there has been an ominous acceptance of the idea of terminating the lives of senior citizens because they are useless or unwanted. This is the same as Hitler's philosophy of eliminating people whom he judged unwanted or mentally or physically defective. Unfortunately, Hitler's idea has survived his death.

All human life, whether young or old, productive or dependent, is sacred. Positive Women should renew their efforts for a constitutional amendment to protect our very young and our very old from the Supreme Court and from Hitler's philosophy.

[...]

Here is a starting checklist of goals that can be restored to America if Positive Women will apply their dedicated efforts:

1. The right of a woman to be a full-time wife and mother and to have this right recognized by laws that obligate her husband to provide the primary financial support and a home for her and their children.
2. The responsibility of parents (not the government) for the care of preschool children.
3. The right of parents to insist that the schools:
   a. permit voluntary prayer,
   b. teach the "fourth R," right and wrong, according to the precepts of Holy Scriptures,
   c. use textbooks that do not offend the religious and moral values of the parents,
   d. use textbooks that honor the family, monogamous marriage, woman's role as wife and mother, and man's role as provider and protector,
   e. teach such basic educational skills as reading and arithmetic before time and money are spent on frills,
   f. permit children to attend school in their own neighborhood, and
   g. separate the sexes for gym classes, athletic practice and competition, and academic and vocational classes, if so desired.

4. The right of employers to give job preference (where qualifications are equal) to a wage earner supporting dependents.

5. The right of a woman engaged in physical-labor employment to be protected by laws and regulations that respect the physical differences and different family obligations of men and women.

6. The right to equal opportunity in employment and education for all persons regardless of race, creed, sex, or national origin.

7. The right to have local governments prevent the display of printed or pictorial materials that degrade women in a pornographic, perverted, or sadistic manner.

8. The right to defend the institution of the family by according certain rights to husbands and wives that are not given to those choosing immoral lifestyles.

9. The right to life of all innocent persons from conception to natural death.

10. The right of citizens to live in a community where state and local government and judges maintain law and order by a system of justice under due process and punishment that is swift and certain.

11. The right of society to protect itself by designating different roles for men and women in the armed forces and police and fire departments, where necessary.

12. The right of citizens to have the federal government adequately provide for the common defense against aggression by any other nation.

All things are possible to those who take as their text:

They that wait upon the Lord shall renew their strength; they shall mount up with wings as eagles; they shall run, and not be weary; and they shall walk, and not faint.

Source

Phyllis Schlafly, *The Power of the Positive Woman* (New Rochelle, NY: Arlington House, 1977), 139, 159–60, 161–63, 175–76. Reprinted by permission of Phyllis Schlafly.

Further Reading

Critchlow, Donald T. *Phyllis Schlafly and Grassroots Conservatism: A Woman's Crusade.* Princeton: Princeton University Press, 2005.

Williams, Daniel K. *God's Own Party: The Making of the Christian Right.* New York: Oxford University Press, 2010.

FRANCIS SCHAEFFER,
A CHRISTIAN MANIFESTO (1981)

With his shoulder-length hair and goatee, Francis Schaeffer (1912– 1984) looked more like a hippie than a conservative activist. For years,

he led an intentional community in Switzerland known as L'Abri (French for "The Shelter") where students and seekers of various kinds discussed theology, philosophy, art, and history. In Schaeffer, historically separatist conservatives found a model for a new worldliness and intellectual engagement with modern life.

In *A Christian Manifesto* (from which this selection comes) and elsewhere, Schaeffer decried the rise of secular humanism in Western culture, a development that threatened not only Christianity but civilization itself. Fundamentalists had often sounded this alarm, usually going on to advocate a retreat from public life in order to maintain the purity of the faithful. However, Schaeffer differed from other conservatives by insisting on the importance of a Christian presence in politics to save the nation from the consequences of unbelief. He was particularly provoked by the issue of abortion, feeling that it represented the triumph of a heartless, materialistic worldview. The most powerful leaders of the new evangelical politics, including Tim LaHaye and Jerry Falwell, acknowledged him as a crucial spur to their own activities.

Often characterized as part of a movement defending "traditional" values or wanting to "turn back the clock," Schaeffer in fact made full use of the modern publishing industry, modern visual media (as in *Whatever Happened to the Human Race?*, the film series he created with C. Everett Koop), and modern colleges and universities, where he often spoke to admiring audiences. Although more recent religious conservatives have distanced themselves from the religious right's combative style, many of them have been deeply shaped by this dynamic blend of tradition and innovation.

Francis Schaeffer, *A Christian Manifesto*

The basic problem of the Christians in this country in the last eighty years or so, in regard to society and in regard to government, is that they have seen things in bits and pieces instead of totals.

They have very gradually become disturbed over permissiveness, pornography, the public schools, the breakdown of the family, and finally abortion. But they have not seen this as a totality—each thing being a part, a symptom, of a much larger problem. They have failed to see that all of this has come about due to a shift in world view—that is, through a fundamental change in the overall way people think and view the world and life as a whole. This shift has been *away from* a world view that was at least vaguely Christian in people's memory (even if they were not individually Christian) *toward* something completely different—toward a world view based upon the idea that the final reality is impersonal matter or energy shaped into its present form by impersonal chance. They have not seen that this world view has taken the place of the one that had previously dominated Northern European culture, including the United States, which was at least Christian in memory, even if the individuals were not individually Christian.

These two world views stand as totals in complete antithesis to each other in content and also in their natural results—including sociological and governmental results, and specifically including law.

It is not that these two world views are different only in how they understand the nature of reality and existence. They also inevitably produce totally different results. The operative word here is *inevitably*. It is not just that they happen to bring forth different results, but it is absolutely *inevitable* that they will bring forth different results.

Why have the Christians been so slow to understand this? There are various reasons but the central one is a defective view of Christianity. This has its roots in the Pietist movement under the leadership of P. J. Spener in the seventeenth century. Pietism began as a healthy protest against formalism and a too abstract Christianity. But it had a deficient, "platonic" spirituality. It was platonic in the sense that Pietism made a sharp division between the "spiritual" and the "material" world—giving little, or no, importance to the "material" world. The totality of human existence was not afforded a proper place. In particular it neglected the intellectual dimension of Christianity.

Christianity and spirituality were shut up to a small, isolated part of life. The totality of reality was ignored by the pietistic thinking. Let me quickly say that in one sense Christians should be pietists in that Christianity is not just a set of doctrines, even the right doctrines. *Every* doctrine is in some way to have an effect upon our lives. But the poor side of Pietism and its resulting platonic outlook has really been a tragedy not only in many people's individual lives, but in our total culture.

True spirituality covers all of reality. There are things the Bible tells us as absolutes which are sinful—which do not conform to the character of God. But aside from these the Lordship of Christ covers *all* of life and *all* of life equally. It is not only that true spirituality covers all of life, but it covers all parts of the spectrum of life equally. In this sense there is nothing concerning reality that is not spiritual.

Related to this, it seems to me, is the fact that many Christians do not mean what I mean when I say Christianity is true, or Truth. They are Christians and they believe in, let us say, the truth of creation, the truth of the virgin birth, the truth of Christ's miracles, Christ's substitutionary death, and His coming again. But they stop there with these and other individual truths.

When I say Christianity is true I mean it is true to total reality—the total of what is, beginning with the central reality, the objective existence of the personal-infinite God. Christianity is not just a series of truths but *Truth*—Truth about all of reality. And the holding to that Truth intellectually—and then in some poor way living upon that Truth, the Truth of what is—brings forth not only certain personal results, but also governmental and legal results.

Now let's go over to the other side—to those who hold the materialistic final reality concept. They saw the complete and total difference between the two positions more quickly than Christians. There were the Huxleys, George Bernard Shaw (1856–1950), and many others who understood a long time ago that there are two total concepts of reality and that it was one total reality against the other and not just a set of isolated and separated differences. The *Humanist Manifesto I*,[1] published in 1933, showed with crystal clarity their comprehension of the totality of what is involved. It was to our shame that Julian (1887–1975) and Aldous Huxley (1894–1963), and the others like them, understood much earlier than Christians that these two world views are two total concepts of reality standing in antithesis to each other. We should be utterly ashamed that this is the fact.

They understood not only that there were two totally different concepts but that they would bring forth two totally different conclusions, both for individuals and for society. What we must understand is that the two world views really do bring forth with inevitable certainty not only personal differences, but also total differences in regard to society, government, and law.

There is no way to mix these two total world views. They are separate entities that cannot be synthesized. Yet we must say that liberal theology, the very essence of it from its beginning, is an attempt to mix the two. Liberal theology tried to bring forth a mixture soon after the Enlightenment and has tried to synthesize these two views right up to our own day. But in each case when the chips are down these liberal theologians have always come down, as naturally as a ship coming into home port, on the side of the nonreligious humanist. They do this with certainty because what their liberal theology really is is humanism expressed in theological terms instead of philosophic or other terms.

An example of this coming down naturally on the side of the nonreligious humanists is the article by Charles Hartshorne in the January 21, 1981, issue of *The Christian Century*, pages 42–45. Its title is, "Concerning Abortion, an Attempt at a Rational View." He begins by equating the fact that the human fetus is alive with the fact that mosquitoes and bacteria are also alive. That is, he begins by assuming that human life is not unique. He then continues by saying that *even after the baby is born* it is not fully human until its social relations develop (though he says the

1. *Humanist Manifestos I and II* (New York: Prometheus Books, 1973).

infant does have some primitive social relations an unborn fetus does not have). His conclusion is, "Nevertheless, I have little sympathy with the idea that infanticide is just another form of murder. Persons who are already functionally persons in the full sense have more important rights even than infants." He then, logically, takes the next step: "Does this distinction apply to the killing of a hopelessly senile person or one in a permanent coma? For me it does." No atheistic humanist could say it with greater clarity. It is significant at this point to note that many of the denominations controlled by liberal theology have come out, publicly and strongly, in favor of abortion.

Dr. Martin E. Marty is one of the respected, theologically liberal spokesmen. He is an associate editor of *The Christian Century* and Fairfax M. Cone distinguished service professor at the University of Chicago divinity school. He is often quoted in the secular press as the spokesman for "mainstream" Christianity. In a *Christian Century* article in the January 7–14, 1981, issue (pages 13–17 with an addition on page 31), he has an article entitled: "Dear Republicans: A Letter on Humanisms." In it he brilliantly confuses the terms "being human," humanism, the humanities and being "in love with humanity." Why does he do this? As a historian he knows the distinctions of those words, but when one is done with these pages the poor reader who knows no better is left with the eradication of the total distinction between the Christian position and the humanist one. I admire the cleverness of the article, but I regret that in it Dr. Marty has come down on the nonreligious humanist side, by confusing the issues so totally.

It would be well at this point to stress that we should not confuse the very different things which Dr. Marty did confuse. *Humanitarianism* is being kind and helpful to people, treating people humanly. The *humanities* are the studies of literature, art, music, etc.—those things which are the products of human creativity. *Humanism* is the placing of Man at the center of all things and making him the measure of all things.

Thus, Christians should be the most humanitarian of all people. And Christians certainly should be interested in the humanities as the product of human creativity, made possible because people are uniquely made in the image of the great Creator. In this sense of being interested in the humanities it would be proper to speak of a Christian humanist. This is especially so in the past usage of that term. This would then mean that such a Christian is interested (as we all should be) in the product of people's creativity. In this sense, for example, Calvin could be called a Christian humanist because he knew the works of the Roman writer Seneca so very well.[2] John Milton and many other Christian poets could

2. This must not be confused with the humanistic elements which were developing slightly earlier in the Renaissance. Francis A. Schaeffer, *How Should We Then Live?* (Old Tappan, NJ: Fleming H. Revell Co., 1976), pp. 58–78.

also be so called because of their knowledge not only of their own day but also of antiquity.

But in contrast to being humanitarian and being interested in the humanities Christians should be inalterably opposed to the false and destructive humanism, which is false to the Bible and equally false to what Man is.

Along with this we must keep distinct the "humanist world view" of which we have been speaking and such a thing as the "Humanist Society," which produced the *Humanist Manifestos I and II* (1933 and 1973). The Humanist Society is made up of a relatively small group of people (some of whom, however, have been influential—John Dewey, Sir Julian Huxley, Jacques Monod, B. F. Skinner, etc.). By way of contrast, the humanist world view includes many thousands of adherents and today controls the consensus in society, much of the media, much of what is taught in our schools, and much of the arbitrary law being produced by the various departments of government.

The term humanism used in this wider, more prevalent way means Man beginning from himself, with no knowledge except what he himself can discover and no standards outside of himself. In this view Man is the measure of all things, as the Enlightenment expressed it.

Nowhere have the divergent results of the two total concepts of reality, the Judeo-Christian and the humanist world view, been more open to observation than in government and law.

We of Northern Europe (and we must remember that the United States, Canada, Australia, New Zealand and so on are extensions of Northern Europe) take our *form-freedom balance* in government for granted as though it were natural. There is form in acknowledging the obligations in society, and there is freedom in acknowledging the rights of the individual. We have form, we have freedom; there is freedom, there is form. There is a balance here which we have come to take as natural in the world. It is not natural in the world. We are utterly foolish if we look at the long span of history and read the daily newspapers giving today's history and do not understand that the form-freedom balance in government which we have had in Northern Europe since the Reformation and in the countries extended from it is unique in the world, past and present.

That is not to say that no one wrestled with these questions before the Reformation nor that no one produced anything worthwhile. One can think, for example, of the Conciliar Movement in the late medieval church and the early medieval parliaments.[3] Especially one must consider the ancient English Common Law. And in relation to that Common Law (and all English Law) there is Henry De Bracton. I will mention more about him in a moment.

3. See *How Should We Then Live?*, pp. 40 and 109.

Those who hold the material-energy, chance concept of reality, whether they are Marxist or non-Marxist, not only do not know the truth of the final reality, God, they do not know who Man is. Their concept of Man is what Man is not, just as their concept of the final reality is what final reality is not. Since their concept of Man is mistaken, their concept of society and of law is mistaken, and they have no sufficient base for either society or law.

They have reduced Man to even less than his natural finiteness by see-ing him only as a complex arrangement of molecules, made complex by blind chance. Instead of seeing him as something great who is significant even in his sinning, they see Man in his essence only as an intrinsically competitive animal, that has no other basic operating principle than nat-ural selection brought about by the strongest, the fittest, ending on top. And they see Man as acting in this way both individually and collectively as society.

Even on the basis of Man's finiteness having people swear in court *in the name of humanity,* as some have advocated, saying something like, "We pledge our honor before all mankind"[4] would be insufficient enough. But reduced to the materialistic view of Man, it is even less. Al-though many nice words may be used, in reality law constituted on this basis can only mean brute force.

In this setting Jeremy Bentham's (1748–1842) Utilitarianism can be and must be all that law means. And this must inevitably lead to the conclusion of Oliver Wendell Holmes Jr. (1841–1935): "The life of the law has not been logic: it has been experience."[5] That is, there is *no* basis for law except Man's limited, finite experience. And especially with the Darwinian, survival-of-the-fittest concept of Man (which Holmes held) that must, and will, lead to Holmes' final conclusion: law is "the majority vote of that nation that could lick all others."[6]

The problem always was, and is, What is an adequate base for law? What is adequate so that the human aspiration for freedom can exist without anarchy, and yet provides a form that will not become arbitrary tyranny?

In contrast to the materialistic concept, Man in reality is made in the image of God and has real humanness. This humanness has produced varying degrees of success in government, bringing forth governments that were more than only the dominance of brute force.

And those in the stream of the Judeo-Christian world view have had something more. The influence of the Judeo-Christian world view can be perhaps most readily observed in Henry De Bracton's influence on British

---

4. See Will and Ariel Durant's book *The Lessons of History* (New York: Simon & Schuster, 1968), pp. 84–86.
5. *American Law Review,* XIV (1880), p. 233.
6. *Harvard Law Review,* XL (1918).

Law. An English judge living in the thirteenth century, he wrote *De Legi-bus et Consuetudinibus* (c. 1250).

Bracton, in the stream of the Judeo-Christian world view, said:

> And that he [the King] ought to be under the law appears clearly in the analogy of Jesus Christ, whose vice-regent on earth he is, for though many ways were open to Him for His ineffable redemption of the human race, the true mercy of God chose this most powerful way to destroy the devil's work, he would not use the power of force but the reason of justice.[7]

In other words, God in His sheer power could have crushed Satan in his revolt by the use of that sufficient power. But because of God's character, justice came before the use of power alone. Therefore Christ died that justice, rooted in what God is, would be the solution. Bracton codified this: Christ's example, because of who He is, is our standard, our rule, our measure. Therefore power is not first, but justice is first in society and law. The prince may have the power to control and to rule, but he does not have the right to do so without justice. This was the basis of English Common Law. The Magna Charta (1215) was written within thirty-five years (or less) of Bracton's *De Legibus* and in the midst of the same universal thinking in England at that time.

The Reformation (300 years after Bracton) refined and clarified this further. It got rid of the encrustations that had been added to the Judeo-Christian world view and clarified the point of authority—with authority resting in the Scripture rather than church *and* Scripture, or state *and* Scripture. This not only had meaning in regard to doctrine but clarified the base for law.

That base was God's written Law, back through the New Testament to Moses' written Law; and the content and authority of that written Law is rooted back to Him who is the final reality. Thus, neither church nor state were equal to, let alone above, that Law. The base for law is not divided, and no one has the right to place anything, including king, state or church, above the content of God's Law.

What the Reformation did was to return most clearly and consistently to the origins, to the final reality, God; but equally to the reality of Man—not only Man's personal needs (such as salvation), but also Man's social needs.

What we have had for four hundred years, produced from this clarity, is unique in contrast to the situation that has existed in the world in forms of government. Some of you have been taught that the Greek city

7. Henry De Bracton, Translation of *De Legibus et Consuetudinibus* (Cambridge, Mass.: Harvard-Belknap, 1968). See James L. Fisk, *The Law and Its Timeless Standard* (Washington: Lex Rex Institute).

states had our concepts in government. It simply is not true.[8] All one has to do is read Plato's *Republic* to have this come across with tremendous force.

When the men of our State Department, especially after World War II, went all over the world trying to implant our form-freedom balance in government downward on cultures whose philosophy and religion would never have produced it, it has, in almost every case, ended in some form of totalitarianism or authoritarianism.

The humanists push for "freedom," but having no Christian consensus to contain it, that "freedom" leads to chaos or to slavery under the state (or under an elite). Humanism, with its lack of *any* final base for values or law, always leads to chaos. It then naturally leads to some form of authoritarianism to control the chaos. Having produced the sickness, humanism gives more of the same kind of medicine for a cure. With its mistaken concept of final reality, it has no intrinsic reason to be interested in the individual, the human being. Its natural interest is the two collectives: the state and society.

Source

Francis Schaeffer, *A Christian Manifesto* (Wheaton, IL: Crossway, 1981), 17–30. Used by permission of Crossway, a publishing ministry of Good News Publishers, Wheaton, IL 60187, www.crossway.org

Further Reading

Hankins, Barry. *Francis Schaeffer and the Shaping of Evangelical America*. Grand Rapids, MI: Eerdmans, 2008.

Martin, William. *With God on Our Side: The Rise of the Religious Right in America*. New York: Broadway, 1996.

Worthen, Molly. *Apostles of Reason: The Crisis of Authority in American Evangelicalism*. New York: Oxford University Press, 2014.

JOHN SHELBY SPONG, "BLESSING GAY AND LESBIAN COMMITMENTS" (1988)

Sex and marriage have long been contentious subjects at the intersection of American religion and politics. During the nineteenth century, the federal government outlawed the polygamous marriages recognized by the Church of Jesus Christ of Latter-Day Saints (Mormons). As shown in the 1878 *Reynolds* decision earlier in this book, the Supreme Court rejected the Mormons' claim that they were exercising their religious freedom, asserting instead that monogamy was a crucial foundation for "Government of the People" and therefore

8. See Will and Ariel Durant's *The Lessons of History*, pp. 70–75.

a legitimate concern of civil authority. During the 1960s, religious views shaped the argument over interracial marriage, which had been banned by many states. In upholding Virginia's ban, a judge in the case of *Loving v. Virginia* opined that "Almighty God created the races . . . and he placed them on separate continents. The fact that he separated the races shows that he did not intend for the races to mix." His ruling was overturned by the Supreme Court in 1968, bringing an end to state proscriptions of marital unions across the color line.

The fight over same-sex marriage in recent decades, then, was not entirely unique, but rather part of a protracted American debate about the political significance of love, sex, and family. The push for same-sex marriage emerged as a consequence of the gay liberation movement that gained strength in the 1960s and 1970s, but it also became possible because of changes in heterosexual practices. For instance, the prevalence of birth control separated sex from reproduction, making children less central as the rationale for wedlock. Despite these trends, many religious groups, particularly evangelical Christians and Catholics, have opposed same-sex marriage as a violation of Christian teaching.

In this selection from his book *Living in Sin?* John Shelby Spong (b. 1931) makes the case for Christians to accept gay and lesbian unions. Spong, for many years the Episcopal Bishop of Newark, has gained a reputation as a leading voice for liberal Christianity. Seeking to make the faith more relevant to modern culture, he has rejected doctrines such as the Virgin Birth and the Resurrection as well as many traditional Christian ideas about morality. Spong's views have attracted opposition from conservatives who accuse him of disregarding the Bible. Yet some radical LGBT activists have criticized the same-sex marriage movement as itself an essentially conservative betrayal of a subversive queer culture that affirms, among other things, the "promiscuous life of gay bars, pornography, and one-night stands" dismissed by Spong. In the end, the contests over marriage show how the most intimate individual acts have become public concerns for religious and political communities.

John Shelby Spong, "Blessing Gay and Lesbian Commitments"

Everything I now know about homosexuality, through conversations with gay and lesbian people, the books I have read, and the experts with whom I have talked, has led me to the conclusion that a homosexual orientation is a minority but perfectly natural characteristic on the human spectrum of sexuality. It is not something one chooses, it is something one is. It is set before birth and is abnormal only in the sense that it is a minority orientation and not the statistical norm for our society. The evidence for this I have noted in chapter 5. Gays and lesbians, like all people, have unique gifts and contributions to offer the human family, some of which might well be present in them because of, not in spite of, their sexual orientation. But it is hard to discover gifts that celebrate one's being when the atmosphere in which one lives is laced with a murderous, oppressive hostility toward who one is.

When people are oppressed by either the external bonds of slavery or the internal bonds of prejudice, their natural creativity is inhibited. It is suffocated in the struggle just to survive. To the ancient Egyptians, Jewish slaves were inconsequential, dull people to whom the lowest of menial tasks were assigned. Jews were considered by their oppressors to be unfit for anything else. How surprised the Egyptians would have been to discover that in the Jewish people they enslaved lurked the genes that would produce two of the world's great religions; the genius minds of Albert Einstein, Sigmund Freud, and Karl Marx; and the life-giving gifts of Eddie Cantor, Jack Benny, Itzhak Perlman, Leon Uris, and Herman Wouk. But the world could not be the beneficiary of these gifts until that slavery was ended. One wonders what genius and grace has been denied the world because of our prejudice against homosexuals. What might have been gained is hinted at by considering that such extraordinary people as Leonardo da Vinci, Michelangelo, Christopher Marlowe, Erasmus, Dostoyevsky, Tchaikovsky, Francis Bacon, W. H. Auden, Richard the Lion Hearted, Lord Byron, Herman Melville, Maynard Keynes, Walt Whitman, and, some would argue, John Milton were gay.

If my conclusions about gay and lesbian people are valid, then the whole of society must be seen as guilty of a cruel oppression of this courageous minority. The time has surely come not just to tolerate, or even to accept, but to celebrate and welcome the presence among us of our gay and lesbian fellow human beings.

One way to do that is for the church to admit publicly its own complicity in their oppression, based on its vast ignorance and prejudice. It is time to overcome that dark chapter of church history by living new chapters with an attitude that embraces yesterday's exile, practices the inclusiveness of God's love, and celebrates the unique gifts of all of God's diverse children. The one act that above all others will best show a serious intention to change the church's attitude will be for the church to state its willingness and eager desire to bless and affirm the love that binds two persons of the same gender into a life-giving relationship of mutual commitment. That ritual act alone will announce to the homosexual world and to ourselves a shift that will be believed. No matter how that liturgy is discussed or defined, the media, the critics, and the world at large will hear it and talk about it as the marriage of homosexuals. But before we decide what to call this service, we need to understand what it is and what it is not. The central clue to this is to discover what the church does and does not do in marriage.

The church does not, in fact, marry anyone. People marry each other. The state, not the church, defines the nature of legal marriage. It does so by giving to married couples the right of joint property ownership. It is not within the power of the church to change this legal fact, though its implications need to be addressed. What the church does in holy matrimony is hear people's public vows to love each other, to live in a faithful relationship, and to be mutually supportive and caring in all of life's vicissitudes. Then the church adds to that vow of commitment its blessing. That blessing is really the church's only contribution. The church blesses the commitment to be a couple that issues from the vows of the two people who stand before "God and this company." That blessing conveys ecclesiastical sanction on the relationship and the official willingness of the church and, through the church, of society to support, undergird, and stabilize in every way possible the life of the newly formed couple. The hope of the church is that this sanction and the resultant public support might enable the vows exchanged in good faith before the altar to have an increased chance of being kept.

If the conveying of blessing and official approval is the church's gift to give, then surely that can be given to any relationship of love, fidelity, commitment, and trust that issues in life for the two people involved. We have not in the past as a church withheld blessing from many things. We have blessed fields when crops were planted, houses when newly occupied, pets in honor of Saint Francis, and even the hounds at a Virginia fox hunt. We have blessed MX missiles called "Peacemakers" and warships whose sole purpose was to kill and destroy, calling them, in at least one instance, *Corpus Christi*—the Body of Christ. Why would it occur to us to withhold our blessing from a human relationship that produces a more complete person in each of the partners, because of their life together? Surely the only possible answer to that question is that the church has shared in the habitual prejudice of the ages. Now I call on the church to step out of this prejudice and bless relationships between human beings that are marked by love, fidelity, and the hope of a lifetime of mutual responsibility. What this service is called can then be left to the people involved, and they can then urge the state to accord such relationships the legal benefits of marriage.

Only when official and public sanction is given to gay and lesbian couples will our society begin to think of them as units rather than as individuals and begin to relate to them in a way that enforces and undergirds that unity. Such simple things as inviting gay and lesbian couples to social functions and to family gatherings and sharing in the celebration of the anniversaries and other holy moments that mark their lives together would solidify the gay or lesbian couple just as it does the heterosexual married couple. Many gay and lesbian couples feel compelled to limit their associations to other homosexual persons with whom they can live their private lives in comfort.

Heterosexual marriages today, as this book has already noted, are under great duress. They are shattering in one out of two instances. That is so despite all the energy expended by the church and society to recognize, bless, and affirm those marriage unions. It is an enormous tribute to the commitment of gay and lesbian people to recognize that they have succeeded in forging long-lasting and in some cases permanent bonds without the support of church, state, or society; indeed in most cases they have done so in the face of active hostility from all three sources.

The heterosexual community needs to see and experience homosexual unions that are marked by integrity and caring and are filled with grace and beauty. The heterosexual majority seems to assume that the only form homosexual lovemaking takes is the promiscuous life of gay bars, pornography, and one-night stands. They are ever ready to condemn that behavior pattern as morally unacceptable—and so it is. But two things seem to have been overlooked by those who make these judgments. First, promiscuity, pick-up bars, pornography, and one-night stands are not unknown in the heterosexual world. That kind of behavior is destructive no matter what the sexual orientation of those who live out that style of life. Second, heterosexual people have the publicly accepted, blessed, and affirmed alternative of marriage that has as yet not been available to the homosexual population. If there is no such positive alternative for homosexual persons, then what is the church's expectation for them? If the church or society refuses to recognize or promote any positive alternative in which love and intimacy can sustain a gay or lesbian couple, then those institutions are guilty of contributing to the very promiscuity that they condemn.

A willingness on the part of church and society to accept, bless, affirm, and encourage long-term faithful relationships among gay and lesbian people would be just and proper. But above all it would indicate to the homosexual minority that there is a recognized alternative to the loneliness of celibacy on the one hand and the irresponsibility of sexual promiscuity on the other.

The fact is that the homosexual population has recognized and supported committed couples, long ahead of the church. In numbers far greater than the "straight" majority suspects, gay people have forged this alternative for themselves with no official help or sanction from anyone. Though those homosexual persons alienated from the church might not welcome the church's Johnny-come-lately arrival on this scene, I believe that the vast majority who crave a sign of society's acceptance of their existence would, if not for themselves then for others. But whether welcomed or not, this is a step the church must take *for the church's sake*. We need to be cleansed from our sin. Then we can send a message to the homosexual population that, first, we have recognized our need for repentance and, second, we are ready at last to offer our resources to turn the attitude of the world away from its traditional stance of rejection, away from intolerance, away even from a grudging acceptance, until finally we can begin to celebrate the presence and the contributions of gay people and of gay couples as well as heterosexual people and couples in our common life.

Being public and articulate about what we believe concerning gay couples and designing a liturgy to place those convictions into the context of public worship is, in my opinion, a major mandate for justice before the church today. Unbeknownst to figures in the hierarchy of the church, the blessing of gay unions is being conducted as a private pastoral rite in congregations of all traditions across this land, at this very moment. In Canada, I am told, the gay and lesbian population invites pastors to do house blessings for them, which includes a blessing of those who live therein. For gay and lesbian couples there, this has served as the church's blessing upon their relationships. It is both a clandestine and an ingenious ploy, but in the future the church will need to be more open and more honest about its participation in it. The grapevine is quite active in informing the gay population of where they can go to receive this ministry of the church.

Gay and lesbian clergy are themselves opening the doors of their churches to their brothers and sisters. None of the proposed liturgies being developed today has yet received the sanction of any ecclesiastical tradition, save the Universal Fellowship of Metropolitan Community Churches, a relatively new denomination founded to minister primarily but not exclusively to gay men and lesbians. Given the virulent negativity that still exists, it may well take another decade before official acceptance is accorded. But ten years is an astonishingly brief time for a change of this magnitude. It will be a signal achievement to achieve it in a decade or less. Until that time I hope that the debate this proposal receives will be a factor in the continuing process of consciousness-raising, and I hope more ordained clergy will be bold enough to add this resource to their private pastoral ministries, until the day arrives when it becomes part of the church's public liturgy.

People do change, and the knowledge explosion continues each day. I am a living example of these facts. Ten years ago I would have been shocked and aghast at the things I am writing at this moment. Five years ago I still had to be pushed to take an inclusive position. However, scientific data that made me aware that my prejudice grew out of ignorance combined with the witness of gay and lesbian people, some of whom were clergy, to educate me. When I became open to new possibilities, then the humanity of representatives of the homosexual world was able to touch my humanity. They loved me and they invited me into the integrity and life-giving power present in their relationships. It was my recognition of the meaning and validity at work in their mutually committed lives that enabled me to accept the new data and to walk slowly but surely away from the prejudice of a lifetime.

If I can make such a journey, so can the church. If not this year, then next year, but it is inevitable that it will come. I only know that when we finally free ourselves from our prejudices we will have a hard time understanding how we had been so blind in the first place. Can anyone imagine a world that would say that Willie Mays, Hank Aaron, or David Winfield cannot play major league baseball because they are black? Well, Jackie Robinson and Satchel Paige could imagine that, for they experienced it first hand. Can anyone imagine the Metropolitan Opera without Leontyne Price? The negativity toward blessing gay and lesbian unions will someday be like the assumption that baseball is a game for white males only, or that a black woman from Mississippi could not hope to sing at the Met. That stance will die and be one more embarrassing relic in the museum of cultural and ecclesiastical prejudices. I look forward to that day. I hope I contribute to its early arrival.

The time to move in this direction is certainly now. The witness of contemporary theology is stimulating us to think about liberation and self-affirmation. The insights of contemporary psychology encourage the expression of natural and basic human drives through creative and responsible outlets. Contemporary health concerns demand the redefinition of responsible social behavior. The growing body of data about sexual orientation charges us to rethink our assumptions. We need only to add the courageous and responsible voice of the official church. That voice will affirm God's Word in creation that "it is not good for man [woman] to live alone." It will affirm God's Word in Jesus Christ that all are invited to come unto him to find the rest of acceptance. It will affirm God's Word in the Spirit that in the body of Christ, whatever language we understand will be the language through which God's love will be proclaimed to us (Acts 2). It is this Word of God that calls us to act now.

Source

John Shelby Spong, *Living in Sin? A Bishop Rethinks Human Sexuality* (San Francisco: Harper and Row, 1988), 198–205. Copyright © 1989 by the Rt. Rev. John Shelby Spong. Reprinted by permission of HarperCollins Publishers.

Further Reading

Erzen, Tanya. *Straight to Jesus: Sexual and Christian Conversions in the Ex-Gay Movement.* Berkeley: University of California Press, 2006.

Jakobsen, Janet R., and Ann Pellegrini. *Love the Sin: Sexual Regulation and the Limits of Religious Tolerance.* New York: New York University Press, 2003.

Petro, Anthony M. *After the Wrath of God: AIDS, Sexuality, and American Religion.* New York: Oxford University Press, 2015.

EMPLOYMENT DIVISION v. SMITH (1990)

The *Smith* decision is one of the most controversial rulings on religious freedom that the Supreme Court has ever handed down. The case resulted from the actions of two members of the Native American Church who, after using the hallucinogen peyote as part of a religious ritual, were fired from their jobs at a drug rehabilitation center. The lawsuit centered on the issue of whether religious practitioners could be exempt from specific laws that conflicted with their faith. Before *Smith*, the court had given wide latitude to minority religious rights. For instance, in the 1963 *Sherbert v. Verner* case, the justices ruled that an employer had to accommodate the religious beliefs of a Seventh-Day Adventist who observed Saturday, rather than the usual Christian Sunday, as a holy day.

In his *Smith* opinion, Justice Antonin Scalia restricted the scope of religious freedom. "The free exercise of religion," he wrote, "means ... the right to believe and profess," but not necessarily the right to engage in practices prohibited by government. As precedents, Scalia cited two cases in this anthology: *Reynolds*, which rejected polygamy as a permissible religious practice, and *Gobitis*, which held that Jehovah's Witnesses could not refuse to salute the flag (*Gobitis* was a curious choice, given that it was contradicted a few years later by *Barnette*).

Outrage over the *Smith* case brought together a wide range of political actors, from conservative evangelicals to left-leaning civil libertarians. This coalition led Congress to pass the Religious Freedom Restoration Act (RFRA) in 1993, a law intended to repudiate *Smith* in favor of the more capacious view of religious freedom invoked by *Sherbert*. In a continuing struggle between the judicial and legislative branches, the Supreme Court ruled RFRA unconstitutional as it applied to the states, but many states then passed their own versions of the law. Most recently, the RFRA statutes have been invoked by opponents of same-sex marriage and universal health care, providing vivid examples of ongoing shifts in the meaning of religious freedom.

Employment Division v. Smith

JUSTICE SCALIA delivered the opinion of the Court.

This case requires us to decide whether the Free Exercise Clause of the First Amendment permits the State of Oregon to include religiously inspired peyote use within the reach of its general criminal prohibition on use of that drug, and thus permits the State to deny unemployment benefits to persons dismissed from their jobs because of such religiously inspired use.

Oregon law prohibits the knowing or intentional possession of a "controlled substance" unless the substance has been prescribed by a medical practitioner. The law defines "controlled substance" as a drug classified in Schedules I through V of the Federal Controlled Substances Act, as modified by the State Board of Pharmacy. Persons who violate this provision by possessing a controlled substance listed on Schedule I are "guilty of a Class B felony." As compiled by the State Board of Pharmacy under its statutory authority, Schedule I contains the drug peyote, a hallucinogen derived from the plant *Lophophora williamsii Lemaire.*

Respondents Alfred Smith and Galen Black (hereinafter respondents) were fired from their jobs with a private drug rehabilitation organization because they ingested peyote for sacramental purposes at a ceremony of the Native American Church, of which both are members. When respondents applied to petitioner Employment Division (hereinafter petitioner) for unemployment compensation, they were determined to be ineligible for benefits because they had been discharged for work-related "misconduct."

[. . .]

The Free Exercise Clause of the First Amendment, which has been made applicable to the States by incorporation into the Fourteenth Amendment, provides that "Congress shall make no law respecting an establishment of religion, or *prohibiting the free exercise thereof* . . ." (emphasis added). The free exercise of religion means, first and foremost, the right to believe and profess whatever religious doctrine one desires. Thus, the First Amendment obviously excludes all "governmental regulation of religious *beliefs* as such." The government may not compel affirmation of religious belief, punish the expression of religious doctrines it believes to be false, impose special disabilities on the basis of religious views or religious status, or lend its power to one or the other side in controversies over religious authority or dogma.

But the "exercise of religion" often involves not only belief and profession but the performance of (or abstention from) physical acts: assembling with others for a worship service, participating in sacramental use of bread and wine, proselytizing, abstaining from certain foods or certain modes of transportation. It would be true, we think (though no case of ours has involved the point), that a State would be "prohibiting the free exercise [of religion]" if it sought to ban such acts or abstentions only when they are engaged in for religious reasons, or only because of the religious belief that they display. It would doubtless be unconstitutional, for example, to ban the casting of "statues that are to be used for worship purposes," or to prohibit bowing down before a golden calf.

Respondents in the present case, however, seek to carry the meaning of "prohibiting the free exercise [of religion]" one large step further. They contend that their religious motivation for using peyote places them beyond the reach of a criminal law that is not specifically directed at their religious practice, and that is concededly constitutional as applied to those who use the drug for other reasons. They assert, in other words, that "prohibiting the free exercise [of religion]" includes requiring any individual to observe a generally applicable law that requires (or forbids) the performance of an act that his religious belief forbids (or requires). As a textual matter, we do not think the words must be given that meaning. It is no more necessary to regard the collection of a general tax, for example, as "prohibiting the free exercise [of religion]" by those citizens who believe support of organized government to be sinful, than it is to regard the same tax as "abridging the freedom . . . of the press" of those publishing companies that must pay the tax as a condition of staying in business. It is a permissible reading of the text, in the one case as in the other, to say that if prohibiting the exercise of religion (or burdening the activity of printing) is not the object of the tax but merely the incidental effect of a generally applicable and otherwise valid provision, the First Amendment has not been offended.

Our decisions reveal that the latter reading is the correct one. We have never held that an individual's religious beliefs excuse him from compliance with an otherwise valid law prohibiting conduct that the State is free to regulate. On the contrary, the record of more than a century of our free exercise jurisprudence contradicts that proposition. As described succinctly by Justice Frankfurter in *Minersville School Dist. Bd. of Ed.* v. *Gobitis,* 310 U. S. 586, 594–595 (1940): "Conscientious scruples have not, in the course of the long struggle for religious toleration, relieved the individual from obedience to a general law not aimed at the promotion or restriction of religious beliefs. The mere possession of religious convictions which contradict the relevant concerns of a political society does not relieve the citizen from the discharge of political responsibilities (footnote omitted)." We first had occasion to assert that principle in *Reynolds* v. *United States,* 98 U. S. 145 (1879), where we rejected the claim that criminal laws against polygamy could not be constitutionally applied to those whose religion commanded the practice. "Laws," we said, "are made for the government of actions, and while they cannot interfere with mere religious belief and opinions, they may with practices. . . . Can a man excuse his practices to the contrary because of his religious belief? To permit this would be to make the professed doctrines of religious belief superior to the law of the land, and in effect to permit every citizen to become a law unto himself."

[. . .]

The only decisions in which we have held that the First Amendment bars application of a neutral, generally applicable law to religiously motivated action have involved not the Free Exercise Clause alone, but the Free Exercise Clause in conjunction with other constitutional protections, such as freedom of speech and of the press, see *Cantwell v. Connecticut,* 310 U. S., at 304–307 (invalidating a licensing system for religious and charitable solicitations under which the administrator had discretion to deny a license to any cause he deemed nonreligious); *Murdock v. Pennsylvania,* 319 U. S. 105 (1943) (invalidating a flat tax on solicitation as applied to the dissemination of religious ideas); *Follett v. McCormick,* 321 U. S. 573 (1944) (same), or the right of parents, acknowledged in *Pierce v. Society of Sisters,* 268 U. S. 510 (1925), to direct the education of their children, see *Wisconsin v. Yoder,* 406 U. S. 205 (1972) (invalidating compulsory school-attendance laws as applied to Amish parents who refused on religious grounds to send their children to school). Some of our cases prohibiting compelled expression, decided exclusively upon free speech grounds, have also involved freedom of religion, cf. *Wooley v. Maynard,* 430 U. S. 705 (1977) (invalidating compelled display of a license plate slogan that offended individual religious beliefs); *West Virginia Bd. of Education v. Barnette,* 319 U. S. 624 (1943) (invalidating compulsory flag salute statute challenged by religious objectors). And it is easy to envision a case in which a challenge on freedom of association grounds would likewise be reinforced by Free Exercise Clause concerns. Cf. *Roberts v. United States Jaycees,* 468 U. S. 609, 622 (1984) ("An individual's freedom to speak, to worship, and to petition the government for the redress of grievances could not be vigorously protected from interference by the State [if] a correlative freedom to engage in group effort toward those ends were not also guaranteed").

The present case does not present such a hybrid situation, but a free exercise claim unconnected with any communicative activity or parental right. Respondents urge us to hold, quite simply, that when otherwise prohibitable conduct is accompanied by religious convictions, not only the convictions but the conduct itself must be free from governmental regulation. We have never held that, and decline to do so now. There being no contention that Oregon's drug law represents an attempt to regulate religious beliefs, the communication of religious beliefs, or the raising of one's children in those beliefs, the rule to which we have adhered ever since *Reynolds* plainly controls.

[. . .]

Values that are protected against government interference through enshrinement in the Bill of Rights are not thereby banished from the political process. Just as a society that believes in the negative protection accorded to the press by the First Amendment is likely to enact laws that affirmatively foster the dissemination of the printed word, so also a society that believes in the negative protection accorded to religious belief can be expected to be solicitous of that value in its legislation as well. It is therefore not surprising that a number of States have made an exception to their drug laws for sacramental peyote use. But to say that a nondiscriminatory religious-practice exemption is permitted, or even that it is desirable, is not to say that it is constitutionally required, and that the appropriate occasions for its creation can be discerned by the courts. It may fairly be said that leaving accommodation to the political process will place at a relative disadvantage those religious practices that are not widely engaged in; but that unavoidable consequence of democratic government must be preferred to a system in which each conscience is a law unto itself or in which judges weigh the social importance of all laws against the centrality of all religious beliefs.

* * *

Because respondents' ingestion of peyote was prohibited under Oregon law, and because that prohibition is constitutional, Oregon may, consistent with the Free Exercise Clause, deny respondents unemployment compensation when their dismissal results from use of the drug. The decision of the Oregon Supreme Court is accordingly reversed.

It is so ordered.

Source

Employment Division v. Smith, 494 U.S. 872 (1990).

Further Reading

Flowers, Ronald B. *That Godless Court? Supreme Court Decisions on Church-State Relationships.* 2nd ed. Louisville: Westminster John Knox Press, 2005.

Sullivan, Winnifred Fallers. *The Impossibility of Religious Freedom.* Princeton: Princeton University Press, 2005.

Global Religion, Global Politics

For historians, the very recent past is often the period of time most resistant to analysis. We are still too close, too fully enmeshed in the events of the last few decades to know what is truly significant and what is merely a passing fad. In many ways, the concerns that appear throughout this book continue to resonate in the twenty-first century. Courts and legislatures struggle to define the First Amendment's protection of the "free exercise of religion." Americans continue to look to their faith traditions for guidance on thorny conundrums of war, race, and sexuality. Interest groups across the political spectrum assert the nation's religious or secular character and try to specify what that would mean.

Two newly prevalent issues have emphasized the global dimensions of these themes. One is the role of Islam in American religion and politics. Although the Muslim faith had been a subject of American political discourse at least since the 1979 Iranian Revolution, it moved to the forefront after the terrorist attacks by al Qaeda on September 11, 2001. Americans considered Islam at several levels: in part as a military question (how could the United States defeat Muslim terrorist groups such as al Qaeda and ISIS?), in part as an international political question (was Islam compatible with democratic government?), and in part as a question of diversity at home (where did Muslim citizens fit in the American religious mosaic?).

Another new area of focus is on ecology and the environment. This trend, too, has a longer history going back to the environmental movement of the 1970s, but it has broadened and accelerated since then, especially with accumulating scientific evidence of climate change. Environmental problems upend the usual ways of thinking about politics that privilege humans and nations, while also challenging theologies that posit a stark separation between spiritual and material realms. The debates over Islam and over environmental responsibility are just two examples of the ways that religion and politics continue to intersect in shaping the contours of twenty-first-century public life.

———

GEORGE W. BUSH,
"FREEDOM AT WAR WITH FEAR" (2001)

On September 11, 2001, terrorists associated with the radical Islamist group al Qaeda hijacked four airplanes. They flew two into the two towers of the World Trade Center in Manhattan and one into the Pentagon building outside Washington, DC (the fourth plane crashed in rural Pennsylvania). This attack, coordinated by al Qaeda leader Osama bin Laden, was an unprecedented domestic calamity that killed nearly 3,000 people. These events came to be known as 9/11, and soon led to the wide-ranging War on Terror that included American military operations in Afghanistan and Iraq, a vast expansion of government techniques of security and surveillance, and ideological conflicts over the limits of freedom and toleration.

"Freedom at War with Fear," excerpted here, was the first extended reflection on 9/11 delivered by President George W. Bush (b. 1946). In reading the speech, one must imagine a nation still shocked and confused by the devastation that had occurred only nine days earlier. Bush tries to frame these inexplicable events and to suggest how Americans might come to terms with them, individually and collectively. Two influences in particular shaped the president's remarks. The first was the outlook of neoconservatives such as speechwriter Michael Gerson (who penned much of Bush's address), Vice President Richard Cheney, and Defense Secretary Donald Rumsfeld. These influential advisers advocated an aggressive use of American military might against suspected terrorists and the nations that harbored them. The second was the power of a dualistic evangelical worldview. The president had often described how Jesus Christ turned his life around by saving him from his alcoholism. In some ways his address after 9/11 invokes that same sense of stark alternatives: freedom versus fear, us versus the terrorists. Those opposite poles, the speech suggests, are not mere political choices but part of a larger cosmic order ("God is not neutral").

Religion comes into the speech in another way, in the rhetorical inclusion of Islam in the nation's religious landscape. Anti-Muslim sentiment in America rose precipitously after the hijackings and threatened the sense of national unity that Bush sought to nurture. The president's address therefore insists on the legitimacy of Islam as part of a diverse American culture. In some ways, a vision of Christians, Jews, and Muslims under the protection of a common God invokes the irenic "tri-faith" spirit of the 1940s, though at that earlier moment the three faiths were Protestants, Catholics, and Jews. Things changed quickly in the months and years after this speech, but to a remarkable degree it laid out the debates over religion, politics, and American values that would define the Bush-era War on Terror.

George W. Bush, "Freedom at War with Fear"

Mr. Speaker, Mr. President Pro Tempore, members of Congress, and fellow Americans:

In the normal course of events, Presidents come to this chamber to report on the state of the Union. Tonight, no such report is needed. It has already been delivered by the American people.

We have seen it in the courage of passengers, who rushed terrorists to save others on the ground—passengers like an exceptional man named Todd Beamer. And would you please help me to welcome his wife, Lisa Beamer, here tonight. (Applause.)

We have seen the state of our Union in the endurance of rescuers, working past exhaustion. We have seen the unfurling of flags, the lighting of candles, the giving of blood, the saying of prayers—in English, Hebrew, and Arabic. We have seen the decency of a loving and giving people who have made the grief of strangers their own.

My fellow citizens, for the last nine days, the entire world has seen for itself the state of our Union—and it is strong. (Applause.)

Tonight we are a country awakened to danger and called to defend freedom. Our grief has turned to anger, and anger to resolution. Whether we bring our enemies to justice, or bring justice to our enemies, justice will be done. (Applause.)

I thank the Congress for its leadership at such an important time. All of America was touched on the evening of the tragedy to see Republicans and Democrats joined together on the steps of this Capitol, singing "God Bless America." And you did more than sing; you acted, by delivering $40 billion to rebuild our communities and meet the needs of our military.

Speaker Hastert, Minority Leader Gephardt, Majority Leader Daschle and Senator Lott, I thank you for your friendship, for your leadership and for your service to our country. (Applause.)

And on behalf of the American people, I thank the world for its outpouring of support. America will never forget the sounds of our National Anthem playing at Buckingham Palace, on the streets of Paris, and at Berlin's Brandenburg Gate.

We will not forget South Korean children gathering to pray outside our embassy in Seoul, or the prayers of sympathy offered at a mosque in Cairo. We will not forget moments of silence and days of mourning in Australia and Africa and Latin America.

Nor will we forget the citizens of 80 other nations who died with our own: dozens of Pakistanis; more than 130 Israelis; more than 250 citizens of India; men and women from El Salvador, Iran, Mexico and Japan; and hundreds of British citizens. America has no truer friend than Great Britain. (Applause.) Once again, we are joined together in a great cause—so honored the British Prime Minister has crossed an ocean to show his unity of purpose with America. Thank you for coming, friend. (Applause.)

On September the 11th, enemies of freedom committed an act of war against our country. Americans have known wars—but for the past 136 years, they have been wars on foreign soil, except for one Sunday in 1941. Americans have known the casualties of war—but not at the center of a great city on a peaceful morning. Americans have known surprise attacks—but never before on thousands of civilians. All of this was brought upon us in a single day—and night fell on a different world, a world where freedom itself is under attack.

Americans have many questions tonight. Americans are asking: Who attacked our country? The evidence we have gathered all points to a collection of loosely affiliated terrorist organizations known as al Qaeda. They are the same murderers indicted for bombing American embassies in Tanzania and Kenya, and responsible for bombing the USS Cole.

Al Qaeda is to terror what the mafia is to crime. But its goal is not making money; its goal is remaking the world—and imposing its radical beliefs on people everywhere.

The terrorists practice a fringe form of Islamic extremism that has been rejected by Muslim scholars and the vast majority of Muslim clerics—a fringe movement that perverts the peaceful teachings of Islam. The terrorists' directive commands them to kill Christians and Jews, to kill all Americans, and make no distinction among military and civilians, including women and children.

This group and its leader—a person named Osama bin Laden—are linked to many other organizations in different countries, including the Egyptian Islamic Jihad and the Islamic Movement of Uzbekistan. There are thousands of these terrorists in more than 60 countries. They are recruited from their own nations and neighborhoods and brought to camps in places like Afghanistan, where they are trained in the tactics of terror. They are sent back to their homes or sent to hide in countries around the world to plot evil and destruction.

The leadership of al Qaeda has great influence in Afghanistan and supports the Taliban regime in controlling most of that country. In Afghanistan, we see al Qaeda's vision for the world.

Afghanistan's people have been brutalized—many are starving and many have fled. Women are not allowed to attend school. You can be jailed for owning a television. Religion can be practiced only as their leaders dictate. A man can be jailed in Afghanistan if his beard is not long enough.

The United States respects the people of Afghanistan—after all, we are currently its largest source of humanitarian aid—but we condemn the Taliban regime. (Applause.) It is not only repressing its own people, it is threatening people everywhere by sponsoring and sheltering and supplying terrorists. By aiding and abetting murder, the Taliban regime is committing murder.

And tonight, the United States of America makes the following demands on the Taliban: Deliver to United States authorities all the leaders of al Qaeda who hide in your land. (Applause.) Release all foreign nationals, including American citizens, you have unjustly imprisoned. Protect foreign journalists, diplomats and aid workers in your country. Close immediately and permanently every terrorist training camp in Afghanistan, and hand over every terrorist, and every person in their support structure, to appropriate authorities. (Applause.) Give the United States full access to terrorist training camps, so we can make sure they are no longer operating.

These demands are not open to negotiation or discussion. (Applause.) The Taliban must act, and act immediately. They will hand over the terrorists, or they will share in their fate.

I also want to speak tonight directly to Muslims throughout the world. We respect your faith. It's practiced freely by many millions of Americans, and by millions more in countries that America counts as friends. Its teachings are good and peaceful, and those who commit evil in the name of Allah blaspheme the name of Allah. (Applause.) The terrorists are traitors to their own faith, trying, in effect, to hijack Islam itself. The enemy of America is not our many Muslim friends; it is not our many Arab friends. Our enemy is a radical network of terrorists, and every government that supports them. (Applause.)

Our war on terror begins with al Qaeda, but it does not end there. It will not end until every terrorist group of global reach has been found, stopped and defeated. (Applause.)

Americans are asking, why do they hate us? They hate what we see right here in this chamber—a democratically elected government. Their leaders are self-appointed. They hate our freedoms—our freedom of religion, our freedom of speech, our freedom to vote and assemble and disagree with each other.

They want to overthrow existing governments in many Muslim countries, such as Egypt, Saudi Arabia, and Jordan. They want to drive Israel out of the Middle East. They want to drive Christians and Jews out of vast regions of Asia and Africa.

These terrorists kill not merely to end lives, but to disrupt and end a way of life. With every atrocity, they hope that America grows fearful, retreating from the world and forsaking our friends. They stand against us, because we stand in their way.

We are not deceived by their pretenses to piety. We have seen their kind before. They are the heirs of all the murderous ideologies of the 20th century. By sacrificing human life to serve their radical visions—by abandoning every value except the will to power—they follow in the path of fascism, and Nazism, and totalitarianism. And they will follow that path all the way, to where it ends: in history's unmarked grave of discarded lies. (Applause.)

[. . .]

The course of this conflict is not known, yet its outcome is certain. Freedom and fear, justice and cruelty, have always been at war, and we know that God is not neutral between them. (Applause.)

Fellow citizens, we'll meet violence with patient justice—assured of the rightness of our cause, and confident of the victories to come. In all that lies before us, may God grant us wisdom, and may He watch over the United States of America.

Thank you. (Applause.)

Source

George W. Bush, "Address to a Joint Session of Congress and the American People," September 20, 2001. http://georgewbush-whitehouse.archives.gov/news/releases/2001/09/20010920–8.html

Further Reading

Anker, Elisabeth R. *Orgies of Feeling: Melodrama and the Politics of Freedom.* Durham, NC: Duke University Press, 2014.

Asad, Talal. *On Suicide Bombing.* New York: Columbia University Press, 2007.

Heilbrunn, Jacob. *They Knew They Were Right: The Rise of the Neocons.* New York: Anchor, 2008.

INGRID MATTSON, "AMERICAN MUSLIMS HAVE A 'SPECIAL OBLIGATION'" (2001)

Muslims' presence in America goes back hundreds of years. Recently, scholars have unearthed evidence that some of the slaves brought to the New World practiced Islam, though little trace of that tradition remains. Throughout the twentieth century, a trickle of Muslim immigrants came from Europe, the Middle East, and India, whether for economic opportunity or to escape political unrest. This early immigration, however, was minuscule in comparison to the Muslim presence since the 1960s. The liberalization of immigration law in 1965, combined with roiling upheavals in many Muslim countries, has led to substantial numbers of new arrivals in the United States. Most American practitioners of Islam come from South Asia and Iran.

Alongside this immigration is an African American tradition that began as an unorthodox sect called the Nation of Islam (NOI), led by Elijah Muhammad and counting Malcolm X and Muhammad Ali among its adherents. Over time, the group chose to drop the NOI label and move closer to mainstream Islamic doctrine, thereby adding an African American presence to America's mosques (meanwhile, Louis Farrakhan carried on Elijah Muhammad's more idiosyncratic teachings in a revived Nation of Islam).

The attacks of September 11, committed by terrorists claiming to act in the name of Islam, brought new attention to the religion. American Muslims faced verbal hostility and sometimes physical violence, but many bravely insisted on the compatibility of their faith with the nation's values. Here Ingrid Mattson (b. 1963), a Muslim religious activist, professor, and sometime presidential adviser, articulates her sense of unease with the dualistic public discourse advanced by George W. Bush and other political and religious leaders.

Ingrid Mattson, "American Muslims Have a 'Special Obligation'"

The terrorist attack on September 11th exacerbated a double-bind American Muslims have been feeling for some time. So often, it seems, we have to apologize for reprehensible actions committed by Muslims in the name of Islam. We tell other Americans, "People who do these things (oppression of women, persecution of religious minorities, terrorism) have distorted the 'true' Islam."

And so often we have to tell other Muslims throughout the world that America is not as bad as it appears. We say, "These policies (support for oppressive governments, enforcement of sanctions responsible for the deaths of almost 1 million Iraqi children, vetoing any criticism of Israel at the United Nations) contradict the 'true' values of America."

But frankly, American Muslims have generally been more critical of injustices committed by the American government than of injustices committed by Muslims. This has to change.

For the last few years, I have been speaking publicly in Muslim forums against the injustice of the Taliban. This criticism of a self-styled Muslim regime has not always been well received. Some Muslims have felt that public criticism of the Taliban harms Muslim solidarity. Others have questioned my motives, suggesting that I am more interested in serving a feminist agenda than an Islamic one. My answer to the apologists has always been—who has the greatest duty to stop the oppression of Muslims committed by other Muslims in the name of Islam? The answer, obviously, is Muslims.

I have not previously spoken about suicide attacks committed by Muslims in the name of Islam. I did not avoid the subject—it simply did not cross my mind as a priority among the many issues I felt needed to be addressed. This was a gross oversight. I should have asked myself, Who has the greatest duty to stop violence committed by Muslims against innocent non-Muslims in the name of Islam? The answer, obviously, is Muslims.

American Muslims, in particular, have a great responsibility to speak out. The freedom, stability, and strong moral foundation of the United States are great blessings for all Americans, particularly for Muslims.

Moreover, we do not have cultural restrictions that Muslims in some other countries have. In America, Muslim women have found the support and freedom to reclaim their proper place in the life of their religious community. And Muslims have pushed and been allowed to democratize their governing bodies. Important decisions, even relating to theological and legal matters, are increasingly made in mosques and Islamic organizations by elected boards or the collective membership.

But God has not blessed us with these things because we are better than the billions of humans who do not live in America. We do not deserve good health, stable families, safety and freedom more than the millions of Muslims and non-Muslims throughout the world who are suffering from disease, poverty, and oppression.

Muslims who live in America are being tested by God to see if we will be satisfied with a self-contained, self-serving Muslim community that resembles an Islamic town in the Epcot global village, or if we will use the many opportunities available to us to change the world for the better— beginning with an honest critical evaluation of our own flaws.

Because we have freedom and wealth, we have a special obligation to help those Muslims who do not—by speaking out against the abuses of Muslim "leaders" in other countries.

In his speech to the nation, President Bush argued that American Muslim leaders and other moderates represent the true voice of Islam. This is true, and we therefore need to raise our voices louder.

So let me state it clearly: I, as an American Muslim leader, denounce not only suicide bombers and the Taliban, but those leaders of other Muslim states who thwart democracy, repress women, use the Qur'an to justify un-Islamic behavior and encourage violence. Alas, these views are not only the province of a small group of terrorists or dictators. Too many rank-and-file Muslims, in their isolation and pessimism, have come to hold these self-destructive views as well.

The problem is that other Muslims may not listen to us, no matter how loud our voices. Surely President Bush wants the moderate voices not only to be raised, but to be heard. American Muslim leaders will be heard only if they are recognized as authentic interpreters of Islam among the global community. This will be very difficult to achieve, because our legitimacy in the Muslim world is intimately linked with American foreign policy. An understanding of some important developments in Islamic history and theology will clarify this apparently odd dependence.

According to Islamic doctrine, after the death of the Prophet Muhammad, no Muslim has the right to claim infallibility in interpreting the faith. There is no ordination, no clergy, no unquestioned authority. This does not mean that all opinions are equal, nor that everyone has the ability to interpret religious and legal doctrine. Solid scholarship and a deep understanding of the tradition are essential. But not all scholars are considered authoritative. Most Muslims will accept the opinions only of scholars who demonstrate that they are truly concerned about the welfare of ordinary people. People simply will not listen to scholars who seem to be mostly interested in serving the interests of the government.

Throughout Muslim history, religious leaders who advocated aggression against the state were usually marginalized. After all, most Muslims did not want to be led into revolution—they simply wanted their lives to be better. The most successful religious leaders were those who, in addition to serving the spiritual needs of the community, acted as intermediaries between the people and state. There have been times, however, when hostile forces attacked or occupied Muslim lands—for example, the Mongol invasions, (Christian) Crusades, European colonialism, and the Soviet invasion of Afghanistan. At those times, people needed revolutionary leaders; those who were unable to unite the people against aggression were irrelevant.

The question we need to ask is, at this point in history, what do Muslims need to hear from their leaders? What voices will they listen to?

In the midst of a global crisis, it seems that American Muslims are being asked to choose between uncritical support for rebels acting in the name of Islam, and uncritical support for any actions taken by the American government. Osama bin Laden has divided the world into two camps: those who oppose the oppression of the Muslim people, and those who aid in that oppression. President Bush has divided the world into two camps: those who support terrorism, and those who fight terrorism.

Where does this leave American Muslim leaders who oppose the oppression of the Muslim people and who want to fight terrorism? In the increasingly strident rhetoric of this war, we may be considered traitors by both sides.

Nevertheless, we must continue to speak. We have to speak against oppressive interpretations of Islam and against emotional, superficial, and violent apocalyptic depictions of a world divided. And in our desire to show ourselves to be patriotic Americans, we cannot suppress our criticisms of the United States when we have them.

We have to do this, not only because it is the right thing to do, but also because if we do not, the Muslim world will remain deaf to our arguments that peaceful change is possible, and that revolt and ensuing lawlessness almost always cause the greatest harm to the people.

It is in the best interest of the United States that we be permitted to continue to speak. In many parts of the world, those who speak out against corruption and unfair government policies are jailed, tortured, and killed. In such circumstances, very few people—only those who are willing to risk losing their property, their families, their security, and their lives—will continue to speak out. Only the radicals will remain.

Source

Ingrid Mattson, "American Muslims Have a 'Special Obligation,'" http://ingrid mattson.org/article/american-muslims-have-a-special-obligation/. Used by permission of Ingrid Mattson.

Further Reading

Alsultany, Evelyn. *Arabs and Muslims in the Media: Race and Representation after 9/11*. New York: New York University Press, 2012.

Curtis, Edward E., IV. *Muslims in America: A Short History*. New York: Oxford University Press, 2009.

GhaneaBassiri, Kambiz. *A History of Islam in America*. New York: Cambridge University Press, 2010.

SAM HARRIS,
THE END OF FAITH (2004)

In the mid-2000s a flurry of best-selling books launched a vigorous assault on religion and its adherents. Most prominent among these polemics were Sam Harris's *The End of Faith* (excerpted here), Daniel Dennett's *Breaking the Spell*, Richard Dawkins's *The God Delusion*, and Christopher Hitchens's *God Is Not Great*. The authors of these texts, collectively dubbed the New Atheists, billed themselves as the defenders of reason and science against the dangerous irrationality of faith.

Unbelief and antireligious sentiment have long histories in American culture, as shown in the Stanton reading in this volume. However, some recent shifts have revitalized the tradition. The New Atheism was in part a reaction to the events of September 11 and the rise of radical Islam, which offered horrific evidence of religion's capacity for violence. Harris and his fellow unbelievers were also responding critically to the continuing power of conservative evangelicalism in the public sphere. Finally, the New Atheism developed amid increasing numbers of so-called nones, that is, those Americans who identify their religious affiliation as "none." Though few of the nones are militant atheists, their prevalence helped produce a climate in which New Atheist ideas could flourish.

More than most New Atheists, Sam Harris (b. 1967) criticizes moderate religion along with fundamentalist or extremist varieties, a marked contrast with the approaches of believers Bush or Mattson elsewhere in this section. Indeed, critics have accused Harris of demonizing his religious opponents and creating an atheism just as closed-minded and judgmental as the spiritual fanaticism he deplores. Regardless of the real or perceived flaws in his ideas, the New Atheists' prominence in contemporary intellectual culture shows that while many Americans find meaning in practicing religion, others find meaning in rejecting it.

Sam Harris, *The End of Faith*

The idea that any one of our religions represents the infallible word of the One True God requires an encyclopedic ignorance of history, mythology, and art even to be entertained—as the beliefs, rituals, and iconography of each of our religions attest to centuries of cross-pollination among them. Whatever their imagined source, the doctrines of modern religions are no more tenable than those which, for lack of adherents, were cast upon the scrap heap of mythology millennia ago; for there is no more evidence to justify a belief in the literal existence of Yahweh and Satan than there was to keep Zeus perched upon his mountain throne or Poseidon churning the seas.

According to Gallup, 35 percent of Americans believe that the Bible is the literal and inerrant word of the Creator of the universe. Another 48 percent believe that it is the "inspired" word of the same—still inerrant, though certain of its passages must be interpreted symbolically before their truth can be brought to light. Only 17 percent of us remain to doubt that a personal God, in his infinite wisdom, is likely to have authored this text—or, for that matter, to have created the earth with its 250,000 species of beetles. Some 46 percent of Americans take a literalist view of creation (40 percent believe that God has guided creation over the course of millions of years). This means that 120 million of us place the big bang 2,500 years *after* the Babylonians and Sumerians learned to brew beer. If our polls are to be trusted, nearly 230 million Americans believe that a book showing neither unity of style nor internal consistency was authored by an omniscient, omnipotent and omnipresent deity.

A survey of Hindus, Muslims, and Jews around the world would surely yield similar results, revealing that we, as a species, have grown almost perfectly intoxicated by our myths. How is it that, in this one area of our lives, we have convinced ourselves that our beliefs about the world can float entirely free of reason and evidence?

It is with respect to this rather surprising cognitive scenery that we must decide what it means to be a religious "moderate" in the twenty-first century. Moderates in every faith are obliged to loosely interpret (or simply ignore) much of their canons in the interests of living in the modern world. No doubt an obscure truth of economics is at work here: societies appear to become considerably less productive whenever large numbers of people stop making widgets and begin killing their customers and creditors for heresy. The first thing to observe about the moderate's retreat from scriptural literalism is that it draws its inspiration not from scripture but from cultural developments that have rendered many of God's utterances difficult to accept as written. In America, religious moderation is further enforced by the fact that most Christians and Jews do not read the Bible in its entirety and consequently have no idea just how vigorously the God of Abraham wants heresy expunged. One look at the book of Deuteronomy reveals that he has something very specific in mind should your son or daughter return from yoga class advocating the worship of Krishna:

> If your brother, the son of your father or of your mother, or your son or daughter, or the spouse whom you embrace, or your most intimate friend, tries to secretly seduce you, saying, "Let us go and serve other gods," unknown to you or your ancestors before you, gods of the peoples surrounding you, whether near you or far away, anywhere throughout the world, you must not consent, you must not listen to him; you must show him no pity, you must not spare him or conceal his guilt. No, you must kill him, your hand must strike the first blow in putting him to death and the hands of the rest of the people following. You must stone him to death, since he has tried to divert you from Yahweh your God. . . . (Deuteronomy 13:7–11)

While the stoning of children for heresy has fallen out of fashion in our country, you will not hear a moderate Christian or Jew arguing for a "symbolic" reading of passages of this sort. (In fact, one seems to be explicitly blocked by God himself in Deuteronomy 13:1—"Whatever I am now commanding you, you must keep and observe, adding nothing to it, taking nothing away.") The above passage is as canonical as any in the Bible, and it is only by ignoring such barbarisms that the Good Book can be reconciled with life in the modern world. This is a problem for "moderation" in religion: it has nothing underwriting it other than the unacknowledged neglect of the letter of the divine law.

The only reason anyone is "moderate" in matters of faith these days is that he has assimilated some of the fruits of the last two thousand years of human thought (democratic politics, scientific advancement on every front, concern for human rights, an end to cultural and geographic isolation, etc.). The doors leading out of scriptural literalism do not open from the *inside*. The moderation we see among nonfundamentalists is not some sign that faith itself has evolved; it is, rather, the product of the many hammer blows of modernity that have exposed certain tenets of faith to doubt. Not the least among these developments has been the emergence of our tendency to value evidence and to be convinced by a proposition to the degree that there is evidence for it. Even most fundamentalists live by the lights of reason in this regard; it is just that their minds seem to have been partitioned to accommodate the profligate truth claims of their faith. Tell a devout Christian that his wife is cheating on him, or that frozen yogurt can make a man invisible, and he is likely to require as much evidence as anyone else, and to be persuaded only to the extent that you give it. Tell him that the book he keeps by his bed was written by an invisible deity who will punish him with fire for eternity if he fails to accept its every incredible claim about the universe, and he seems to require no evidence whatsoever.

Religious moderation springs from the fact that even the least educated person among us simply *knows* more about certain matters than anyone did two thousand years ago—and much of this knowledge is incompatible with scripture. Having heard something about the medical discoveries of the last hundred years, most of us no longer equate disease processes with sin or demonic possession. Having learned about the known distances between objects in our universe, most of us (about half of us, actually) find the idea that the whole works was created six thousand years ago (with light from distant stars already in transit toward the earth) impossible to take seriously. Such concessions to modernity do not in the least suggest that faith is compatible with reason, or that our religious traditions are in principle open to new learning: it is just that the utility of ignoring (or "reinterpreting") certain articles of faith is now overwhelming. Anyone being flown to a distant city for heart-bypass surgery has conceded, tacitly at least, that we have learned a few things about physics, geography, engineering, and medicine since the time of Moses.

So it is not that these texts have maintained their integrity over time (they haven't); it is just that they have been effectively edited by our neglect of certain of their passages. Most of what remains—the "good parts"—has been spared the same winnowing because we do not yet have a truly modern understanding of our ethical intuitions and our capacity for spiritual experience. If we better understood the workings of the human brain, we would undoubtedly discover lawful connections between our states of consciousness, our modes of conduct, and the various ways we use our attention. What makes one person happier than another?

Why is love more conducive to happiness than hate? Why do we generally prefer beauty to ugliness and order to chaos? Why does it feel so good to smile and laugh, and why do these shared experiences generally bring people closer together? Is the ego an illusion, and, if so, what implications does this have for human life? Is there life after death? These are ultimately questions for a mature science of the mind. If we ever develop such a science, most of our religious texts will be no more useful to mystics than they now are to astronomers.

While moderation in religion may seem a reasonable position to stake out, in light of all that we have (and have not) learned about the universe, it offers no bulwark against religious extremism and religious violence. From the perspective of those seeking to live by the letter of the texts, the religious moderate is nothing more than a failed fundamentalist. He is, in all likelihood, going to wind up in hell with the rest of the unbelievers. The problem that religious moderation poses for all of us is that it does not permit anything very critical to be said about religious literalism. We cannot say that fundamentalists are crazy, because they are merely practicing their freedom of belief; we cannot even say that they are mistaken in *religious* terms, because their knowledge of scripture is generally unrivaled. All we can say, as religious moderates, is that we don't like the personal and social costs that a full embrace of scripture imposes on us. This is not a new form of faith, or even a new species of scriptural exegesis; it is simply a capitulation to a variety of all-too-human interests that have nothing, in principle, to do with God. Religious moderation is the product of *secular* knowledge and scriptural *ignorance*—and it has no bona fides, in religious terms, to put it on a par with fundamentalism. The texts themselves are unequivocal: they are perfect in all their parts. By their light, religious moderation appears to be nothing more than an unwillingness to fully submit to God's law. By failing to live by the letter of the texts, while tolerating the irrationality of those who do, religious moderates betray faith and reason equally. Unless the core dogmas of faith are called into question—i.e., that we know there is a God, and that we know what he wants from us—religious moderation will do nothing to lead us out of the wilderness.

The benignity of most religious moderates does not suggest that religious faith is anything more sublime than a desperate marriage of hope and ignorance, nor does it guarantee that there is not a terrible price to be paid for limiting the scope of reason in our dealings with other human beings. Religious moderation, insofar as it represents an attempt to hold on to what is still serviceable in orthodox religion, closes the door to more sophisticated approaches to spirituality, ethics, and the building of strong communities. Religious moderates seem to believe that what we need is not radical insight and innovation in these areas but a mere dilution of Iron Age philosophy. Rather than bring the full force of our creativity and rationality to bear on the problems of ethics, social cohesion, and even spiritual experience, moderates merely ask that we relax our standards of adherence to ancient superstitions and taboos, while otherwise maintaining a belief system that was passed down to us from men and women whose lives were simply ravaged by their basic ignorance about the world. In what other sphere of life is such subservience to tradition acceptable? Medicine? Engineering? Not even politics suffers the anachronism that still dominates our thinking about ethical values and spiritual experience.

Imagine that we could revive a well-educated Christian of the fourteenth century. The man would prove to be a total ignoramus, except on matters of faith. His beliefs about geography, astronomy, and medicine would embarrass even a child, but he would know more or less everything there is to know about God. Though he would be considered a fool to think that the earth is flat, or that trepanning[1] constitutes a wise medical intervention, his religious ideas would still be beyond reproach. There are two explanations for this: either we perfected our religious understanding of the world a millennium ago—while our knowledge on all other fronts was still hopelessly inchoate—or religion, being the mere maintenance of dogma, is one area of discourse that does not admit of progress. We will see that there is much to recommend the latter view.

With each passing year, do our religious beliefs conserve more and more of the data of human experience? If religion addresses a genuine sphere of understanding and human necessity, then it should be susceptible to *progress;* its doctrines should become more useful, rather than less. Progress in religion, as in other fields, would have to be a matter of *present* inquiry, not the mere reiteration of past doctrine. Whatever is true now should be *discoverable* now, and describable in terms that are not an outright affront to the rest of what we know about the world. By this measure, the entire project of religion seems perfectly backward. It cannot survive the changes that have come over us—culturally, technologically, and even ethically. Otherwise, there are few reasons to believe that we will survive *it.*

Moderates do not want to kill anyone in the name of God, but they want us to keep using the word "God" as though we knew what we were talking about. And they do not want anything too critical said about people who *really* believe in the God of their fathers, because tolerance, perhaps above all else, is sacred. To speak plainly and truthfully about the state of our world—to say, for instance, that the Bible and the Koran both

---

1. Trepanning (or trephining) is the practice of boring holes in the human skull. Archaeological evidence suggests that it is one of the oldest surgical procedures. It was presumably performed on epileptics and the mentally ill as an attempt at exorcism. While there are still many reasons to open a person's skull nowadays, the hope that an evil spirit will use the hole as a point of egress is not among them.

contain mountains of life-destroying gibberish—is antithetical to tolerance as moderates currently conceive it. But we can no longer afford the
luxury of such political correctness. We must finally recognize the price
we are paying to maintain the iconography of our ignorance.

Source

Sam Harris, *The End of Faith* (New York: Norton, 2004), 16–23. Copyright ©
  2004 by Sam Harris. Used by permission of W. W. Norton & Company, Inc.

Further Reading

Cimino, Richard, and Christopher Smith. *Atheist Awakening: Secular Activism
  and Community in America.* New York: Oxford University Press, 2014.
Pew Research Center. "America's Changing Religious Landscape." May 12, 2015.
  http://www.pewforum.org/2015/05/12/americas-changing-religious-land
  scape/. Accessed July 6, 2015.

WENDELL BERRY,
"FAUSTIAN ECONOMICS" (2008)

Since the 1970s, the environmental movement and a series of ecological crises have brought concerns about the natural world into
American political discourse. In 2005, the effects of Hurricane Ka-
trina on the Gulf Coast showed how socially produced inequality
could exacerbate natural disasters. In 2010, the *Deepwater Horizon*
oil spill produced an extended debate about the public responsibilities
of multinational corporations. Looming largest in the early twenty-
first century is the problem of climate change, which most scientists
believe has been dangerously accelerated by the use of fossil fuels.

At one level, environmental politics centers on material things, such
as trees and coal and electric cars. Americans have, however, also understood their relationship to the natural world in theological terms.
So it was that Oklahoma senator James Inhofe denied the very possibility of human-induced climate change, stating that regardless of
the activities of mere mortals, "God is still up there, and He promised
to maintain the seasons." Conversely, climate change activists such as
Bill McKibben have insisted on the responsibility of Christians to care
for God's creation by enacting better environmental policies.

The Kentucky writer and farmer Wendell Berry (b. 1934) has been
one of the leading critics of capitalism and its ecological consequences.
Berry's outlook, often called agrarian, takes local communities and
small-scale agriculture as the virtuous heart of American life. His politics are somewhat difficult to map on a liberal-conservative spectrum:
his environmentalism and opposition to war ally him with the left,
while his defenses of family and tradition sometimes sound like those

of partisans on the right. As for religion, Berry discusses it mostly as a repository of ethical and cultural wisdom. In this essay, he defends the Christian focus on human limits and discusses the implications of those limits for our political choices about Earth's future.

Wendell Berry, "Faustian Economics"

The general reaction to the apparent end of the era of cheap fossil fuel, as to other readily foreseeable curtailments, has been to delay any sort of reckoning. The strategies of delay, so far, have been a sort of willed oblivion, or visions of large profits to the manufacturers of such "bio-fuels" as ethanol from corn or switchgrass, or the familiar unscientific faith that "science will find an answer." The dominant response, in short, is a dogged belief that what we call the American Way of Life will prove somehow indestructible. We will keep on consuming, spending, wasting, and driving, as before, at any cost to anything and everybody but ourselves.

This belief was always indefensible—the real names of global warming are Waste and Greed—and by now it is manifestly foolish. But foolishness on this scale looks disturbingly like a sort of national insanity. We seem to have come to a collective delusion of grandeur, insisting that all of us are "free" to be as conspicuously greedy and wasteful as the most corrupt of kings and queens. (Perhaps by devoting more and more of our already abused cropland to fuel production we will at last cure ourselves of obesity and become fashionably skeletal, hungry but—thank God!— still driving.)

The problem with us is not only prodigal extravagance but also an assumed limitlessness. We have obscured the issue by refusing to see that limitlessness is a godly trait. We have insistently, and with relief, defined ourselves as animals or as "higher animals." But to define ourselves as animals, given our specifically human powers and desires, is to define ourselves as *limitless* animals—which of course is a contradiction in terms. Any definition is a limit, which is why the God of Exodus refuses to define Himself: "I am that I am."

Even so, that we have founded our present society upon delusional assumptions of limitlessness is easy enough to demonstrate. A recent "summit" in Louisville, Kentucky, was entitled "Unbridled Energy: The Industrialization of Kentucky's Energy Resources." Its subjects were "clean-coal generation, biofuels, and other cutting-edge applications," the conversion of coal to "liquid fuels," and the likelihood that all this will be "environmentally friendly." These hopes, which "can create jobs and boost the nation's security," are to be supported by government "loan guarantees . . . investment tax credits and other tax breaks." Such talk we recognize as completely conventional. It is, in fact, a tissue of clichés that is now the common tongue of promoters, politicians, and journalists. This language does not allow for any computation or speculation as to the *net* good of anything proposed. The entire contraption of "Unbridled Energy" is supported only by a rote optimism: "The United States has 250 billion tons of recoverable coal reserves—enough to last 100 years even at double the current rate of consumption." We humans have inhabited the earth for many thousands of years, and now we can look forward to surviving for another hundred by doubling our consumption of coal? *This* is national security? The world-ending fire of industrial fundamentalism may already be burning in our furnaces and engines, but if it will burn for a hundred more years, that will be fine. Surely it would be better to intend straightforwardly to contain the fire and eventually put it out! But once greed has been made an honorable motive, then you have an economy without limits. It has no place for temperance or thrift or the ecological law of return. It will do anything. It is monstrous by definition.

In keeping with our unrestrained consumptiveness, the commonly accepted basis of our economy is the supposed possibility of limitless growth, limitless wants, limitless wealth, limitless natural resources, limitless energy, and limitless debt. The idea of a limitless economy implies and requires a doctrine of general human limitlessness: *all* are entitled to pursue without limit whatever they conceive as desirable—a license that classifies the most exalted Christian capitalist with the lowliest pornographer.

This fantasy of limitlessness perhaps arose from the coincidence of the Industrial Revolution with the suddenly exploitable resources of the New World—though how the supposed limitlessness of resources can be reconciled with their exhaustion is not clear. Or perhaps it comes from the contrary apprehension of the world's "smallness," made possible by modern astronomy and high-speed transportation. Fear of the smallness of our world and its life may lead to a kind of claustrophobia and thence, with apparent reasonableness, to a desire for the "freedom" of limitlessness. But this desire, paradoxically, reduces everything. The life of this world is small to those who think it is, and the desire to enlarge it makes it smaller, and can reduce it finally to nothing.

However it came about, this credo of limitlessness clearly implies a principled wish not only for limitless possessions but also for limitless knowledge, limitless science, limitless technology, and limitless progress. And, necessarily, it must lead to limitless violence, waste, war, and destruction. That it should finally produce a crowning cult of political limitlessness is only a matter of mad logic.

The normalization of the doctrine of limitlessness has produced a sort of moral minimalism: the desire to be efficient at any cost, to be unencumbered by complexity. The minimization of neighborliness, respect, reverence, responsibility, accountability, and self-subordination—this is the culture of which our present leaders and heroes are the spoiled children.

Our national faith so far has been: "There's always more." Our true religion is a sort of autistic industrialism. People of intelligence and ability seem now to be genuinely embarrassed by any solution to any problem that does not involve high technology, a great expenditure of energy, or a big machine. Thus an X marked on a paper ballot no longer fulfills our idea of voting. One problem with this state of affairs is that the work now most needing to be done—that of neighborliness and caretaking—cannot be done by remote control with the greatest power on the largest scale. A second problem is that the economic fantasy of limitlessness in a limited world calls fearfully into question the value of our monetary wealth, which does not reliably stand for the real wealth of land, resources, and workmanship but instead wastes and depletes it.

That human limitlessness is a fantasy means, obviously, that its life expectancy is limited. There is now a growing perception, and not just among a few experts, that we are entering a time of inescapable limits. We are not likely to be granted another world to plunder in compensation for our pillage of this one. Nor are we likely to believe much longer in our ability to outsmart, by means of science and technology, our economic stupidity. The hope that we can cure the ills of industrialism by the homeopathy of more technology seems at last to be losing status. We are, in short, coming under pressure to understand ourselves as limited creatures in a limited world.

This constraint, however, is not the condemnation it may seem. On the contrary, it returns us to our real condition and to our human heritage, from which our self-definition as limitless animals has for too long cut us off. Every cultural and religious tradition that I know about, while fully acknowledging our animal nature, defines us specifically as *humans*— that is, as animals (if the word still applies) capable of living not only within natural limits but also within cultural limits, self-imposed. As earthly creatures, we live, because we must, within natural limits, which we may describe by such names as "earth" or "ecosystem" or "watershed" or "place." But as humans, we may elect to respond to this necessary placement by the self-restraints implied in neighborliness, stewardship, thrift, temperance, generosity, care, kindness, friendship, loyalty, and love.

In our limitless selfishness, we have tried to define "freedom," for example, as an escape from all restraint. But, as my friend Bert Hornback has explained in his book *The Wisdom in Words*, "free" is etymologically related to "friend." These words come from the same Indo-European root, which carries the sense of "dear" or "beloved." We set our friends free by our love for them, with the implied restraints of faithfulness or loyalty. And this suggests that our "identity" is located not in the impulse of selfhood but in deliberately maintained connections.

Thinking of our predicament has sent me back again to Christopher Marlowe's *Tragical History of Doctor Faustus*. This is a play of the Renaissance; Faustus, a man of learning, longs to possess "all Nature's treasury," to "Ransack the ocean . . . / And search all corners of the newfound world . . ." To assuage his thirst for knowledge and power, he deeds his soul to Lucifer, receiving in compensation for twenty-four years the services of the sub-devil Mephistophilis, nominally Faustus's slave but in fact his master. Having the subject of limitlessness in mind, I was astonished on this reading to come upon Mephistophilis's description of hell. When Faustus asks, "How comes it then that thou art out of hell?" Mephistophilis replies, "Why, this is hell, nor am I out of it." And a few pages later he explains:

> Hell hath no limits, nor is circumscribed
> In one self place, but where we [the damned] are is hell,
> And where hell is must we ever be.

For those who reject heaven, hell is everywhere, and thus is limitless. For them, even the thought of heaven is hell.

It is only appropriate, then, that Mephistophilis rejects any conventional limit: "Tut, Faustus, marriage is but a ceremonial toy. If thou lovest me, think no more of it." Continuing this theme, for Faustus's pleasure the devils present a sort of pageant of the seven deadly sins, three of which—Pride, Wrath, and Gluttony—describe themselves as orphans, disdaining the restraints of parental or filial love.

Seventy or so years later, and with the issue of the human definition more than ever in doubt, John Milton in Book VII of *Paradise Lost* returns again to a consideration of our urge to know. To Adam's request to be told the story of creation, the "affable Archangel" Raphael agrees "to answer thy desire / Of knowledge *within bounds* [my emphasis] . . . ," explaining that

> Knowledge is as food, and needs no less
> Her temperance over appetite, to know
> In measure what the mind may well contain;
> Oppresses else with surfeit, and soon turns
> Wisdom to folly, as nourishment to wind.

Raphael is saying, with angelic circumlocution, that knowledge without wisdom, limitless knowledge, is not worth a fart; he is not a humorless archangel. But he also is saying that knowledge without measure, knowledge that the human mind cannot appropriately use, is mortally dangerous.

I am well aware of what I risk in bringing this language of religion into what is normally a scientific discussion. I do so because I doubt that we can define our present problems adequately, let alone solve them, without some recourse to our cultural heritage. We are, after all, trying now to deal with the failure of scientists, technicians, and politicians to "think up" a version of human continuance that is economically probable and ecologically responsible, or perhaps even imaginable. If we go back into our tradition, we are going to find a concern with religion, which at a minimum shatters the selfish context of the individual life, and thus forces a consideration of what human beings are and ought to be.

This concern persists at least as late as our Declaration of Independence, which holds as "self-evident, that all men are created equal; that they are endowed by their Creator with certain unalienable rights . . ." Thus among our political roots we have still our old preoccupation with our definition as humans, which in the Declaration is wisely assigned to our Creator; our rights and the rights of all humans are not granted by any human government but are innate, belonging to us by birth. This insistence comes not from the fear of death or even extinction but from the ancient fear that in order to survive we might become inhuman or monstrous.

And so our cultural tradition is in large part the record of our continuing effort to understand ourselves as beings specifically human: to say that, as humans, we must do certain things and we must not do certain things. We must have limits or we will cease to exist as humans; perhaps we will cease to exist, period. At times, for example, some of us humans have thought that human beings, properly so called, did not make war against civilian populations, or hold prisoners without a fair trial, or use torture for any reason.

Some of us would-be humans have thought too that we should not be free at anybody else's expense. And yet in the phrase "free market," the word "free" has come to mean unlimited economic power for some, with the necessary consequence of economic powerlessness for others. Several years ago, after I had spoken at a meeting, two earnest and obviously troubled young veterinarians approached me with a question: How could they practice veterinary medicine without serious economic damage to the farmers who were their clients? Underlying their question was the fact that for a long time veterinary help for a sheep or a pig has been likely to cost more than the animal is worth. I had to answer that, in my opinion, so long as their practice relied heavily on selling patented drugs, they had no choice, since the market for medicinal drugs was entirely controlled by the drug companies, whereas most farmers had no control at all over the market for agricultural products. My questioners were asking in effect if a predatory economy can have a beneficent result. The answer too often is No. And that is because there is an absolute discontinuity between the economy of the seller of medicines and the economy of the buyer, as there is in the health industry as a whole. The drug industry is interested in the survival of patients, we have to suppose, because surviving patients will continue to consume drugs.

Now let us consider a contrary example. Recently, at another meeting, I talked for some time with an elderly, and some would say an old-fashioned, farmer from Nebraska. Unable to farm any longer himself, he had rented his land to a younger farmer on the basis of what he called "crop share" instead of a price paid or owed in advance. Thus, as the old farmer said of his renter, "If he has a good year, I have a good year. If he has a bad year, I have a bad one." This is what I would call community economics. It is a sharing of fate. It assures an economic continuity and a common interest between the two partners to the trade. This is as far as possible from the economy in which the young veterinarians were caught, in which the powerful are limitlessly "free" to trade, to the disadvantage, and ultimately the ruin, of the powerless.

It is this economy of community destruction that, wittingly or unwittingly, most scientists and technicians have served for the past two hundred years. These scientists and technicians have justified themselves by the proposition that they are the vanguard of progress, enlarging human knowledge and power, and thus they have romanticized both themselves and the predatory enterprises that they have served.

As a consequence, our great need now is for sciences and technologies of limits, of domesticity, of what Wes Jackson of the Land Institute in Salina, Kansas, has called "homecoming." These would be specifically human sciences and technologies, working, as the best humans always have worked, within self-imposed limits. The limits would be the accepted contexts of places, communities, and neighborhoods, both natural and human.

I know that the idea of such limitations will horrify some people, maybe most people, for we have long encouraged ourselves to feel at home on "the cutting edges" of knowledge and power or on some "frontier" of human experience. But I know too that we are talking now in the presence of much evidence that improvement by outward expansion may no longer be a good idea, if it ever was. It was not a good idea for the farmers who "leveraged" secure acreage to buy more during the 1970s. It has proved tragically to be a bad idea in a number of recent wars. If it is a good idea in the form of corporate gigantism, then we must ask, For whom? Faustus, who wants all knowledge and all the world for himself, is a man supremely lonely and finally doomed. I don't think Marlowe

was kidding. I don't think Satan is kidding when he says in *Paradise Lost,*
"Myself am Hell."

If the idea of appropriate limitation seems unacceptable to us, that
may be because, like Marlowe's Faustus and Milton's Satan, we confuse
limits with confinement. But that, as I think Marlowe and Milton and
others were trying to tell us, is a great and potentially a fatal mistake.
Satan's fault, as Milton understood it and perhaps with some sympathy,
was precisely that he could not tolerate his proper limitation; he could
not subordinate himself to anything whatever. Faustus's error was his
unwillingness to remain "Faustus, and a man." In our age of the world
it is not rare to find writers, critics, and teachers of literature, as well as
scientists and technicians, who regard Satan's and Faustus's defiance as
salutary and heroic.

On the contrary, our human and earthly limits, properly understood,
are not confinements but rather inducements to formal elaboration and
elegance, to *fullness* of relationship and meaning. Perhaps our most serious cultural loss in recent centuries is the knowledge that some things,
though limited, are inexhaustible. For example, an ecosystem, even that
of a working forest or farm, so long as it remains ecologically intact, is
inexhaustible. A small place, as I know from my own experience, can
provide opportunities of work and learning, and a fund of beauty, solace,
and pleasure—in addition to its difficulties—that cannot be exhausted in
a lifetime or in generations.

To recover from our disease of limitlessness, we will have to give up
the idea that we have a right to be godlike animals, that we are potentially omniscient and omnipotent, ready to discover "the secret of the universe." We will have to start over, with a different and much older premise: the naturalness and, for creatures of limited intelligence, the necessity,
of limits. We must learn again to ask how we can make the most of
what we are, what we have, what we have been given. If we always have
a theoretically better substitute available from somebody or someplace
else, we will never make the most of anything. It is hard to make the most
of one life. If we each had two lives, we would not make much of either.
Or as one of my best teachers said of people in general: "They'll never be
worth a damn as long as they've got two choices."

To deal with the problems, which after all are inescapable, of living
with limited intelligence in a limited world, I suggest that we may have
to remove some of the emphasis we have lately placed on science and
technology and have a new look at the arts. For an art does not propose
to enlarge itself by limitless extension but rather to enrich itself within
bounds that are accepted prior to the work.

It is the artists, not the scientists, who have dealt unremittingly with the
problem of limits. A painting, however large, must finally be bounded by

a frame or a wall. A composer or playwright must reckon, at a minimum, with the capacity of an audience to sit still and pay attention. A story, once begun, must end somewhere within the limits of the writer's and the reader's memory. And of course the arts characteristically impose limits that are artificial: the five acts of a play, or the fourteen lines of a sonnet. Within these limits artists achieve elaborations of pattern, of sustaining relationships of parts with one another and with the whole, that may be astonishingly complex. And probably most of us can name a painting, a piece of music, a poem or play or story that still grows in meaning and remains fresh after many years of familiarity.

We know by now that a natural ecosystem survives by the same sort of formal intricacy, ever-changing, inexhaustible, and no doubt finally unknowable. We know further that if we want to make our economic landscapes sustainably and abundantly productive, we must do so by maintaining in them a living formal complexity something like that of natural ecosystems. We can do this only by raising to the highest level our mastery of the arts of agriculture, animal husbandry, forestry, and, ultimately, the art of living.

It is true that insofar as scientific experiments must be conducted within carefully observed limits, scientists also are artists. But in science one experiment, whether it succeeds or fails, is logically followed by an-other in a theoretically infinite progression. According to the underlying myth of modern science, this progression is always replacing the smaller knowledge of the past with the larger knowledge of the present, which will be replaced by the yet larger knowledge of the future.

In the arts, by contrast, no limitless sequence of works is ever implied or looked for. No work of art is necessarily followed by a second work that is necessarily better. Given the methodologies of science, the law of gravity and the genome were bound to be discovered by somebody; the identity of the discoverer is incidental to the fact. But it appears that in the arts there are no second chances. We must assume that we had one chance each for *The Divine Comedy* and *King Lear*. If Dante and Shake-speare had died before they wrote those poems, nobody ever would have written them.

The same is true of our arts of land use, our economic arts, which are our arts of living. With these it is once-for-all. We will have no chance to redo our experiments with bad agriculture leading to soil loss. The Appalachian mountains and forests we have destroyed for coal are gone forever. It is now and forevermore too late to use thriftily the first half of the world's supply of petroleum. In the art of living we can only start again with what remains.

And so, in confronting the phenomenon of "peak oil," we are really confronting the end of our customary delusion of "more." Whichever way we turn, from now on, we are going to find a limit beyond which there will be no more. To hit these limits at top speed is not a rational choice. To start slowing down, with the idea of avoiding catastrophe, *is* a rational choice, and a viable one if we can recover the necessary political sanity. Of course it makes sense to consider alternative energy sources, provided *they* make sense. But also we will have to re-examine the economic structures of our lives, and conform them to the tolerances and limits of our earthly places. Where there is no more, our one choice is to make the most and the best of what we have.

Source

Wendell Berry, "Faustian Economics," *Harper's*, May 2008, 35–42. http://harpers.org/archive/2008/05/faustian-economics/. Copyright © 2008 Harper's Magazine. All rights reserved. Reproduced from the May issue by special permission.

Further Reading

McKibben, Bill. *The End of Nature.* New York: Random House, 1989.

Stoll, Mark. *Inherit the Holy Mountain: Religion and the Rise of American Environmentalism.* New York: Oxford University Press, 2015.